THE PUZZLE OF PRISON ORDER

DAVID SKARBEK

THE PUZZLE OF PRISON ORDER

Why Life Behind Bars Varies Around the World

OXFORD
UNIVERSITY PRESS

OXFORD
UNIVERSITY PRESS

Oxford University Press is a department of the University of Oxford. It furthers
the University's objective of excellence in research, scholarship, and education
by publishing worldwide. Oxford is a registered trade mark of Oxford University
Press in the UK and certain other countries.

Published in the United States of America by Oxford University Press
198 Madison Avenue, New York, NY 10016, United States of America.

Library of Congress Cataloging-in-Publication Data
Names: Skarbek, David, author.
Title: The puzzle of prison order : why life behind bars varies around the world / David Skarbek.
Description: New York, NY : Oxford University Press, [2020] | Includes bibliographical references and index. |
Identifiers: LCCN 2019054862 (print) | LCCN 2019054863 (ebook) |
ISBN 9780190672492 (hardback) | ISBN 9780190672508 (paperback) |
ISBN 9780190672522 (epub) | ISBN 9780190090234
Subjects: LCSH: Prisons—Cross-cultural studies. | Imprisonment—Cross-cultural studies. |
Prisoners—Cross-cultural studies. |
Criminal justice, Administration of—Cross-cultural studies.
Classification: LCC HV9443 .S53 2020 (print) | LCC HV9443 (ebook) | DDC 365—dc23
LC record available at https://lccn.loc.gov/2019054862
LC ebook record available at https://lccn.loc.gov/2019054863

1 3 5 7 9 8 6 4 2

Paperback printed by LSC Communications, United States of America
Hardback printed by Bridgeport National Bindery, Inc., United States of America

*In memory of
my mother and grandfather*

CONTENTS

LIST OF FIGURES

LIST OF TABLES

ACKNOWLEDGMENTS

I have been extremely fortunate while working on this book to have had engaging and thoughtful colleagues at both King's College London and Brown University. Discussions with them have done much to shape the way that I think about institutions, governance, and prison. Several people provided helpful feedback on a previously published article that informs this book's analysis. Thanks for doing so to John Alcorn, Sacha Darke, Henry Farrell, Danilo Freire, Anna Gwiazda, Nicola Lacey, John Meadowcroft, Michael Munger, Mark Pennington, and Emily Skarbek. I have also benefited a great deal from those who were generous enough to give their time in commenting on some or all of this manuscript. Thanks to Nicholas Barnes, Yoram Barzel, Christopher Blattman, Peter Boettke, Rosolino Candela, Ben Crewe, Daniel D'Amico, Sacha Darke, Sharon Dolovich, Gianna Englert, Danilo Freire, Rosemary Gartner, Scott Gerber, Dana Hayward, Calla Hummel, Marek Kaminski, Philip Keefer, Candace Kruttschnitt, Phillip Magness, Adam Martin, John Meadowcroft, Kristian Mjåland, Michael Munger, Jennifer Peirce, John Pratt, Livia Schubiger, Anja Shortland, Daniel Skarbek, Emily Skarbek, Richard Snyder, and Rusty Young.

I also benefited tremendously from presenting this material in a variety of venues, each of which yielded thoughtful challenges, questions, and suggestions. I am grateful to the participants in talks at Harvard University, King's College London, MIT, New York University, the Ostrom Workshop at Indiana University Bloomington, Stanford University, Texas A&M, Texas Tech, Trinity College, University of Bergen, University of California Berkeley, University College London, University of Connecticut, University of Glasgow, University of Oxford, and the University of Reading. Thanks to

Nicola Lacey for organizing a panel on this topic at the London School of Economics, and to the other panelists, Insa Koch and Lisa McKenzie. I received valuable feedback at the University of California Los Angeles–Michigan Prison Law and Policy Roundtable; thanks to all of the participants and to the organizers, Sharon Dolovich and Margo Schlanger. Thanks to the Center for the Study of Law & Society at University of California Berkeley for hosting me as a Visiting Scholar, where I finished final edits on the book. I received helpful suggestions while presenting parts of this work at the annual meetings of the American Society of Criminology, Law & Society Association, the Public Choice Society, and the Society for Institutional & Organizational Economics.

At Oxford University Press, I am enormously grateful for the invaluable guidance and suggestions from my editor, David McBride. Two anonymous reviewers provided feedback that helped me to write a more cogent and coherent book. Thanks also to the skillful work of the production staff. Thanks to the Earhart Foundation for providing financial support for parts of this project. At the Political Theory Project at Brown University, I am grateful to my colleague John Tomasi for providing such a productive venue to pursue this research. Daniel D'Amico is an endless source of thoughtful and thought-provoking conversation. I am also grateful to Alytheia Laughlin and Katherine Bonadies for outstanding professional support.

My greatest thanks go to my partner Emily. She is an endless source of support and encouragement and a helpful critic in the best possible way, pushing me to refine, revise, and reexamine my argument at each step. What a joy to share my life with her.

1

Why Does Prison Social Order Vary?

Reality is disconcerting in a prison; what seems right is often wrong, and apparently absurd things have a logic that stems from their circumstances.

Drauzio Varella, Brazilian prison doctor[1]

We must see the prison as a society within a society.

Gresham M. Sykes[2]

I n the popular telling of Charles Darwin's famous trip aboard the *Beagle*, he discovered the idea of evolution by observing finches at the Galápagos Islands.[3] Despite the fact that the archipelago was tightly clustered and subject to similar weather conditions, the birds' beaks differed in significant ways, varying in length, width, shape, and strength from island to island. Darwin's genius was to recognize that these beaks were actually fine-tuned to local conditions. They were just the right shape to access the nuts and seeds found in each island's local ecology. Each finch faced the general problem of foraging for food, but each population needed different beaks to do this well. In *The Origin of Species*, Darwin marveled at how this evolutionary process generated species that took "endless forms most beautiful and most wonderful."[4]

Though prisons do not share the same inspirational qualities as the diversity of species, I am pursuing a similar intellectual enterprise: the study of institutional diversity. The goal of this book is to understand the diversity that exists in a wide-ranging sample of prisons from around the world and through time. While institutions do not evolve with the efficiency of finches, all prisoners face the general problem of order and the need for governance, and the solutions that they devise depend significantly on local conditions. This book catalogs, describes, and explains specimens of prisoner governance institutions found among the world's incarcerated populations.

Prisons often appear as either distant, obscure places or perhaps as wholly unique ones. Nevertheless, navigating life behind bars means solving many of the same problems that have always plagued humankind. Imagine for a moment that you have been incarcerated. How would you stay safe? The strategies you chose would depend on where you were locked up. For example, in Andersonville, a Civil War prisoner-of-war camp, officials left the prisoners to fend for themselves. One prisoner's diary records the fear that plagued the camp. He writes, "Suspicious-looking chaps move through parts of the prison. Presently the cry of 'thief,' 'raiders,' and suppressed voices are heard, like men in a struggle. Again cries of 'catch him,' 'murder,' 'Oh, God, they've killed me!' . . . For a time the desperadoes vanish, then reappear. The disturbance kept up all night; we did not feel safe to lie down unless someone of our tent watched."[5] By stark contrast, in better-managed prisons, Norwegian prisoners not only feel far less vulnerable, but also maintain norms of civility. In one modern Nordic prison, for instance, one observer explains, "Inmates expect basic courtesies of one another when passing on the gravel roads around the island. Violent confrontations are strongly frowned upon by inmates because violence attracts the officers' attention."[6] Some prisoners solve the problem of violence; others do not. It is important that we know why.

How would you gain access to resources in prison? Most prisoners want the same things that we all want, such as good food, clean water, effective healthcare, and opportunities for education and recreation. At some facilities, prisoners can simply rely on officials to provide these things. Norwegian mass murderer Anders Behring Breivik lives in relative opulence. His single-occupancy cell is a three-room unit with windows, access to television, radio, and newspapers. His belongings include a treadmill, fridge, and Sony PlayStation.[7] He is pursuing a college degree through a distance-learning program and participated in a gingerbread-house baking contest at Christmas time. In other places, prisoners are not so fortunate. Again, at Andersonville, officials provided incredibly few necessities. It was the deadliest camp operating during the war—about a third of prisoners perished. Those who survived suffered through constant hunger, disease, and privation. One medical officer provides a graphic account of the lack of even basic sanitary conditions, writing that

> as the forces of the prisoners were reduced by confinement, want of exercise, improper diet, and by scurvy, diarrhea, and dysentery, they were unable to evacuate their bowels within the stream or along its banks, and the excrements were deposited at the very doors of their tents. The vast majority appeared to lose all repulsion to filth, and both sick and well disregarded all the laws of hygiene and personal cleanliness.[8]

Unfortunately, this is not the sole exception; even in modern prisons, officials often provide few essentials.

Still, even when prison officials do not provide crucial resources, prisoners can sometimes turn to the private enterprise system for relief. For example, in the late 1960s, a prison in Tijuana, Mexico, was home to a flourishing, free-market economy. Under the watchful but laissez-faire hand of officials, there was a proliferation of market activity. The economy included six prisoner-run grocery shops, two restaurants, a tortilla shop, and food carts that sold tacos, soda, ice cream, and fruit.[9] Prisoners could buy better sleeping arrangements, including a bedroll, a cot, or a spot on a bunk bed.

Wealthy prisoners could even purchase their own private apartment inside the prison.[10] In one Venezuelan prison, the captives have managed to gain significant access to resources. One journalist describes a festive scene that sounds more like debauchery than deprivation. He writes, "Bikini-clad female visitors frolic under the Caribbean sun in an outdoor pool. Marijuana smoke flavors the air. Reggaetón booms from a club filled with grinding couples. Paintings of the Playboy logo adorn the pool hall. Inmates and their guests jostle to place bets at the prison's raucous cockfighting arena."[11] In general, surviving prison requires gaining access to necessary resources. Some prisoners overcome this challenge with ease; other fail to do so and suffer, or even perish.

Who would you rely on to govern social life among prisoners? As the Norway examples suggest, officials are sometimes the primary source of governance for prisoners. In fact, in Nordic prison systems there are just as many members of prison staff as there are prisoners. Staff have also received extensive training and have a prominent presence in facilities. They oversee and govern social interactions. In Latin American prisons, the limited presence—or total absence—of official governance has given rise to a wide range of diverse prisoner-run institutions. In the Venezuelan prison just described, prisoners armed with assault rifles patrol the prison. The prisoner-leader who runs the facility appointed them. According to one prisoner, the "prisoners here run the show, and that makes life inside a bit easier for us all."[12] Another prisoner, a convicted murderer and one of the prison's pastors, says that self-rule has not led to destitution and violence. On the contrary, he claims, "our prison is a model institution," and another prisoner suggests, "there's more security in here than out on the street."[13] A report by the Inter-American Commission on Human Rights likewise finds that at one Mexican prison, the prisoners actually elect their own prisoner-leaders. Many prisoners view this system favorably, and the report explains that prisoners "emphasized that everyone tries to maintain stability within the prison and that the prisoners respect one another and follow the inside rules."[14] However, democracy doesn't take hold everywhere. In one Ecuadorian prison, cellblock mafias collude with guards to rule the prisoner community.[15] The mafias regulate the underground economy—in particular the drug trade—as well as abuse and extort weaker prisoners.[16] These anecdotes provide just a glimpse at the tremendous variation in the ways in which social order is established and maintained—or not—in prisons around the world.

The differences that we see across various prisons are even more curious when one considers that the basic features of a prison are essentially the same regardless of where we look. Prisoners, who have either been charged with or convicted of a crime, are forced to relocate to a facility for confinement. Once there, the captive must usually interact with other people in the same situation. They suffer the pains of imprisonment, which often include deprivation of liberty, goods and services, heterosexual relationships, autonomy, and security. Prisoners tend to come from relatively disadvantaged socio-economic backgrounds. All prison systems are based on coercion, and prisoners have no voluntary exit option.[17] In his seminal book on the topic, sociologist Gresham Sykes argued that all prisons also shared remarkably similar social structures.[18] However, the study of prison social order since the 1950s has shown that this is not true. Prisons are home to a wide range of social orders.

Why does life in prison vary so much? Why do the organizations and networks that prisoners turn to for stability and safety come in such different forms depending on when and where we look? Why does the informal prisoner community rise to considerable importance in some places but remain inconsequential in others? We should care about how prisoners solve these problems. The inability to control violence and to establish social order is a direct threat to the quality of life of the more than 10 million people in prisons worldwide currently.[19] This is just a small fraction of the total number of people who have served, or will serve, time in their lifespan. Even if you think it could never happen to you personally, it might very well happen to your friend, sibling, or child. How would you want them treated? More generally, when prisons degrade their residents it is a disservice to the effectiveness and legitimacy that must be the foundation of a good criminal justice system. Practically speaking, we should care about prison conditions because most prisoners are released. In the United States, 93 percent of prisoners will eventually come home.[20] Do we want them to have invested in improving themselves and their post-incarceration prospects or do we want them to have been subject to the often brutal and capricious choices of tyrannical prisoners or prison staff? Prisons are also not isolated communities. They have porous walls. In California, prison gangs are the de facto government for street gangs across the state. They tax drug sales, adjudicate disputes, and regulate violence. In doing so, they help crime flourish in our neighborhoods. In Brazil, the *Primeiro Comando da Capital* prison gang has such a powerful reach into the free world that it was able to coordinate a massive assault against urban transport, police, and banking infrastructure, bringing São Paulo to a standstill for four days.[21] In short, even if we do not see prisoners on a daily basis, what happens on the inside matters for the rest of us in society.

More generally, prisoners confront many of the same foundational questions that people in all societies face. They must find ways to control who uses violence and to what end. They need to decide how resources are used, how to manage inequities, and how to control disruptive and predatory members of the group. They face the fundamental problem of political economy: how to create institutions that are strong enough to protect property rights but constrain these institutions so that political power is not used to violate people's rights. As with communities in the free world, prisoners sometimes succeed and often fail. We have much to learn about politics and economics by studying how prisoners struggle toward solving these problems.[22]

THE PROBLEM OF ORDER

Governance institutions define and protect property rights, offer personal security, enforce agreements, facilitate trade, and aid in the production of collective and public goods. They are the "rules of the game" in a society.[23] Studies of governance institutions outside of prison consistently confirm their importance for economic and social outcomes.[24] When governance institutions are effective, markets flourish. Standards of living improve, markets innovate, and individuals funnel their energy into activities that are socially beneficial. When governance institutions work poorly, markets fail and economies stagnate. Markets are static, domineering, or benefit only a limited segment of society. In the worst cases, institutions create incentives that encourage people to act in predatory ways.[25] People defraud customers, act opportunistically, steal, and use violence to intimidate, control, and exploit others. Good governance institutions are the foundation of peaceful, prosperous societies that encourage people to truck, barter, and exchange. Poor institutional environments undermine social order by encouraging people to act in wasteful and destructive ways.

The government is a major supplier of governance institutions. Courts of law and police officers help make one's property more secure. Market regulation and licensing requirements can give confidence in the trustworthiness of a business.[26] However, governments do not produce all of the governance on which people rely. Even in developed countries, much of the governance that people base their social interactions on is produced by other entities. A wide range of private businesses and professional associations create rules that certify the quality and trustworthiness of members and assure transactions.[27] Alternative dispute resolution services facilitate commerce in the shadow of the law. For people who use these services, government courts are too slow or too costly to rely on, so instead they turn to the expertise of private dispute resolution services. Commercial companies likewise develop technologies and services that allow citizens to protect themselves from crime.[28] Thus, the governance that people rely on in their everyday lives comes from a rich mosaic of different sources.

The same needs for governance that exist throughout society also arise in prison. Members of prison staff are often the most visible source of governance. Official procedures can make prisons safer and more secure. Guards oversee social interactions. Officials provide food, clothing, housing, and healthcare. Staff watch prisoners and discourage fights, uprisings, and other disruptions. When violence breaks out, correctional officers wield lethal and less-lethal weapons to restore order. The architecture of a prison can also enhance security and control.[29] The same bars that keep a prisoner locked in his or her cell also keep other prisoners out. Surveillance cameras document prison activity and encourage good behavior from both prisoners and staff members alike. Many prisons segregate those people officials believe would be especially dangerous to others. In these ways, official governance institutions can define and enforce property rights over possessions and enhance physical safety.

Yet, as the examples presented earlier suggest, officials in many prisons do not provide the governance institutions that prisoners deem important or necessary. Instead, prisoners must govern themselves. The need for extralegal governance institutions arises for several reasons. Many prisoners view their peers as untrustworthy and threatening. Prisons tend to attract those people who are most willing, on average, to break the law. Their residents are more likely to have histories of violence, as both perpetrators and victims. Prisoners tend to have lower levels of self-control, and they are more likely to act impulsively. They are least willing to wait patiently for future benefits.[30] Prisoners are often correct to be suspicious of their peers and it will often be worth investing in self-protection efforts. This can entail finding better ways to hide valuables, making weapons for self-defense, or forming alliances with other prisoners who can provide mutual support and protection.

Prisoners sometimes govern themselves because officials lack the ability to govern them.[31] For officials to secure a person's property, they must be able to certify who has the legitimate claim to it. Yet, in many Latin American prisons, for example, it is difficult or impossible for officials to do so because staff have few resources. Any claim of legal title likewise requires the state be willing to enforce the claim, but prison officials will not always do so, such as with contraband. If prisoners do not trust officials, then officials may need to invest in establishing a credible claim to protect— instead of prey upon—prisoners or their property. However, in prisons rife with abuse or corruption, prisoners might be wise to fear officials.

Perhaps most importantly, prisoners require extralegal governance institutions because officials do not facilitate economic activity. Most prisons outlaw prisoner-to-prisoner trading (although these rules are often ignored and unenforced). Even though a prison commissary might provide access to some goods, prisoners still lack access to a large number of other goods and services, including alcohol, cellphones, drugs, sex, tattoos, and tobacco.[32] Since these are often in high demand, prisoners can profit by supplying them. However, because of the illicit nature of contraband, prisoners cannot officially rely on prison officers to protect the items involved or to regulate the transaction. Likewise, disputes over contraband cannot be resolved through formal complaint procedures. A prisoner involved in a drug deal who received a packet of heroin that is not of the quantity or quality that he expected cannot turn for help to (non-corrupt) prison guards.[33] As one Brazilian prisoner explains, "if I sell a rock of crack and the guy doesn't cough up, I got no judge to complain to or promissory note to claim. If I let it go I become a doormat, see, nobody pays me anymore and my supplier doesn't give a rat's ass."[34] In the absence of legal standing, police, and courts of law, prisoners must develop their own extralegal governance institutions to facilitate illicit trade.

The extent to which prisoners rely on officials or on themselves to provide governance varies significantly. It is helpful to think about four ideal types of governance regimes, based on who produces the governance: official governance, co-governance, self-governance, and minimal governance. In an official governance regime, officials are prisoners' main supply of resources, administration, and governance. The Nordic prison systems are a good example of this type of regime because officials provide prisoners with an abundance of material resources and high-quality governance. Prisoners avoid violent conflict because they fear discipline from members of staff. This regime type does not require the total absence of extralegal governance institutions, such as informal norms, which are likely to exist in any social setting. Instead, the key point is that officials are the primary source of governance for most prisoners.

Co-governance regimes exist when prisoners play an important role working with officials to govern the facility. In one Brazilian jail, for example, prisoners facilitate daily prison operations, including dispensing meals, doing repairs, and conducting security-related tasks.[35] They work hand in hand with officials to administer the daily life of the prison. In Texas, prior to the 1980s, officials selected some prisoners to serve as "building tenders." These prisoners would resolve disputes among other prisoners and provide information to guards about what was happening in the unit.[36] These regimes are distinct in that officials and prisoners are explicitly working together to govern.

Self-governance regimes exist when prisoners create important governance institutions that are distinct and autonomous from official institutions. They are different from co-governing regimes because there is a clear separation between prisoners and officials in terms of authority, legitimacy, operation, and organization. For example, prisoner-institutions might govern the underground economy because officials cannot legitimately do so, or prisoners might invest in self-protection efforts because they feel unsafe. These extralegal activities can range from being incredibly decentralized and informal to highly centralized and organized. Historically, prisoners have often relied on the "convict code" to govern social order.[37] A decentralized system of norms guided people about what was acceptable behavior. For example, good convicts don't snitch and they pay back their debts. Adherence to the code raised one's status; violation of the code reduced one's status. Self-governing regimes can also have more centralized institutions. In one Bolivian prison, prisoner associations and committees organize nearly all aspects of the everyday life of the prison, and officials play no significant governance role. Prisoners have written rules, leaders are elected, and property is registered in a centralized record.

Finally, minimal governance regimes exist when neither officials nor prisoners reliably provide resources, competent administration, or effective governance. The descriptions of Andersonville given earlier provide a good sense of what this regime type looks like. In this case, neither officials nor prisoners provided significant resources, competent administration, or high-quality governance. As a result, prisoners were mired in poverty and lawlessness. In short, when governance institutions exist, either officials, prisoners, or both groups provide them. When governance institutions do not emerge in significant ways, neither group has produced them.[38]

HOW WELL DO OFFICIALS GOVERN?

The importance of extralegal governance institutions and the form that they take depends on several key factors. First, the supply and demand for governance shapes the importance of extralegal governance institutions. If the quality of official governance, administration, and resources is high relative to prisoner's demand for it, then prisoners will not invest the time, energy, and resources to create extralegal governance institutions. They have little reason to do so. For example, Nordic prisoners living in relative comfort have far less reason to invest in gaining access to material resources than the impoverished prisoners in many Latin American facilities. If the quality of official governance is low relative to prisoners' demand, then there is greater likelihood that prisoners will create extralegal governance institutions. However, prisoners will not inevitably respond in this way. It must be worth the effort. This depends on the net benefits from producing extralegal governance and on prisoners' ability to overcome the collective action problem of producing governance. Some prisoners might want to free ride on other people's hard work to govern daily life.[39] For instance, a prisoner might prefer that someone else confront a belligerent and disruptive prisoner rather than doing so himself.

To support this argument, I study the prison social order in prisons where the quality of official governance varies substantially. In chapter 2, I discuss a Brazilian jail where the quality of official governance is low and a system of trustees working with officials organizes prison life. I also examine a Bolivian prison where officials provide almost no governance at all and a system of prisoner-created committees and associations—all acting independently of officials—produces order. By contrast, in chapter 3, I examine cases from Nordic prisons where the quality of official governance is far better and officials are the main source of governance for most prisoners. Finally, at the Andersonville prisoner of war camp (discussed in chapter 4), the quality of official governance was remarkably poor, but prisoners still did little to govern. For most of the time it was in operation, prisoners had no reason to invest in collective action because there were few benefits from doing so. These four cases support the argument that there is a negative relationship between the quality of official governance and the importance of extralegal governance. (See the appendix for a longer discussion of research design and methods.)

High-quality governance can be absent for a variety of reasons, including lack of state capacity, unwillingness on the part of officials to provide it, expectations about prisoners' responses, adherence to a particular philosophy of punishment, and run-of-the-mill corruption. In this book, I do not explain why this varies, so I am not making a strong claim about directions of causality. When I discuss official governance institutions, I am referring singularly to the collection of officials who make choices about governance within a prison. So my discussion includes the higher-level bureaucrats and politicians who make decisions about the number of prisons in operation and their budget. It includes mid-level bureaucrats who make choices about the formal rules in a prison system. Finally, it includes the street-level bureaucrats—correctional officers and other prison staff—who make choices on the ground about how official rules are applied. Importantly, I do not unpack how these different people contribute to the end result. That task is too far beyond the scope of this project. Instead, I take these decisions by officials as given and study their consequences.

SIZE, SOCIAL NETWORKS, AND SOCIAL DISTANCE

If prisoners wish to provide governance, they can do so in either more centralized or more decentralized ways (see Table 1.1). Centralized mechanisms are distinctive for their hierarchies of authority, written rules and regulations, corporate entity, permanence, and often a system of mutual responsibility. By contrast, decentralized mechanisms lack a rigid

Table 1.1 Characteristics of Decentralized and Centralized Institutions

Decentralized Institutions	Centralized Institutions
• Little to no rigid, explicit hierarchy	• Clearly defined hierarchies
• Norms emerge through social interactions	• Written rules and regulations created by leaders
• No specific person is in charge of monitoring and enforcing norms	• Specific people are responsible for monitoring and enforcing the rules
• Prisoner relationships are loose, fleeting, and overlapping	• Groups have a corporate identity, permanence, and are mutually exclusive
• Individual reputations matter most	• Group reputation matters more

hierarchy. Prisoners are not required to affiliate with groups, and they are not held accountable for other people's actions. The individual's standing and reputation are what matters most. Decentralized institutions lack clear venues for creating rules and processes for informing prisoners of them, monitoring compliance, and punishing offenses. Each prisoner decides whether he or she wishes to adhere to norms and whether to punish norm violations. Gossip, ostracism, and shaming are common tools of social control.

Important studies by sociologists Diego Gambetta and Federico Varese find that mafias come into existence and wield influence in places where state-produced governance is unavailable or ineffective.[40] To increase their ability to extract tribute, successful mafias often enforce property rights and facilitate trade when the state does not.[41] In the incarceration context, prison gangs in California likewise emerged as a centralized mechanism to govern social and economic life in large, diverse prison populations.[42] However, a need for extralegal governance does not imply that centralized institutions must produce it. If decentralized institutions are effective and relatively cheap to use—which is often the case with shaming, gossip, and ostracism—then prisoners will not bear the cost of creating and operating more centralized mechanisms.[43]

The choices that prison officials make have an important influence on the costs of using decentralized governance. I focus on three ways: the size, social networks, and social distance of the prisoner community.[44] First, if officials incarcerate large populations of people in large prisons, then it is costlier to learn about people's reputations.[45] In large populations, it is harder to know most people's social standing. Threatening to ostracize a prisoner who does not pay back debts is not an effective deterrent if that person has plenty of other people from whom to borrow. This threat will only be persuasive if the community can find a way to alert everyone to who is untrustworthy. Larger groups also tend to be less tightly knit, making ostracism less painful and therefore less of a deterrent. These dynamics suggest that extralegal governance institutions are more likely to be decentralized if the prisoner population is sufficiently small to allow information to flow at relatively low cost.

In the case of women's prisons in California (chapter 5), prisoners rely on a system of norms to govern social and economic affairs. Unlike men's prisons, these norms allow prisoners to seek help from correctional officers. As a result, correctional officers play a more important role than in men's prisons. Some women also form fictive kinships, which can be a source of order. These quasi-families are extraordinarily fluid, overlapping, and interconnected. They lack the clear structure and permanence found in more centralized prisoner governance institutions. Prison families are a useful way to organize when populations are relatively small.

Second, if prison officials incarcerate prisoners close to their home communities, this lowers the cost of prisoners learning information about other people's reputations. Pre-prison social networks mean that other prisoners might know a new person's reputation as soon as he or she arrives. Incarcerated friends and associates can vouch for the new arrival. At the same time, a new prisoner might also know the social standing of other prisoners. Social networks that span prison walls to the community outside can likewise increase the audience to a prisoner's actions. Friends and family at home might learn about how one is behaving while incarcerated. If the social network is likely to persist after incarceration, it makes maintaining these relationships and one's reputation even more important.

In chapter 6, I discuss English prisons, where both relatively small facilities and dense pre-prison social networks combine to make decentralized governance effective. Prisoners typically form loose affiliations based on the shared postcode of the area from which they come. Postcodes are the United Kingdom's equivalent of United States' zip codes, except that instead of covering an average of nearly 8,000 people each, they typically cover only about 15 properties. Prison officials also intentionally house prisoners in facilities close to their homes, so they often know other prisoners upon arrival. Prisoners know that people from their hometown will know how they acted in prison. They will also interact with other prisoners in the future once back in their communities. These factors make information about people's reputation easier to obtain and are the foundation of a decentralized governance system based on focal, regional relationships.

Third, officials make choices when classifying prisoners that affects the prisoner community's social distance—the extent to which people share appearances, beliefs, customs, practices, and other characteristics that define their identity.[46] In chapter 7, I study the gay and transgender housing unit at the Los Angeles County Jail. Due to an unusual classification process, the residents of this unit tend to have "low" social distance, often coming from the same social scene on the outside, having similar lifestyles, visiting the same bars and clubs, and often sharing similar life experiences. On the other hand, in the general population housing units, there tends to be "high" social distance among prisoners. Prisoners there have more varied personal histories, come from different neighborhoods, do not socialize in the same circles, and do not have a strong shared identity. Communities characterized by low social distance can more easily rely on decentralized governance than can those with higher social distance. With low social distance, it is easier to communicate with other people. Such groups share stronger consensus on what constitutes acceptable behavior, what is a violation of the norms, and what is the appropriate response. They are more likely to share other-regarding preferences, face lower costs of deliberating, and have more similar preferences for public goods.[47] They also tend to have an easier time discouraging free riding in the production of public goods.[48]

Each of these cases are very different from the social order that exists in California's state prisons for men. In past work, I argued that when the prison population grows larger and more ethnically diverse, prisoners create centralized, extralegal governance institutions.[49] Prison gangs organize as a "community responsibility system," where all prisoners affiliate with some group, and within a group, all members are responsible for each member's actions. For these systems to be effective, they must accomplish three tasks. First, a group must clearly delineate membership since the group is responsible for other member's actions. Without restricting access, a group would be inundated with opportunistic members who would incur obligations for which the group would be responsible. Second, each group requires a way to monitor members' behavior. They might have written rules about what is acceptable conduct. They might delegate monitoring to specific entities or people within the group. Groups often have a procedure for judging guilt and carrying out punishments. Finally, since these systems emerge to govern life among strangers, prisoners need a way to know with which group a stranger affiliates. For these systems to work best, there must be credible ways of signaling group affiliation that are difficult for non-group members to fake.

Several techniques make these community responsibility systems work effectively. First, to limit internal opportunistic behavior, prisoners exclude membership to people who will be costly to be held accountable for. This includes those prisoners who are considered to be in the lowest social standing, known by disparaging terms like "junky," "snitch," and "cho mo" (prison slang for drug users, informants, and child molesters). In California, sex offenders are subject to systematic assaults by other prisoners until they ask to be removed from the general population.[50] Because community responsibility systems work best when everyone is in a group, these deviant prisoners cannot be tolerated as rogue, unaffiliated prisoners. Second, membership is often somewhat permanent and mutually exclusive to reduce uncertainty about which group is responsible for any particular individual. Fleeting or overlapping membership among groups causes confusion about which group is responsible for a particular prisoner at a particular point in time. A degree of permanence and exclusivity in membership reduces this ambiguity. Finally, in a society of strangers, groups align in ways that make it easier to identify group affiliation. For these reasons, if you were to have a bird's-eye view of a California prison yard, you would see that groups sort themselves by race—making it easy for any one prisoner to know who is aligned with which gangs. Visible tattoos serve the same purpose. These features are prominent because they facilitate centralized extralegal governance. We should not expect to see them in decentralized prison contexts.

To summarize, the governance theory of prison social order suggests several empirical implications about how prison order looks in the real world (see Figure 1.1). The first concerns official governance provision: if officials provide high-quality governance, then prisoners will tend to produce less extralegal governance; if official governance is absent or insufficient, prisoners will tend to produce more extralegal governance. The second

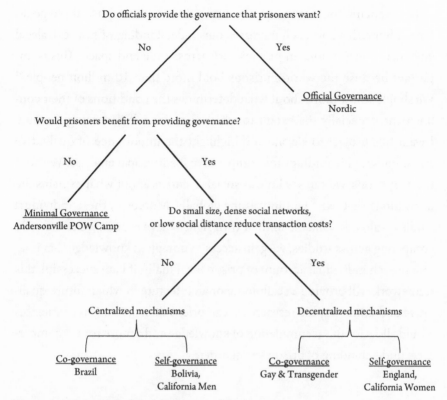

Figure 1.1 A Simplified Representation of the Argument

involves the costs of producing governance: if the benefits from producing governance are low relative to the cost of doing so, prisoners will not produce governance, even in the face of the state's failure to govern. Third, information availability and the size, social networks, and social distance of the population matters: if prisoners can collect information and punish bad behavior relatively cheaply—especially through gossip, ostracism, and shaming—then they will tend to rely on decentralized governance mechanisms. When prison populations are relatively small, have preexisting social networks, and low social distance, prisoners will tend to rely on decentralized extralegal governance. Finally, prisons with decentralized extralegal governance institutions will tend to lack strict racial and ethnic segregation, be more tolerant of sex offenders, and will not operate as a community responsibility system.

In advancing this argument, this book aims to accomplish three goals. First, I hope this approach increases our understanding of how extralegal governance institutions in prisons vary across time and space. This is important because the world's prisons hold more than 10 million people.[51] We should know more about what determines the conditions of their confinement, especially the extent to which they are self-governing. Second, I want this project to elevate and highlight the importance of qualitative and ethnographic findings for comparative institutional analysis. Without these methods, we can say little as social scientists about what explains the institutions that exist within prisons globally. Moreover, these individual studies—already valuable in their own right—have even more to offer. By comparing across studies, we gain access to untapped knowledge that is latent in each individual account of prison life. Finally, if I am successful, this framework will provide a scaffolding or architecture in which future qualitative and ethnographic researchers can orient their work. Over time, this would allow for the accumulation of knowledge and a more robust comparative understanding of prison social order.

PART I

Who Governs?

2

When Prisoners Govern

Brazil and Bolivia

The inmates kept the Big House running and without them
it would have been chaos.

Drauzio Varella, Brazilian prison doctor[1]

Latin American countries have experienced significant increases in
their prison populations since the 1980s. However, the procedures
and practices of confinement there—the way that prisons operate—have
not followed the same trends seen in other countries with growing prison
populations.[2] In the United States, corrections work has become increasingly professionalized. Prison officials bring a vast amount of state and federal funding and cutting-edge technology to the administration of prisons.
These resources facilitate prisoner classification and the regimentation
of daily life. Officials use video cameras to surveil housing units. Prison
officials isolate residents from each other and from family and friends, and

they limit and control prisoner work within the facility closely. A broad range of governmental and non-governmental organizations holds prisons in the United States and Europe accountable to some extent. There is also a high degree of formalization in prison management and procedures. In many parts of Latin America, by contrast, each of these characteristics is significantly less common or entirely absent.

Studying cases of Latin American prisons provides an opportunity to assess one of the main empirical implications of the governance theory of prison social order. In particular, given the extremely low quality of official governance that exists in many of these prisons, the theory predicts that there will be a significant investment in extralegal governance institutions. Of course, not all prisons in Latin America are poorly governed and there is variation both within and across countries. However, I argue that these prison systems tend to have relatively few resources, their administrations are ineffective, overwhelmed, or simply absent, and they do a poor job of governing the prisoner community. As a result, prisoners invest heavily in extralegal governance institutions.

I start by providing a brief overview of material conditions in Latin American prisons and documenting the diversity of extralegal governance institutions that operate within them. The aggregate evidence is consistent with the theory and is the first step in establishing that there is a systematic relationship between official governance and extralegal governance. The next chapter examines prisons where official governance is of a high quality and there are few extralegal governance institutions. Taken together then these two chapters show that there is a correlation between the quality of official governance and the importance of extralegal governance. In addition, each chapter examines specific prisons to show how these relationships operate on the ground. Finally, the evidence available in these cases shows that the mechanisms that emerge are consistent with the underlying intuition of the theory. The combination of aggregate correlations, detailed cases studies, and identification of mechanisms provide support for the governance theory.

In this chapter, I chose to focus on two cases because they vary in the type and quality of governance that officials provide. First, I examine a

Brazilian jail where officials have delegated a large number of administrative responsibilities to prisoners. This research comes from criminologist Sacha Darke who studies Brazilian prisons and jails. In addition to his articles, his book *Conviviality and Survival: Co-Producing Brazilian Prison Order* provides a compelling account of the origins, nature, and challenges facing many Brazilian prisoners. His fieldwork has taken him to more than forty Brazilian prisons and jails, where he has interviewed prisoners and staff and observed prison operations.[3] Second, I discuss Bolivia's San Pedro prison, where officials provide neither governance nor significant material resources. I draw on a variety of sources, including reports from government and non-governmental organizations, journalists, and former prisoners. It is an extreme example of a self-governing prison regime, and officials rarely even enter the facility. Instead, prisoners create associations and committees to govern the community and participate in a thriving prison economy, all of which promote order amid a state-created sphere of statelessness.

THE IMPOVERISHED STATE OF LATIN AMERICAN PRISONS

In general, the quality of official governance in Latin American prisons is far lower than in U.S. and European prisons. Table 2.1 provides some basic measures of prison size and operation for the region's prison systems. The average prison population across the sample of countries is 72,670 people, but there is a significant amount of variation. Prison populations range from a low of only 1,000 people incarcerated in Suriname to more than 659,000 prisoners in Brazil. The average prison use rate is 254 prisoners per 100,000 residents, with a low of 130 in both Bolivia and Guatemala and a high of 586 in El Salvador. The average prison occupancy rate is 159 percent of designed capacity. El Salvador, Guatemala, Bolivia, and Peru have the highest levels of overcrowding—with facilities packed with between two to three-and-a-half times the designed capacity. Brazil's occupancy rate is about 164 percent of designed capacity, and overcrowding has long plagued the system. In 1998, Human Rights Watch concluded that "severe overcrowding is perhaps the most basic, and most chronic, problem

Table 2.1 Descriptive Statistics of Latin American Prison Systems

Country	Prison Population[a]	Prison Use Rate (per 100,000)[a]	Occupancy Rate[a]	Number of Facilities	Average Population per Facility	Prisoners per Staff[b]	Percentage of National Budget[c]
Argentina	72,693	167	106%	285	255	1.6	0.56
Belize	1,443	410	87%	1	1,443	4.9	
Bolivia	14,598	130	253%	61	239	11.7	
Brazil	659,020	319	163%	1,424	463	7.7	0.79
Chile	42,639	235	110%	103	414	2.1	0.68
Colombia	115,878	229	147%	136	852	7.8	1.1
Costa Rica	17,440	352	139%	33	528	4.3	0.33
Ecuador	26,421	160	114%	52	508	17.3	0.70
El Salvador	38,159	586	348%	25	1,526	14.7	0.70
Guatemala	22,184	130	296%	22	1,008	8.8	0.50
Guyana	2,113	278	128%	5	423	4.3	
Honduras	17,253	200	162%	27	639	10.0	
Mexico	233,469	192	111%	379	616	6.4	0.23
Nicaragua	10,569	171	128%	9	1,174	8.3	0.45
Panama	17,165	421	121%	24	715	13.8	0.35
Paraguay	12,741	180	178%	16	796	8.3	
Peru	83,639	262	232%	69	1,212	9.0	0.38
Suriname	1,000	183	75%	31	32		
Uruguay	10,228	297	112%	29	353	3.8	
Venezuela	54,738	173	153%	58	944		0.21

a. World Prison Brief 2018.

b. Based on data about prison staff numbers from United Nations Office on Drugs and Crime. Data are from 2015 or are the most recent estimate available.

c. Inter-American Commission on Human Rights (2011, 21–22). Data is missing for some countries.

plaguing Brazil's prison system."[4] The size of prisons varies too. Across the sample, there is an average of 707 people per facility, with five countries (El Salvador, Belize, Peru, Nicaragua, and Guatemala) exceeding an average of 1,000 prisoners per facility. The ratio of prisoners to members of staff is largest in Ecuador (17.3 to 1), El Salvador (14.7 to 1), Panama (13.8 to 1), Bolivia (11.7 to 1), and Honduras (10 to 1). The staffing levels are highest in Argentina, Chile, Uruguay, and Costa Rica. Finally, for those countries where data is available, only one spends more than 1 percent of the national budget on the prison system, and on average, prisons receive only 0.5 percent of the national budget.

These data give some sense of the size and use of Latin American prisons, but they do not say much about the conditions of life inside of them. For instance, I do not have data on what percentage of prisoners across these systems receive adequate food, water, healthcare, and clothing from prison officials. Likewise, we do not know how safe these prisons are. The consensus in the literature is that Latin American prisons are often in a decrepit state, but we do not have systematic data documenting this across countries.[5] In lieu of that, I'll briefly mention findings from a variety of studies and reports that give a snapshot of some of these dimensions.[6]

In a 2007 survey of 1,615 Mexican prisoners, 53 percent reported that the food was insufficient, 41 percent reported it was of poor or very poor quality, and 29 percent reported they did not have sufficient clean drinking water.[7] In Peru, half of the prisoners did not have access to health services, with an average of just one doctor for every 885 prisoners.[8] Prisoners relied heavily on their families to bring them food (90 percent of respondents), medicine (49 percent), money (64 percent), and clothes or shoes (85 percent).[9] At the Penitenciaría del Litoral, Ecuador's largest federal prison, one scholar reports, "food and medicine always ran in short supply. The inmates themselves protested bitterly over the horrendous quality of their meals, as well as the general absence of medicine throughout the complex."[10]

The inability to maintain even the most basic level of cleanliness compounds the misery of poverty and overcrowding. One Brazilian prisoner told Human Rights Watch, "Everything is dirty and infested. There are little bugs there—*muquirana*—that live in your clothes and make your skin itch all night. It's impossible to sleep. Every Friday [the staff] have a 'geral' (full search). There is a big patio there. Everyone is forced to strip naked and wait in the patio, often in the cold. They turn on a hose and wash down everything. But it doesn't keep the bugs away."[11] Access to clean water, soap, and showers are also limited. When showers are available, they often consist only of a pipe coming out of a wall with no showerhead and no hot water.[12] In 2003, in Venezuela's El Rodeo prison, there was no working plumbing and improper electrical wiring caused several deaths.[13] Because of overcrowding, prisoners often install drapes and partitions to create some privacy, but given the poor quality of electrical work, this can present a serious fire risk.[14] Prisoners in Paraguayan prisons describe a similar setting: decaying buildings, suffocating overcrowding, lack of hygiene, and little access to food and healthcare.[15] One prisoner likened their treatment to animals, saying "there is no difference between a zoo and this place, but animals have mothers and I am alone."[16] A study of Mexican prisons concludes that, "almost all of the prisons in the study were in a sorry state, with deteriorating installations and furnishings and limited prisoner access to basic goods and services."[17]

Sociologist Loïc Wacquant, writing about the Brazilian prison system, describes "the appalling state of the country's prisons, which are more akin to *concentration camps for the dispossessed*, or public enterprises for the industrial storage of social refuse, than to judicial institutions serving any identifiable penological function."[18] He describes a prison system in crisis: "staggering overcrowding resulting in abominable living conditions and catastrophic hygiene, characterized by lack of space, air, light and food . . . denial of access to legal assistance and basic health care, the result of which has been the dramatic acceleration of the spread of tuberculosis and the HIV virus."[19]

Prisons are often extremely understaffed. Table 2.1 shows that for the entire sample, there is an average of eight prisoners for each member of staff, but this overstates staff presence in two ways. First, it includes all employees, not just those in a custodial role. Some people hired as guards instead work in administrative positions.[20] Second, many of these prison systems both have a high proportion of staff on medical leave and face chronic absenteeism.[21] There is also significant variation in staffing within countries. For example, in Ecuador's largest federal prison, there were approximately 32 guards responsible for about 4,000 prisoners.[22] Perhaps as a way to cope with being outnumbered, anthropologist Chris Garces explains, "the guards quickly employ force to maintain their aura of sovereign violence. They often fire their weapon of choice, the sawed-off shotgun, in a dramatic display."[23] Human Rights Watch's visit to a Brazilian facility in Rio Grande do Norte found that three members of staff were responsible for 646 prisoners.[24] In Venezuela in 2006, eight staff guarded more than 1,400 prisoners.[25] In 2009, the United Nations Committee Against Torture found that, on a visit to a lockup in Rio de Janeiro, there were only six officials responsible for 1,405 prisoners.[26] At a prison in Recife, Pernambuco, five prison officers oversaw a population of 4,200 prisoners.[27] Wacquant reports that only twelve guards worked at any time at Casa de Detenção of São Paulo, and they were responsible for overseeing about 1,700 prisoners.[28]

Visitors to Latin American prisons often see the lack of resources and formal control and assume that this leads to chaos, violence, or complete destitution. Human Rights Watch argued, "with the meagre guard presence in many prisons, there is very little to prevent tougher, stronger, richer and more well-connected inmates from threatening, intimidating and sometimes violently abusing their more vulnerable fellows."[29] While violence and abuse do occur, this is not always the case. Prisoners have an incentive to respond to harsh conditions. Sacha Darke and Maria Lúcia Karam, criminologists and Latin American prison experts, explain that despite their plight, "for the majority of prisoners life goes on with some degree of everyday normality—meals are distributed, rubbish is collected, families visit at the weekend, minor illnesses get treated, disputes are usually avoided or settled."[30]

In the face of limited resources, undertrained or absent officials, and poor governance institutions, prisoners often govern themselves. The literature on Latin American prisons documents numerous forms of prisoner governance.[31] These include *directivas* (directors) in Bolivia; the *cabos/delegados de pabellón* (heads/dormitory delegates), *jefes de patio o pasillo* (heads of patio or corridor)/*gremio* (management), and *polipresos* (inmate police) in Venezuela; the *nueva mafia* (new mafia) in Honduras; *delegados* (delegates) in Peru; the *comités de orden y disciplina* (committees of order and discipline) of Guatemala; the "cellblock bosses" of Mexico; the "internal chiefs" of Colombia; the *capataces* (foremen) of Paraguay; the *comités* and *representantes* (representatives) of the Dominican Republic; and the *limpiezas* (cleaners) of Argentina. In 2012, a Mexican human rights commission likewise found that 60 percent of Mexican prisons are "self-governed."[32] In Honduras, at the national penitentiary Marco Aurelio Soto, anthropologist Jon Carter describes what it feels like to enter the prisoner-run barracks: "crossing the threshold for the first time was like walking through an electrical current, where one body of law recedes and another begins."[33] As these examples show, extralegal governance is not limited to only a few places. These diverse governance mechanisms vary in their effectiveness and desirability, but they are alike in that prisoners play a major role in governing the conditions of their own confinement. These are not one-off examples within a generally well-functioning prison system. They are endemic. In Latin America, extralegal governance is not extraordinary.

CO-GOVERNANCE IN A BRAZILIAN JAIL

Prisoners sometimes play a part in contributing to a prison's administrative needs. In the United States, this is now relatively rare; over the last 70 years, there has been a significant decline in the extent to which prisoners help run U.S. prisons.[34] However, prisoners often administer Brazilian jails capably, playing a key role in maintaining the physical structure of the facility and running the day-to-day operations.[35] Partly because of low staffing levels, thousands of Brazilian prisoners have jobs as prison *apoios* (support staff).[36] According to official data from June 2011, more than 15,000 prisoners worked as support staff in the São Paulo prison system (about 9 percent of prisoners) and 270 as support staff in Rio de Janeiro (about 1 percent of prisoners).[37] There are also numerous unofficial positions created for prisoner leaders and trustees.

One example where this occurs is in a jail lockup in Rio de Janeiro, called Polinter prison (which has since closed). The jail held about 600 people, and prisoners outnumbered members of staff by 10 to 1.[38] The facility consisted of two wings, with nine dormitories.[39] There was a general wing and a *seguro* wing (a segregation wing), for prisoners who would not be safe in the general population. Each cell had a prisoner leader, called the *representante de cela* (cell representative) and each of the two jail wings had a *representante geral* (general representative). Officials did not appoint these representatives. Other prisoners chose them, either through elections, by a prisoner being considered the most experienced in the jail, or with someone arising as a "natural leader."[40] These representatives worked with prison officials to co-govern the jail.

A prisoner who took on such a leadership role did not gain significant material benefits. In the secured wing of the prison, being a representative provided the advantage of enjoying more time outside of the dormitory during the day, but few other benefits. These positions did not create substantial material inequalities. Importantly, strong, influential prisoners did not unilaterally declare themselves the leader.[41] Prisoners held representatives accountable for fulfilling their responsibilities. The representatives "owe their position to the confidence of the *coletivo* [the collective] as much as to other prisoner representatives."[42] Forty-five prisoner trustees, knowns as *colaboradores* (collaborators), were responsible for nearly all of the administrative operations of the jail, including receiving and transferring new prisoners.

One of the most important tasks was to decide which prisoners should reside in the jail and which new arrivals were dangerous and disruptive enough to be sent to a higher-security facility. If a new arrival would not be accepted by the prisoners (for example, because he was a sex offender), then he was sent to the segregation wing.[43] The *Povão de Israel* (People of Israel), a group that formed for prisoners not affiliated with a criminal gang, governed this part of the jail. Unlike with some Brazilian prison gangs, affiliation with the *Povão de Israel* is limited entirely to within the prison setting. The group has little influence outside of the prison and membership did not oblige prisoners to continue working for the group after release.[44]

Trustees in the jail performed a wide range of custodial tasks. They were in charge of cleaning the jail, cooking and distributing meals, making repairs to the facility, serving as porters, and providing medicine, cooking utensils, toiletries, and bedding and clothing. Prisoners also built furniture, fixed fans, and even repaired police cars.[45] These prison workers were often collo-quially called *faxinas*, which is derived from the word *faxineiras*—cleaners.[46]

Writing about Brazil's Carandiru prison, prison doctor Drauzio Varella likewise highlights the crucial role that prisoners play in the basic oper-ation of the facility. He explains, "the cleaners were the backbone of the prison. Without understanding their organization, it is impossible to com-prehend the day-to-day events, from the ordinary moments to the most ex-ceptional ones."[47] The cleaners at Carandiru did more than administer the prison. They governed as well. Varella points out that in Brazil "the cleaners were absolutely fundamental in keeping internal violence in check."[48] They created rules for adjudicating disputes. He reports, "If an inmate didn't honour a debt, his creditor couldn't knife him without first consulting the pavilion leader, who would listen to both parties and set a deadline for the resolution of the situation. Before this time was up, woe was the creditor who dared attack a debtor."[49] One prisoner characterizes a prison leader as "the one who keeps a handle on everything that happens in the pavilion. At that moment, they might be digging a tunnel, planning an escape, and a poorly timed stabbing throws a spanner in the works."[50] As in Brazil's Polinter jail, the leaders at Carandiru did not attain their position because they were simply the physically strongest prisoners. Instead, they were the people who had the respect and the skill needed to maintain order in the pavilions.[51]

In Brazil's Polinter jail, prisoners organized mutual aid efforts. They welcomed new prisoners to the facility, helped them find a place to sleep, and provided essential goods like food, toiletries, medicine, and the prison uniform, which consisted of Bermuda shorts, a white T-shirt, and sandals. Cell representatives often collected items left by departing prisoners (who were expected to leave everything but the clothes they were wearing) and gave them to new or needy prisoners.[52] Prisoners who received family visits were typically better off than prisoners who did not, so it is was expected that they would contribute to a *caixinha* (collection box) for needier prisoners. Prisoners used these funds "to provide a welcome kit for new prisoners and bus fares for freed prisoners, and to buy communal items such as cleaning products, electric ovens, cooking utensils, fans, and televisions."[53] One trustee explains, "It's like a religion inside. Those that have the least, that do not have visits, that are ill, the old, they get priority in everything ... I am obligated, if I have visits, to share what I have with him."[54]

Trustees were also in charge of vital security responsibilities. It was their job to handcuff and escort prisoners through the facility. They ensured that everyone was in their cell when required, that prisoners were not excessively loud, did not curse, and were silent after midnight.[55] Trustees were also responsible for end-of-visit strip searches and the evening *confere*, when they did a head count, cell check, and final lockup.[56] Officials mainly communicated with prisoners through their representatives and rarely entered the cell areas.[57]

To give a sense of the trust and authority vested in prisoner trustees, Sacha Darke recounts what happened after a trustee found another prisoner trying to escape, "One of the head [trustees] took him into the office, where I was sitting, and assaulted him in front of the deputy director."[58] After placing the prisoner in a van for immediate transfer to a higher-security facility, the trustee realized that one of the officers escorting the prisoner had forgotten his rifle. Acting swiftly, "as the van was leaving, the second head [trustee] rushed to the arms cabinet, loaded the rifle and passed it to the officer through the window."[59] Trustees were not trivial participants in prison administration, but instead held a high level of trust and freedom among officials.

When the prison director was not on site, the head trustees were left in charge of the jail, including carrying keys to the cellblock and a cell phone in case they needed to speak to the director.[60] A prisoner-representative explained, "We try to do everything to avoid confusion ... to maintain calm for everyone ... There needs to be one person in charge ... one person to talk for everyone, for everyone to obey."[61] Another Brazilian prisoner explained the importance of prisoner co-governance. He notes, "there needs to be someone who organizes, a leadership for everything not to get messy. Because there needs to be rules and norms for everything to function well ... No one eat someone else's food ... have a shower [at the wrong time] . . . take someone else's cup . . . use lots of swear words . . . fight with one another."[62]

The prison officials' primary concern was that the facility was calm and orderly. As long as the prison wings were quiet, the director was happy for management of the wings to be "their business."[63] The prison director notes that, "I try to help them with everything they need . . . In return they give me discipline."[64] Given that officials administer few tasks, there were no strong visual distinctions between the residents and the keepers.[65] In fact, because of these entangled staff-prisoner relations, Darke reports that "one of the most difficult tasks at the beginning of the study was to establish which of the people working there were prisoners and which were police."[66]

This case study of a Brazilian jail lockup provides several initial insights for my broader analysis. First, although it is only one example, it suggests that prisoner governance can be both important and relatively effective. Second, it illustrates that prisoner governance can arise with prisoners and prison officials working together to co-produce governance specifically. Third, it provides details about how and why prisoners play a pivotal role in daily operations. Prisoners fill an administrative gap left by officials, and they do so with the explicit approval and support of prison officials. Prisoners and staff view trustees as legitimate sources of authority, and both groups hold prisoner-leaders accountable. Finally, this case is consistent with the predictions of the governance theory: when officials govern less, prisoners tend to govern more.

SELF-GOVERNANCE IN A BOLIVIAN PRISON

Bolivia's San Pedro Prison provides an opportunity to examine an extreme setting, where prisoners are responsible for essentially all prison services.[67] Guards restrict access to the facility and prevent escape. Other than that, the prisoners rule. Prisoners participate in a thriving market economy— they even once offered tours to curious visitors. Whereas the Brazilian jail example shows that prisoners can complement official mechanisms, this case shows how self-governance institutions operate in near-total isolation from formal institutions. These two cases, when viewed alongside the cases from Nordic prisons that will be described later, are consistent with the theoretical prediction that lower quality official governance correlates with more extensive extralegal governance.

The city of La Paz, Bolivia, is home to nearly 800,000 residents. It is one of the largest cities in the country and the state capital. Many Bolivians, and not just prisoners, are familiar with extralegal governance and the informal economy. According to estimates from the World Bank, the shadow economy in Bolivia is the largest in the world, equaling nearly 70 percent of official gross domestic product.[68] San Pedro prison sits on the edge of the Plaza de San Pedro in La Paz. Surrounded by large, foreboding walls that lack aesthetic flair or stylistic flourish, it was designed to hold only 250 prisoners, but various estimates put the prison population at between 1,300 and 2,400 prisoners.[69] A handful of guards stand around its main entrance. Women and children bustle about, waiting to visit incarcerated friends and loved ones. From the outside, it reveals nothing special. But on the inside, we see a world where official governance institutions are almost entirely absent. Indeed, the guards milling about outside do little more than regulate who enters and leaves. Inside, both their presence and influence on the activity of the prison is extremely limited.[70] Thus within the prison, according to the National Lawyers Guild, prisoners "have complete freedom of movement," and San Pedro Prison, they conclude, is "essentially self-governed."[71]

The National Lawyers Guild, a public interest association of legal professionals that reported on the extent to which formal governance is lacking, noted that "the prison administration provides no rehabilitation services, no schools, and minimal health care."[72] It is common for prisoners to have to pay for their own medical services and treatment, and as in other Latin American prisons, the prisoners themselves often also provide it.[73] Prison officials make water and electricity available, but prisoners must pay for their use at the end of their sentences.[74] Members of staff provide a minimal amount of low-quality food on which prisoners can subsist. According to the guild "although the prison provides a gruel-like soup and bread twice a day (and meat twice a week), prisoners report that it tastes bad and causes ulcers and hepatitis."[75] The report notes that the kitchen was filthy. Quite understandably, prisoners seek out alternatives to the gruel, and those who can afford to do so either cook or purchase their own food. Other organizations that have visited the facility come to a similar conclusion about the operation and state of the prison.[76]

The Real Estate Market and Housing Associations

When a new prisoner first enters San Pedro, a reception committee comprised of prisoners will often greet him. The Inter-American Commission on Human Rights explains that the group consists of volunteers who protect the "newcomer from abuse by other prisoners, and advise him of the rules he must respect within the prison, and the rights he will enjoy. The committee works with the newcomer to find him lodging."[77] Religious and charitable organizations also help new arrivals by providing information, money, clothes, antibiotics, and food.[78]

One of the primary governance mechanisms that prisoners rely on is provided by the democratically elected representatives of each of the eight different housing sections within the prison.[79] The prison lacks the homogenous tiers, cells, and pods that exist in newly built U.S. prisons. Instead, prisoners live in a mixture of styles of accommodation and housing. When a new prisoner arrives, he must purchase or rent his own cell. If he cannot, he will end up sleeping on the ground in a corridor or courtyard.[80] Housing sections have committees responsible for resolving disputes and disciplining residents and sometimes several other formal positions, including a representative, treasurer, disciplinary secretary, culture and education secretary, sports secretary, and health secretary. Elections determine who serves on these committees. To be eligible for such a role, the person must have resided in the prison for at least six months, have an unmortgaged cell, and no debt.[81] Note that while these are extralegal institutions, they are also highly formal.

The quality of housing varies significantly within the prison. According to the National Lawyers Guild and the U.S. Department of State, housing prices also vary widely.[82] The least desirable, inexpensive housing consists of bare six-by-nine-foot rooms with no amenities.[83] Some small cells have no ventilation, light, or bed, and some crowded cells require people to sleep sitting up on the floor.[84] The most expensive housing, by contrast, can include multi-story apartments, with internet access and other modern amenities.[85] One prisoner built a second floor to his cell and purchased a piano.[86] Many prisoners have household appliances, such as televisions, stoves, refrigerators, and microwaves.[87]

As in real estate markets on the outside, some prisoners rent and others buy. By purchasing a cell, the prisoner also buys the right to sell it to another prisoner. To do so, an owner will sometimes hire an agent to advertise and negotiate the exchange. Freelance real estate agents work on a commission basis. They advertise available units on restaurant menus and bulletin boards in each housing section.[88] Alternatively, an owner may simply place a "for sale" sign on the unit to indicate its availability.[89] When new prisoners arrive at the prison, officials also offer to sell them a place to live.[90] However, prisoners report that officials charge much more than the market rate within the prison, perhaps as much as 50 percent more than if the cell were purchased from another prisoner.[91] Given that new prisoners are less likely to be knowledgeable about the prison real estate market and officials control the initial access to it, it makes sense that they would attempt to exploit the asymmetric information and charge higher rates.

Purchasing a unit requires payment of a non-refundable fee to the housing section, typically 20 to 25 percent of the purchase price.[92] The fee is supposed to "cover section expenses such as maintenance, administration, cleaning, renovations and the occasional social event such as the Prisoners' Day party every September, when the section delegates cooked a barbecue and hired a band for the inmates."[93] Residents rarely refuse membership to a particular housing section, especially if a prisoner pays the fee and a cell is available.[94] But the more expensive housing sections sometimes require a recommendation in support of an applicant. Some housing sections also have rules such as prohibitions on drug use, the violation of which can result in expulsion.[95]

A simple record-keeping procedure documents the legitimacy of claims to a particular unit. Each cell owner has a property title that notes the cell number, where in the prison it is located, a description of the unit, the name of the previous resident or owner, and the purchase price.[96] The owner retains the original title, but many people also give a copy of the title to the housing section registrar. To transfer a title, prisoners sign a purchase contract in the presence of the housing section delegate, who is responsible for verifying the transaction, stamping the contract with the section's official seal, and collecting the section fee. A witness will also verify the exchange and sign the purchase contract. As the end of a prisoner's sentence approaches, an owner can sell the unit to a newly arriving prisoner or a current resident of the prison.

Some prisoners cannot afford to purchase a cell and must rent part of another prisoner's cell or an entire cell from someone who owns multiple properties. One prisoner explains "I can't afford to buy, so I rent it for 80 bolivianos [about $12] a month. I am awaiting trial. I could be here another three months or two years—nobody knows. I am accused of drug trafficking. I have this cell to myself—it has a kitchenette and a tiny window to see the sun, so I guess it's not that bad."[97] The poorest residents are allowed to live in some housing sections in exchange for performing tasks like cleaning the bathrooms and making repairs.[98] The most impoverished prisoners sleep outside, exposed to the elements and vulnerable to victimization by other prisoners.

Buying or renting a cell provides more than just a place to sleep. Prisoners rely on their cells as a source of protection and to provide a degree of autonomy, privacy, and security in an environment where these are otherwise lacking. The National Lawyers Guild reports that inside San Pedro, the "living units are unlike cells in that there are no bars. If there are locks on the doors, the keys are kept by the prisoner who can lock his unit at any time."[99] As Varella likewise explains, at Brazil's Carandiru prison, "some prisoners would weld a metal ring to the inside of their door, another to the doorjamb and padlock them together to lock themselves in."[100]

Buying real estate also provides access to a community and a particular type of neighbor. The nicer housing sections function much like gated communities do, restricting access for daily visitors.[101] During the day, prisoners can move unrestricted throughout most housing sections, but at night, several of the nicer sections exclude non-residents.[102] The cheaper housing sections, perhaps not surprisingly, do not have gates to keep non-residents out; these areas are of lower quality and cleanliness and many of their residents use drugs. Violence within the prison, according to one resident, clusters in the poorer housing areas. He reports that this is "where all the stabbings occur ... [but] it's perfectly safe during the day. At night is when you have to look out."[103]

The National Lawyers Guild describes how each of these communities tends to operate: "each section has the feel of a neighborhood or even a small village with its own courtyard plaza and shops. The committee in charge of each section manages the section, repairing the sidewalks or painting the walls. Each '*directiva*' sets an assessment charge for prisoners in the section and each committee is responsible for its own budget. Inmates pay for all services."[104] Purchasing a cell provides access to that section's amenities, which in some cases includes billiard tables and inter-sectional soccer tournaments.[105] Many prisoners enjoy gambling on the outcomes of these tournaments, and section leaders have offered skilled players nice cells as a way to recruit the best players and improve their chances of victory.[106] The Coca-Cola Company sponsored some of these sports teams and provided tables, chairs, and umbrellas to the housing section.[107] The prison is also open in a political sense: Bolivian prisoners can vote while incarcerated. Leopoldo Fernández, a politician charged with several serious crimes, ran for vice president while incarcerated at San Pedro.[108] He came in second place, with 27 percent of the votes.

A market for goods and services of all kinds also thrives inside the walls of San Pedro, and it does so out in the open instead of covertly. There is no need to conceal it from officials. The freedom to exchange has several positive effects. An entrepreneur can openly advertise his wares without fear of alerting officials. Advertisements for goods and services are displayed in the courtyards, providing information about what is available. Building permanent structures, accumulating an inventory, or making capital investments is a safer bet when the guards are unlikely to confiscate or destroy them.

The forces of supply and demand operate within the prison walls. One prisoner reports that "everything [is] about money. And I mean *everything.*"[109] He goes on to explain that the prison "apart from being a social microcosm, is also a microeconomy that operates under basic capitalist principles. In fact, it's probably more efficient than the whole Bolivian national economy."[110] Prisoners cannot rely on prison officials "for anything, not even to maintain the buildings, so everything that needed to be done or bought was done or bought by the prisoners themselves. And because of this, anyone who wasn't independently wealthy had to have a job."[111] In addition, for a small fee, people from the outside can bring in a variety of goods and services to sell to prisoners.[112]

Prisoners operate grocery stores, restaurants, food stalls, barbershops, butcher shops, carpentry services, and at least one copying center.[113] One prisoner explains, "not everyone likes the food in the canteen, so we sell snacks and sandwiches here for inmates and for their families when they come to visit . . . The chorizo sandwich with tomato and salad costs three bolivianos . . . With the money I make, I pay my rent and keep a few bolivianos for cigarettes."[114] The prison's economy includes cooks, restaurateurs, painters, carpenters, electricians, accountants, and doctors.[115] Even those residents who lack experience with a specific trade or do not possess a specialized skill can perform simple services for a fee, such as shining shoes, serving as couriers, delivering food, and relaying messages. In short, one prisoner explains, "basically, anything you wanted done or anything you wanted to buy, you could, and if they didn't have it, someone could get it in for you for a small commission."[116]

Conflict Resolution and Civil Society

Though prisoners benefit from access to market opportunities, life in the prison is far from perfect. As in many other prisons, the captives at San Pedro do not tolerate the presence of sex offenders.[117] For example, in one instance a group of prisoners threw a sex offender into a pit and beat him to death.[118] A 2006 report from the U.S. Department of State reports, "Several deaths due to violence in prisons occurred during the year, including the death of a child molester/rapist who was killed by his fellow inmates."[119] Other tragic and disturbing acts of violence have occurred as well. In 1997, for instance, a prisoner raped and murdered a young girl during a New Year's Eve celebration.[120] Prisoners report that violence is relatively rare during the day, but that at night altercations become more frequent. Drug use, which is rampant among some prisoners, often leads to knife fights.[121] According to one observer, the most common reason that stabbings occur is drug users' failure to pay debts to prison drug dealers. However, he observes, "on the whole, [the prison is] fairly ordered."[122]

One way of assessing the degree of order in the prison is to examine the experience of one of its potentially most vulnerable populations: the women and children who choose to live there. According to Article 26 of Bolivia's Law on the Execution of Criminal Sentences, children under the age of six may live with their fathers in the prison; officials have not prevented either older children or wives from joining their families behind bars.[123] According to José Orias, a prison official, "It's a custom that was permitted and no authority wanted to put a stop to it. The previous administrations wanted to ingratiate themselves to the prisoners rather than enforce the law."[124] As a result, entire families now live in San Pedro, and spouses and children can enter and leave the prison (apparently for a small fee paid to the guards) during the day.[125] One journalist writing about these families explains, "the arrangement provides a type of social security that the inmates' immediate families don't get from either their extended families or the state. Without the father working, women must find jobs, not act as caretakers . . . When whole families move in it's often for moral support, to keep the family together, and because, in many instances, they have nowhere else to go."[126] This phenomenon is not unique to Bolivia. One observer of Mexican prisons reports that "it is common for children to be seen running and playing throughout Mexican prisons."[127]

In 2013, there were about 2,100 children living in Bolivian prisons. At San Pedro, there was a total of 236 children, 93 girls and 143 boys.[128] Around Christmas, social workers report that there is an influx of children because "during vacation, they all come to visit an uncle or a brother."[129] One child living in the prison remarks, "I like it here . . . I have friends, there are lots of fruits and my dad's here."[130] A ten year old warns that in the prison, "there are thieves, rapists, murderers . . . In the mornings they're high on drugs, at night sometimes they steal and the young men fight."[131]

Nevertheless, he said, they also "have everything here, free lunches, free bread ... We play soccer, jump into the pool."[132]

Prisoners created a parent's association to assist in caring and providing for the prison's children. The president of the association admits that it is not necessarily the best environment to raise a child because some prisoners abuse drugs and swear, but overall, he says that those people are a minority and their influence is not substantial. In addition to the housing section representatives, the parent's association holds prisoners accountable for their actions when it affects the children. The parent's association president comments that "If anything happens [to the children], we call a meeting, and [the prisoner responsible is] immediately punished ... It is more secure in here than out there."[133] The community forbids prisoners from fighting in the presence of children. Rusty Young, who lived in San Pedro prison, explains that he saw this rule in action. If a fight takes place and children are in the area, the prisoners must stop fighting immediately.[134] He says, "That's one of the most important rules. I saw it happen myself. Mid-fight, they stopped, held their positions when a child went past, then continued belting each other when the child had passed."[135]

One woman, Rosy, has lived in the prison for four years with her five-year-old daughter. After her husband's incarceration for assault, she felt she could not afford to pay the rent and utilities on the outside. "Necessity obligated us," she reflects, "because outside there are so many expenses, and it's not possible to get by alone."[136] She explains, "In the beginning I was afraid. I thought that anything could happen here, but the days went by."[137] The parents in San Pedro strive to protect and care for their children. She says, "everything depends on the parents, how we organise to protect and take care of the children. Outside it's the same."[138] The family lives in a small cell, which cost them about $785 to purchase. Rosy earns about $100 a month making and selling food to prisoners and visitors. Their child, who has lived in the prison for nearly her entire life, says it is fun because she has many friends and can spend time with her father. Rosy notes that the prison is dangerous, but she says that danger is not limited to prison. She observes, "anywhere that you might trust [someone around your child], anything can happen, even within a family."[139]

Despite parents' desire to protect their children, horrific crimes have sometimes taken place. According to Bolivian Prison Director General Ramiro Llanos, in 2013 a 12-year-old girl who was living in the prison approached authorities and reported that her father, uncle, and godfather had raped her for more than four years, and that she was now pregnant.[140] Llanos explains, "If a child is with his father, there's a dual purpose—the child stays close and the child helps work. Sometimes, they use the kids to bring in drugs or alcohol so the children live in environments that harm them . . . There are many cases of fathers raising their daughters in San Pedro and after the father is released, the girls will stay in jail or act as prostitutes."[141]

While the cases of Brazil and Bolivia show that co-governing and self-governing regimes can work, this does not imply that this is the ideal institutional outcome. Some of San Pedro's residents are still incredibly poor, with little food, healthcare, and sometimes no accommodation. Some prisoners become addicted to drugs. The rule of law does not exist for sex offenders, who are sometimes subject to mob justice. The accountability within the system is also limited. Prisoners have recourse to housing section leaders for disputes with other residents, but beyond that, there are few options. For those who can afford it, there is some choice among competing housing sections, so if one section becomes irresponsible or abusive, there is some opportunity for exit. However, moving might be prohibitively costly. For prisoners of limited means, the freedom to choose does not manifest in practice.

In an ideal world, perhaps well-intentioned staff would operate Latin American prisons and prisoners would have access to the resources needed to live safe, healthy, and secure lives while incarcerated. Nevertheless, to assume that this is the relevant alternative institutional regime would be a mistake. We must compare the real world experience with the actual alternatives faced, rather than with some ideal form of prison organization.[142] The most relevant alternative to self-governance in San Pedro is the type of governance provided in some other Latin American prisons. As I have argued, many of these facilities are plagued with overcrowding, health risks, insufficient food, limited movement, and little access to fresh air. Prisoners at San Pedro also fare better than other prisoners in at least one way: prison staff do not subject prisoners to frequent abuse and outright torture.[143]

CONCLUSION

In San Pedro prison, governance emerges in the political realm (in the form of housing associations), in the commercial realm (markets and exchange with the outside world), and in civil society (as with the parent's association). These mechanisms have a variety of positive effects. Because prisoners can earn money engaging in productive economic activity, they have less incentive to steal from, abuse, and prey on others. As the return to productive activity increases, prisoners do more of it. Likewise, the ability to own and modify property creates several positive incentives. First, because prisoners are residual claimants, they capture the benefits of improvements to their cell and their housing section. Unlike U.S. prisons, where prisoners have no ownership over their cell and no market for them exists, San Pedro prisoners can better themselves by bettering their environment. If they make additions or renovations that other people value, then they profit from doing so. Likewise, if they devise better rules to govern their housing section, then their property will be worth more. A second benefit of home ownership is that it provides prisoners a level of control and autonomy over their lives. The ability to lock one's door offers security for a person and his or her property. This allows them to protect and enjoy the resources accumulated through economic activity. This in turn makes prisoners more willing to engage in commercial activity.

The two case studies examined in this chapter provide evidence in support of several key claims of the governance theory. First, they show that in the absence of official governance, prisoners can govern. The aggregate data (see Table 2.1) suggests that Latin American prisons provide relatively low-quality governance, and in prisons across the continent, there is a proliferation of extralegal governance institutions. The case studies from Brazil and Bolivia further support this conclusion and provide details about the specific ways in which prisoners govern. Second, San Pedro prison provides a useful contrast between self-governing and co-governing regimes. While in the Brazilian jail, prisoners worked with officials; at San Pedro, the guards are not even present within the perimeter of the prison. In the Brazilian jail, prisoners are completing tasks assigned "from above." In San Pedro, prisoners' actions are emerging "from below" in response to the needs and problems that prisoners face.

A third insight from these case studies is that they reveal that there are many different institutional responses to the lack of official governance, including in the forms of housing committees, trustees, markets, and parent's associations. It is unlikely that there is a "one size fits all" response to a lack of state governance. Instead of a single institution carrying out a wide range of activities, prisoners tailor self-governance institutions to serve specific needs. There is also a significant degree of overlap and competition between them.[144] For example, prisoners can choose from several different housing sections and from many different food vendors. The ability to choose who provides a particular service sparks competition that can give suppliers an incentive to provide better service.

The governance theory predicts that if staff and resources were provided in abundance, there would be far less investment in extralegal governance institutions. The most useful way to test this would be to find a Bolivian prison that transitioned from offering low-quality official governance to high-quality official governance. The theory predicts that prisoners would invest far less in extralegal governance institutions. Unfortunately, I do not know of a prison that has experienced such a dramatic change. Nevertheless, the general pattern in the United States is consistent with this prediction. Trustee positions like those found in the Brazilian jail were once more common in the United States, but as prisons and the corrections profession have modernized, they have mostly disappeared.[145] In the absence of similar cases in Latin America, in the next chapter I will compare across cases by looking at prisons in Nordic countries, where the quality of official governance is far higher than in the typical Latin American prison and where extralegal institutions are far less important.

When Officials Govern

Nordic Exceptionalism

The punishment is the restriction of liberty; no other rights
have been removed by the sentencing court . . . life inside
will resemble life outside as much as possible.

Principle of the Norwegian Correctional Service[1]

I n 2008, criminologist John Pratt sparked a debate among prison scholars
by arguing that Nordic prison systems are exceptional compared to
the world's other prison systems.[2] Based on field visits to 16 facilities in
Finland, Norway, and Sweden, he argued that they are superior in many
ways: smaller prisons, more interaction between prisoners and staff, better
amenities, more programing, more open prisons, less militarized culture
and practice, and a greater focus on rehabilitation than on punishment.[3]
These are precisely the types of differences that suggest that the quality of

official governance is far better in Nordic prison systems than in the cases from Latin American prisons.[4]

This makes Nordic prison systems a useful case for testing the governance theory. The theory predicts that extralegal governance institutions in these prisons will be far more limited and have far less influence. This chapter provides evidence showing that prisoners in Nordic facilities rely on decentralized systems of norms to govern societal interactions. In contrast to the Latin American prisons discussed in chapter 2, Nordic prisoners spend little time running the daily operation of the prison, engaging in extensive economic exchange, or playing a prominent role in governing social and economic affairs. Combined with the aggregate data and case study evidence in the previous chapter, the data on Nordic prison systems provides further evidence that there is a negative relationship between the quality of official institutions and the importance of extralegal institutions.

Table 3.1 provides country-level data that supports several claims about the superiority of official governance in Nordic prisons. Nordic countries hold an average of only about 3,100 prisoners total, and their rates of prison use are some of the lowest in the developed world, ranging from a high of 59 prisoners per 100,000 residents in Denmark to a low of 37 per 100,000 residents in Iceland. With the slight exception of Finland (105 percent occupancy rate), the prison systems are not overcrowded. On average, they house 69 people per prison facility. There is roughly one prisoner per member of staff.

While there is variation across facilities, even the largest prisons in the region are small by U.S. standards. For example, the typical Californian prison holds more than 3,000 prisoners. By contrast, the largest prisons in Sweden and Norway hold between 350 and 400 prisoners, and most Nordic prisons are designed to hold far fewer.[5] Scholars at the Correctional Service of Norway Staff Academy argue that the optimal prison size in Scandinavian countries is only 250 prisoners.[6] In practice, Norwegian prisons often house far fewer: about 30 percent of prisons hold fewer than 30 prisoners, and only five facilities hold between 51 and 100 prisoners.[7] The smallest Norwegian prison housed only 12 prisoners and was staffed by 19 employees.[8]

Table 3.1 Descriptive Statistics of Nordic Prison Systems

	Prison Population[a]	Prison Use Rate (per 100,000)[a]	Occupancy Rate[a]	Number of Facilities[a]	Average Population per Facility	Prison Staff[b]	Prisoners per Staff
Denmark	3,408	59	96%	57	60	3,326	1.0
Finland	3,174	57	105%	26	122	2,336	1.3
Iceland	124	37	87%	5	25	104	1.1
Norway	3,874	74	89%	54	72	3,509	1.1
Sweden	5,245	53	84%	79	66	7,150	0.7

a. World Prison Brief 2018.
b. United Nations Office on Drugs and Crime: Data are from 2015 or the most recent estimate available.

Officials can govern small prisons more easily. In small facilities, a closer relationship can develop between officers and prisoners.[9] Smaller prisons tend to be less stressful.[10] Prison officials can more easily watch prisoners.[11] Smaller prisons often have less administrative hierarchy, so that information and decisions flow more easily through the hierarchy, leading to greater responsiveness to prisoner needs.[12] Small prisons also make it easier for prisoners to observe quality leadership in action and for staff to watch and learn from effective leaders.[13] Large prisons, on the contrary, tend to require more regimentation and take on an assembly line quality.[14]

In addition, small prisons might be more orderly for reasons not directly tied to staff leadership or effectiveness. For instance, living among fewer people means there are simply fewer people with whom to have disagreements and conflicts. Less overcrowding suggests prisoners have more opportunities for privacy and autonomy. There is often less uncertainty and more stability in social systems that are more intimate. Small facilities allow people to develop personal relationships with others, and having better knowledge of other people can reduce conflict.[15] These are all reasons for why we should expect small prison populations to be governed well (especially when officials have significant resources) and therefore to predict that extralegal institutions will be less important.

Survey responses from prisoners held in 32 higher security Norwegian prisons supports these claims. The survey found that prisoners in small prisons (defined as holding fewer than 50 prisoners) have more positive perceptions of prison life than respondents do in medium (50–100 prisoners) and large prisons (more than 100 prisoners).[16] Prisoners in small prisons more often reported that they had good relationships with front-line staff. In medium and large facilities, prisoners generally had negative comments about staff. Smaller prisons also scored better on questions about treatment by senior management, attitudes toward senior management, and safety, control, and security.[17]

The Nordic countries are also known for their "open" prisons in which prisoners have significant autonomy and freedom in their daily movements and activities.[18] In open prisons, officials reduce the visual displays of imprisonment, opting for less intimidating and less visible barriers.[19] Open prisons often lack barbed wire fences and solid walls with gun towers.[20] Some prisons have no fences at all.[21] They often have common rooms, televisions, and cooking facilities.[22] Prisoners are allowed to use the grounds anytime during the day.[23] In the lowest security facilities, prisoners can leave the facility to shop in local stores.[24] One scholar reports that in these low-security facilities, prisoners have a shared housing area that includes "a clean, bright communal kitchen. Men cook together in order to save money. A bus takes them to a grocery where local citizens wait outside while the men shop."[25]

Nevertheless, many Nordic prisons look more similar to prisons in other Western countries: "closed" prisons that hold people with higher security risks. They are more likely to have high walls topped with barbed wire, security gates monitored by officers, and corridors with locked doors and video security surveillance.[26] While open prisons attract a great deal of attention, closed prisons actually hold a large proportion of prisoners. For example, in Norway, close to two-thirds of prisoners live in closed prisons.[27]

As noted in Table 3.1, Nordic prisons have a much smaller proportion of prisoners to members of staff, about one prisoner for every staff member. These jobs attract high-quality employees, and in Finland and Norway, it is common for there to be an excess supply of applicants.[28] Working in corrections is a more attractive career than it is in many other countries.[29] The fact that students sometimes work as prison officers suggests that the environment in Nordic prisons is more relaxed than that in many other prisons and the work is socially acceptable.[30] Many Nordic prison officers have university and vocational education. For example, about 20 percent of staff in Swedish men's prisons have university degrees[31] and at the beginning of employment, staff members participate in a 20-week in-service training program and take 10-week university courses on sociology and social psychology.[32] In Norway, prison officers receive two years of training at full salary and nearly all have tertiary educational qualifications.[33] By comparison, California correctional officer training lasts 12 weeks and requires only a high-school diploma.[34]

Officer attire can also reveal something about a prison regime's philosophy and approach.[35] The relaxed uniforms worn by many Nordic officers lack the military style of staff uniforms found in many U.S. prisons.[36] This reflects prison authorities' explicit emphasis on the importance of rehabilitation. For instance, a Norwegian fact sheet states that "the punishment is the restriction of liberty; no other rights have been removed ... During the serving of a sentence, life inside will resemble life outside as much as possible ... Progression through a sentence should be aimed as much as possible at returning to the community. The more closed a system is, the harder it will be to return to freedom."[37] According to the Finnish Sentences Enforcement Act of 2002, "punishment is a mere loss of liberty. The enforcement of the sentence must be organized so that the sentence is only loss of liberty."[38]

Nordic prisons also differ from Latin American prisons by offering significantly better material conditions. The quality and availability of food significantly exceeds that provided by officials in Latin America.[39] These facilities tend to lack the "prison smell" commonly found in prisons (which arises for a variety of reasons, including personal hygiene, cigarette smoke, and lack of ventilation).[40] Prisoners can typically wear their own clothes rather than prison uniforms.[41] At Norway's largest prison, residents have access to a gym and can take spinning classes.[42] Some Nordic prisons also have solarium facilities so that prisoners with little access to sunlight do not suffer vitamin D deficiencies.[43] Living conditions reflect conditions on the outside as much as possible.[44]

Compared to many prisons across Latin America, Nordic prisons tend to operate extremely differently in terms of size, scope, services, and amenities.[45] To use Nordic prisons as a test of the governance theory, it is important to establish that they provide higher-quality official governance institutions than Latin American prisons do. The theory predicts that when prisoners have access to better material resources, educational and vocational activities, a larger number of better-trained staff members, small prisons, and clean and sanitary living conditions, they will invest less time, energy, and resources in extralegal governance mechanisms. If Nordic prisons were home to significant extralegal governance institutions, then this would be evidence against my theory. However, the evidence provided here suggests that in the face of high-quality official governance institutions prisoners do not invest significantly in producing extralegal governance.

DECENTRALIZED GOVERNANCE IN A
NORWEGIAN PRISON

Material exceptionalism in Nordic prisons does not eliminate social conflict. In any community—and perhaps especially within a community
that is forced to live together—problems will arise. Yet, there is little evidence that prisoners create and maintain centralized extralegal governance
institutions. In particular, with the possible exception of Denmark, these
prison regimes are not home to prison gangs like those found in Brazil or
California.[46] Writing in 1985, for instance, the director of prison research in
the Norwegian Ministry of Justice concludes, "Scandinavian prison officials
do not have to contend with the violence of organized ethnic gangs."[47]

Instead, social order tends to be based on decentralized, loose-knit
affiliations, usually centered on criminal social networks, personal interests,
age, and attitude toward incarceration.[48] These relationships provide safety
and a source of information about the happenings and operation of the
prison. In *Power and Resistance in Prison*, Thomas Ugelvik documents the
norms governing interactions among prisoners at a maximum-security
prison in Norway.[49] This is a useful case to study for several reasons. First,
it is the largest prison in the country, holding about 400 male prisoners
(about 10 percent of the country's total prison population).[50] While small
by U.S. standards, it is large by Nordic standards. To the extent that larger
prisons are more difficult to manage, conflict is more likely to occur in this
facility. Second, many of the remand prisoners (those held prior to trial
or plea) have been incarcerated for a relatively long time because they
are charged with serious crimes, such as murder, rape, and major drug
trafficking.[51] If convicted, they will receive sentences far longer than the average. These men are not facing minor criminal charges. Third, since these
prisoners come from the relatively multi-cultural city of Oslo, they tend
to be more ethnically diverse than the population of convicted prisoners
in general. In fact, there were prisoners from 54 different countries held
in this prison at the time of the study.[52] Of Norwegian remand prisoners,
60 percent are foreign nationals.[53] We might expect that larger populations
of diverse people facing uncertain futures will experience more conflict. If

we are going to observe a need for more centralized extralegal governance in a Nordic prison, it seems likely that it would be in this one.

What this study finds, however, is that conflict is neither frequent nor especially violent. In fact, the key mechanism for avoiding and resolving conflict between prisoners is highly decentralized and does not usually involve physical violence. Prisoners rely almost entirely on ostracism and shunning, which they typically use for three reasons.[54] First, prisoners view some people as genuinely evil or dangerous. These people are seen to have violated a basic moral code, so other prisoners avoid interacting with them.[55] Second, prisoners shun those who do not adapt well to prison. Some people are overly nervous, complain about their situations excessively, or act pitifully.[56] A common example of this is prisoners with a substance use disorder. Prisoners view them as slaves to the drug, and they disparage those with the most serious and troubling addictions as "junkies."[57]

Third, prisoners ostracize those who for a variety of reasons have low social standing. At the top of the prison social hierarchy are "real" or "proper" prisoners.[58] Those who stick to their values and stand strong in the face of adversity. Prisoners reside lower in the social hierarchy for several reasons. Prisoners often view young prisoners as childish and immature.[59] They do not yet know how to "do time" and are a source of noisiness and chaos, which other prisoners do not appreciate.[60] Prisoners also view sex offenders negatively. However, unlike in many other prisons, sex offenders are not subject to systematic acts of serious violence.[61] One prisoner describes the ostracism of a prisoner who was convicted of a sexual offense: "We found out what he is in for, that he got six years the day before, and then suddenly he is just sitting there, smiling. No one will talk to him; everyone turned their back on him."[62] This type of ostracism is normal and routine.[63] Part of the reason why violence is less common is that prisoners know that officials are watching. One prisoner says, "Paedophiles and rapists should do their time alone, and they should do long stretches. Really long. I mean, you can't hurt him physically, not in here, the officers are guarding him now. But I will hurt him in other ways."[64]

Informants occupy a low place in the social hierarchy.[65] One prisoner who was betrayed explains that he did not seek revenge against the informant even though they lived in the same housing unit. He feared that officials would know it was him and that it would negatively affect his trial and sentencing. He explains, "If anything happens to him, then, of course, they will come straight to me. I wouldn't do it, because I don't want to ruin things for myself . . . I don't want to ruin my case. I don't need to do more time than I'm going to get. But as soon as my sentence is final, then fuck it."[66]

This study provides evidence on several aspects of the governance theory. As the theory predicts, because of both the higher quality of official governance and the relatively small population, prisoners do not create centralized extralegal governance institutions. In the context of close, personal relationships, prisoners use decentralized mechanisms. There is a social hierarchy based on norms of appropriate conduct, and people's standing and esteem depends on their adherence to it. No single person or group is in charge of the prisoner society. Prisoners do not rely on written rules and regulations. There is nothing like the committees that play such a crucial role in San Pedro. Social control is enforced with ostracism and shaming, which prisoners view to be both important and effective. Small prison populations make these mechanisms powerful, and they are cheap, requiring few resources, organization, or collaboration. The counterfactual implication is that if we shipped Nordic prisoners to San Pedro, they would soon invest in many of the same types of extralegal institutions that currently exist there. Likewise, if we transferred Bolivian prisoners to this Norwegian prison, they would not reproduce many of the same organizations and institutions that they currently use.

A CULTURE OF SHARING DRUGS IN PRISON

An alternative explanation for the limited use of extralegal governance institutions might be that there is no underground economy that needs governance. To some extent this is true because Nordic prisons provide significantly better material resources. However, this is not true of contraband, which by definition, is illicit and not legitimately governed by officials. Moreover, drug use is common in Nordic prisons. About 60 percent of prisoners in Norway reported having used drugs in prison in the previous month of incarceration, and perhaps as many as half of the prison population are thought to have a serious drug problem.[67] In Denmark, about 10 percent of daily mandatory random drug tests are positive for illegal drugs.[68] An illicit sphere exists and needs to be governed in some way. The governance theory predicts that small populations of people with dense social networks will use decentralized mechanisms to do so.

In general, it is difficult to stop illicit substance use in prison. Tests designed to detect and deter drug use are not reliable enough to stop consumption all together. Prisoners might know when tests will be administered and find ways to avoid or sabotage the test. Moreover, some drugs leave the body more quickly than others do. In a perverse twist, increasing the frequency of tests can encourage prisoners to switch to harder drugs. For instance, marijuana is detectable in the body for up to a month after use, while heroin is detectable for only a few days. One study of Danish prisons found that following the introduction of mandatory urine tests, some prisoners stopped smoking marijuana and turned to heroin.[69] If officials cannot suppress the use of illegal substances, then prisoners need ways to govern its distribution and use.

In many prisons, when there is a demand for drugs, an illicit market arises that is coordinated by the laws of supply and demand. Residents of Latin American prisons speak of market forces driving the prison economy.[70] One of the earliest ethnographic studies on prison social order, by economist Richard A. Radford, revolves around the dynamics and equilibrium of the prison economy. A captive in a World War II prisoner of war camp, he observed that "a market came into spontaneous operation, and prices were fixed by the operation of supply and demand."[71] However, it would be a mistake to conclude that markets will always govern a prison's underground economy. A fascinating study of drug use in one Norwegian prison reveals that this common method of accessing and distributing drugs is not universal. Sociologist Kristian Mjåland's research reveals a unique way in which prisoners can get drugs without using markets.

Based on observations and interviews over eight months at Norway's Kollen prison, Mjåland finds that prisoners obtain illicit substances through reciprocal sharing arrangements with other prisoners, not market exchanges. Instead, prisoners engage in "a culture of sharing." In this system, when a prisoner obtains illicit substances he shares some of it with others, who in turn, share with him in the future. One prisoner explains that sharing is guided by norms of reciprocity, noting, "you have to give in order to get."[72] The system is open and available for any other prisoner, as long as he reciprocates past sharing.[73] Prisoners at the top of the hierarchy might get the first taste, but in general, this system has a striking degree of inclusiveness.[74] Prisoners sometimes punish the failure to share with violence or the threat of violence, but the main punishments were ostracism, shamming, and losing others' trust.[75]

This sharing system lacks many of the classic characteristics of a market economy. It does not have market-generated money prices and prisoners do not have to pay to participate.[76] Prisoners also do not go into debt to access drugs—a common source of conflict in many prisons. One prisoner explains, "you can't get into debt here, it's *impossible*, that would never happen. If anybody says so, it's nonsense, I have never heard of it."[77] Whereas past studies have suggested that markets will emerge spontaneously, that is not the case here.

Prisoners suggest two possible explanations for why they rely on sharing drugs rather than trading them. First, prisoners share for purely instrumental reasons. One prisoner says that a person "helps those who are able to get drugs for themselves. In order to always have it. So it comes back to you."[78] Sharing among those who will have access to drugs in the future increases a person's access to drugs. This is a good reason to participate, but it does not explain why prisoners in so many other facilities find markets more effective and reliable for maintaining access to drugs. Second, ethical reasons motivate some prisoners to share. One prisoner says, "it's also a kind of duty ... That people expect you to do it because they would have."[79] What is different about this situation that encourages prisoner to be more generous and to work within a culture of sharing?

To understand this, it is helpful to think about the benefits that we typically believe markets provide.[80] Profits reward people for effort and risk-taking. Higher prices elicit greater supply and discourage demand. Prices signal where resources are more highly valued and provide an incentive for people to reallocate resources accordingly. Voluntary exchanges increase wealth because both parties exchange something they value less for something they value more. Money frees us from the inefficiency of barter. If these problems are not present, then nonmarket alternatives may be a more effective way to accomplish social coordination over the use of resources.[81] This is especially true when relying on decentralized enforcement is easy and effective.

There are several reasons why market exchange does not offer significant benefits to this prisoner community. First, most of the illicit substances are not smuggled in from the outside. Instead, staff members are the major source of drugs. The facility provides two types of drugs (buprenorphine and benzodiazepine) to residents as part of an opioid treatment program. Prisoners receive treatment if they were enrolled in such a program prior to incarceration.[82] Many prisoners who are not enrolled in the treatment regime have a desire for opioids because they deliver a calming high and they are not as easily detected by drug tests as other substances are.[83]

Since officials indirectly provide the substance—which was reported to be dispensed daily with a "very stable" stream—higher prices are not needed to increase the quantity supplied.[84] Officials deliver the opioid maintenance treatment in a highly controlled setting. Two members of staff oversee the process, which involves bringing in one or two prisoners to a medical room, breaking the tablets into smaller pieces and placing them under the prisoner's tongue to dissolve. The process takes about 10 minutes.[85] Prisoners must drink water before and after they receive the pills, and a staff member inspects the person's mouth afterwards to ensure he has consumed the pills. Nevertheless, a substantial number of prisoners are able to retain the tablets undissolved and distribute them back on the prison wings.[86]

Interestingly, officials also give large doses of the drugs. Prisoners believe that they receive excessive dosages. Even though one 8mg tablet of buprenorphine can allegedly affect up to thirty people, staff give an average daily dose of 18mg to residents.[87] Many of the prisoners, Mjåland reports, "claimed that their doses were far too high, and that they easily could take less buprenorphine without suffering withdrawal symptoms, especially if they also snorted some of the buprenorphine they hid away, or if they took a full dose every other day."[88]

After a prisoner has successfully smuggled some of the drug back to the housing area, he could simply store the excess dose for future use. However, prisoners felt that storage was dangerous because of the risk of discovery by officials.[89] High storage costs create an incentive for a prisoner to transfer the drug to someone who would consume it right away. While in most other prisons this would lead to an economic exchange, here prisoners turn to sharing.

Prisoners at Kollen prison can rely on sharing more easily than prisoners in other prisons because it is easier for them to enforce norms. Within the housing areas for those in the treatment program, there are 10 cells, usually holding between 20 and 30 people, and a shared kitchen.[90] The small population and open living arrangement makes it easy for residents to see who gets treatment and to keep track of who shares and who does not. Prisoners can communicate to other people in the unit who fails to share. Moreover, many of the prisoners knew each other outside of prison as part of the local drug scene or from previous incarceration experiences.[91] A person's reputation might be known upon arrival, and a person's actions would affect his reputation after he was released. Related to this, the population in the treatment facility is highly similar: all males, typically ranging in age from 25 to 45, and all ethnic Norwegians who lived in a nearby city.[92] Compared to groups that are more culturally, ethnically, or nationally diverse, this group of drug users would likely have more agreement about what constitutes fair play.

Finally, and related to this last point, there is less uncertainty about what it means to share in this context. Prisoners are typically sharing the same substances, just at different times. Sharing would be more contentious if it involved different items with multiple characteristics because it would raise the question of what is a fair share. For sharing to be sustainable, people should not feel that they are consistently getting a bad deal because they give away something that is more valuable than what they receive. Sharing the same item over time—and within a community of knowledgeable participants—reduces this problem. The system of sharing seems to work quite well. One prisoner reports, "There are many drugs in this prison right now. It's never been as much as now. It's crazy. I have never seen drugs as accessible before."[93] Another explains, "It's predictable. The stuff is often still wet when we get it!"[94]

This unique facility provides a nice complement to the Norwegian prison discussed earlier. In that case, the combination of high-quality governance and small prison population meant that prisoners did not invest significantly in extralegal governance. This is consistent with the theory's predictions. In this case, the high quality of official governance cannot directly govern the organization of the illicit drug market. In lieu of that, the unique prisoner demographics make reliance on decentralized mechanisms preferable. Prisoners can manage this system well because it is a small prison population, with dense social networks, and low social distance. It is precisely here where norms and reputations should work best—and they do. Given the absence of other problems that markets can solve and the low cost for use of decentralized governance mechanisms, it makes sense that prisoners rely on a culture of sharing rather than a market economy.

CONCLUSION

There are clear differences between the resources and quality of official governance in Nordic prison systems and prisons across Latin America. Nordic facilities have far more material resources, significantly more staff relative to prisoners, and their facilities house far smaller populations. Consistent with the governance theory, in both cases, prisoners rely on a decentralized system of norms about what constitutes acceptable behavior in the social hierarchy. These norms are an emergent phenomenon, rather than constructed from the top down. No prisoners have the responsibility to monitor and punish rule violations. Instead, prisoners use ostracism and shaming to enforce good behavior. Nordic countries have a far more decentralized and muted response to the pains of imprisonment than other prison systems.

The lack of centralized extralegal governance mechanisms is a response to the relative abundance of material resources provided and the quality of official administration and governance. Whereas Latin American prisoners invest significant time and effort gaining access to food, clothing, water, and healthcare, Nordic prisoners do not. The trustees in the Brazilian jail discussed previously spent many hours working with officials to administer the jail. Nordic prisoners do not. Prisoners at San Pedro have committees to write rules, resolve disputes, and punish rule breakers. Nordic prisoners do not. In Nordic prisons, officials provide these competently so the presence and influence of extralegal mechanisms is greatly diminished. It only manifests in two main situations: in the close, personal relationships of the prisoner community and in the illicit sphere where drugs are shared.

Taken together, the aggregate data and case studies in chapters 2 and 3 support one of the main predictions of the governance theory: there is a negative association between prisoners' investments in extralegal governance and how well officials govern. The case study evidence also provides rich detail on how and why prisoners respond in different ways. Even if we had better aggregate data to test this relationship across many more cases, this degree of detail would be necessary. Aggregate data can tell us something about *what* happened, but often not *why* it happened. To understand the causal mechanism, we need the thick description found in ethnographic studies of prisons. This chapter has drawn on two ethnographies to describe institutional variation in Nordic prisons and, more broadly, to compare the institutional response in Nordic and Latin American cases. Both prisoners face the same types of problems—maintaining social order, gaining access to resources, governing illicit activity—but they come up with different solutions. This is not accidental or random. Variation in the quality of official governance is a major part of the explanation.

While the evidence is consistent with the theory's predictions, it is important to point out ways in which the evidence and analysis could be stronger. In particular, I have examined variation across cases, rather than within and across cases.[95] It would be more helpful if I had evidence on cases where there was substantial variation in the quality of official governance within prisons in both Latin American and Nordic countries. For example, we could make stronger claims if we were able to observe cases where a poorly governed Bolivian prison adopts Nordic-style governance and where a Nordic prison resorts to Bolivian-style neglect. The governance theory would predict a decline in extralegal governance in the former case and a rise in the latter case. That type of additional within-case variation would provide the opportunity for a more thorough assessment of the theory.

A challenge that arises from comparing across cases is that it becomes more difficult to rule out potential confounding factors. An obvious objection, for instance, is that Norway and Bolivia are incredibly different countries, and any number of these differences could be the true cause of differences in extralegal governance within their prisons. While that is a valid concern, the specific focus on prisons should mitigate our worries to some extent. Prisons, by definition and practice, are unique places. We should expect to find far fewer differences between prisons in different countries than between those countries in general. The narrower our analytical focus, the less problematic general country-level differences become. Moreover, while it is true that there are significant differences in how countries operate their prison systems, that variation is precisely what my argument aims to exploit.

Nevertheless, given these concerns, it is worth examining whether my analysis overlooks confounding variables that might be driving differences in extralegal governance across these cases. There are two alternative hypotheses at the country level that seem plausible: differences in trust and religiosity. It might be that Latin American prisoners have higher levels of trust. If so, they might be more successful at organizing extralegal governance institutions. According to the World Values Survey, this is not true. When asked about trust, more than 70 percent of people in Norway agree that "most people can be trusted," compared to less than 10 percent in Brazil (no data are available for Bolivia).[96] The average for Finland, Norway, and Sweden is 67 percent. For a sample of Latin American countries, including Brazil, Chile, Colombia, Ecuador, El Salvador, Guatemala, and Peru, that average drops to 11.6 percent. In short, there is far less generalized trust in Latin American countries than in Nordic countries. It is not likely that extralegal governance thrives in Latin American prisons because their prisoners are more trusting. The direction of causality might go in the other direction. Bolivian prisoners might invest more in extralegal governance because they are more likely to distrust other prisoners. This intuition is not inconsistent with the governance theory. Lack of trust reflects a greater demand for governance, especially if officials do not provide it. Moreover, if Latin Americans are especially untrusting, and untrustworthy, the robustness of their extralegal governance institutions is a testament to their ingenuity in a difficult environment.

Religiosity might make extralegal governance more likely if religious people are more effective at civic engagement, working with others, or have more brotherly love for others. There is, in fact, a growing evangelical Pentecostal movement in Brazilian prisons.[97] Consistent with the claim that religiosity facilitates extralegal governance, a Gallup poll finds that, on average, 87 percent of Brazilians say that religion is an "important part" of daily life, whereas in Denmark and Sweden, an average of only 18 percent of people do.[98] It might be that religiosity aids production of extralegal governance mechanisms, but there are reasons to be skeptical that this is the main explanation. Even in the face of country-level differences, it might be that people who go to prison are less likely to be devoutly religious than others. Moreover, almost none of the extralegal associations, committees, or trustee arrangements discussed are explicitly organized or operated along religious lines. There is no direct evidence that religion is what makes extralegal governance institutions possible or prominent.

I am skeptical that either of these alternative explanations account for a major part of the variation in extralegal governance institutions across cases. First, country-level explanations seem too far removed from the day-to-day interactions and pressures on prisoners to have strong explanatory value, and the prisoner population is also likely to be systematically different from a country's population. Second, the qualitative evidence discussed in chapters 2 and 3 provide clear and direct evidence about the nature of prisoner self-organization, the challenges they face, and why they invest in extralegal governance. This should receive more weight than the murky and indirect evidence that country-level explanations might offer. Nevertheless, I do suspect that more information or better data could increase our explanatory power. I do not claim to explain all of the variation across these cases. Instead, I argue that the evidence provided thus far shows that the quality of official governance, administration, and resources are crucial factors in explaining extralegal governance across prisons.

The next chapter examines the Andersonville Civil War prisoner of war camp—where neither officials nor prisoners provided much governance. I selected this case because, like San Pedro prison, officials provided incredibly few resources and limited governance. However, unlike the Bolivian case, prisoners did not invest substantially in extralegal governance because they derived few benefits from collective action. The case is also useful because there is within-case variation in the benefits from acting collectively. Prisoners produced (co-)governance for a short time in response to a threat from a group of violent, predatory prisoners. Prior to that crime spree, and after the bandits were defeated, prisoners did not engage in significant collective action efforts.

4

When No One Governs

Andersonville Prisoner of War Camp

It is a singular sight to look down into this inclosure. The suffering within both mind and body is fearful, and one can only compare it to a Hades on Earth.

A visitor to Andersonville[1]

Privation and abuse have made me Selfish and more like a Devil than a man.

A prisoner at Andersonville[2]

n the discussion of Latin American and Nordic prisons, I argued that whether officials provide high-quality governance institutions is a crucial explanation for whether prisoners invest in and develop extralegal governance institutions. However, it would be a mistake to assume that just because prisoners want governance that they can and will produce it. In this chapter, I examine a case where the quality of official governance is poor, but unlike in Latin America, prisoners have little access to resources or the freedom to engage in economic activity to offset the failures of official administration. The American Civil War prisoner of war camp at Andersonville has often been used as "a case study in systems failure," and it provides an opportunity to understand why prisoners sometimes do not invest in significant self-organization activities, even in the face of massive administrative failure.[3]

Andersonville was a Confederate prison housing Union soldiers that operated during the final fifteen months of the war, between February 1864 and May 1865.[4] The squalid conditions, overcrowding, and the high mortality rate made the prison infamous. Soon after the war ended, the North used the horrors of Andersonville as propaganda about the South's brutality. The prison received further attention during the trial of Captain Henry Wirz, who had been third in command at the prison. He was found guilty for war crimes and was publicly executed on gallows that stood where the U.S. Supreme Court would later be built.

The case of Andersonville is worthy of investigation for a few reasons. First, I argue that it shows that the governance framework is not only applicable in contemporary settings, but can explain historical cases as well. Second, for most of the existence of the camp, neither officials nor prisoners provided governance. This makes it a useful case to understand why governance institutions fail to emerge. Moreover, it provides an additional test of the theory. As discussed later, when a group of thieves and murderers began to terrorize the camp, the benefits from collective action increased so prisoners worked with officials to suppress the raiders. Third, it is actually somewhat surprising that so little governance emerges here. The prison camp is full of soldiers, not criminal offenders. It would seem that these people would constitute a more cooperative or trustworthy community. They enter the prison camp with a pre-existing, military social order already built into their community. If any group of prisoners were able to respond to the utter failure of official governance, it would seem that it would be this one. The fact that they do not do so highlights the importance that extreme restrictions on their freedom (and thus few gains from trade) does to smother collective action.

The evidence from this chapter draws from a variety of sources. I use scholarly histories written about the camp. The earliest credible history of the prison is Ovid Futch's 1968 book *History of Andersonville Prison*.[5] Another useful source is William Marvel's *Andersonville: The Last Depot*, which offers a detailed historical account of the prison. Roger Pickenpaugh's *Captives in Blue* likewise provides important details of the everyday life at the camp. I also draw on data from the prison's records on the population size and mortality rate at the camp. Additionally, I use reports and communications in *The War of the Rebellion: A Compilation of the Official Records of the Union and Confederate Armies*, a 127-volume collection that includes correspondence from prison officials, prison inspectors, and medical personnel about the needs and challenges facing the prison. Finally, I draw on excerpts from prisoner diaries, which give insights about the experiences of prisoners living within the stockade. While some of the better known diaries have been shown to be generally unreliable or dubious (such as those by John McElroy and John Ransom), others offer credible and reliable accounts, and historians use them in their scholarship.[6] In particular, I draw on John Northrop's *Chronicles from the Diary of a War Prisoner in Andersonville and Other Military Prisons of the South in 1864* and Eugene Forbes's *Diary of a Soldier and Prisoner of War in the Rebel Prisons*.[7] Taken together, these sources provide a fairly good picture of the problems faced by both captors and captives.

ANDERSONVILLE PRISONER OF WAR CAMP

During the Civil War, the Confederate military captured more than 211,000 Union soldiers, releasing about 8 percent of them shortly after capture.[8] The remainder were taken to prisoner of war camps throughout the South. More than 150 such camps existed across the North and South.[9] While the quality of life in these camps varied, it was typically a harrowing experience. Of the nearly 195,000 men who were incarcerated by the South, more than 30,000 of them died while in custody—about 15 percent of all prisoners.[10] The men who survived suffered through a painful and dangerous experience.

Andersonville (which officials formally referred to as Camp Sumter) was built in Anderson, Georgia, about 120 miles south of Atlanta.[11] The village was home to about 20 people, and the only access was via a small train depot nearby.[12] Confederate officials needed a new prison camp because of the desperate state of conditions at other facilities, especially at Belle Island in Richmond.[13] They also feared that advancing Northern armies or a prisoner uprising would unleash havoc in any neighboring populated areas or that escaped prisoners would overthrow the Confederate government.[14] When Andersonville opened, it received prisoners from nearly 40 locations, with the largest numbers coming from camps in Virginia (Danville and Richmond), Georgia (Albany, Atlanta, Macon, and Thomasville), North Carolina (Plymouth), and Mississippi (Meridian).[15]

Officials initially identified several other sites for the prison, but they decided against each of them, deeming them too populated. Officials also faced a political backlash from residents who feared having so many enemy combatants so close to home.[16] However, a significant downside to choosing an isolated location like Anderson was that it was difficult, costly, and time-consuming to get supplies to the prison, especially given the increased scarcity of supplies and the challenges confronting a government at war.[17]

Construction of the prison began on January 10, 1864, aided by the impressed labor of enslaved people from local plantations.[18] Officials initially planned to build a stockade that could hold 6,000 prisoners. However, as planning continued, and with the arrival and input of General John Henry Winder, they decided to increase the designed capacity to 10,000 prisoners.[19] The stockade walls were 15 feet high and dotted with sentry towers, which prisoners would refer to as "pigeon roosts."[20]

Building the prison was itself a challenge because officials lacked basic materials, competent labor, and even simple tools.[21] Government officials often diverted necessary resources to the front lines of the war. The blockade of Southern ports worsened the problem.[22] As the arrival date for prisoners neared, the camp still lacked essentially all key operational components: there was no barracks, no canteen, no organized supply chain for food and other provisions, and no sewage waste system. Historian William Marvel details the extent of unpreparedness, noting the camp "still had no baking pans, no flour or meal, no beef, and only ten thousand pounds of bacon—enough to last only three days . . . . [the prison] lacked a single wagon, team, or harness, nor any doors, for that matter, or nails."[23] Later, the commander of the post, Colonel Alexander W. Persons, would justify some of the camp's failures by describing the condition of the prison when he arrived: "By the want of tools, such axes, spades, shovels, picks, &c., this post was greatly embarrassed. In the interior of the prison not an ax, hoe, spade, shovel, &c., could be had when in the same were quartered about 8,000 prisoners."[24]

Andersonville officials were clearly frustrated at their inability to obtain needed supplies. Their correspondence with quartermasters and other officials throughout the South reveals the desperate state of things and their frustrated efforts. In April 1864, Captain Winder pleads with one quartermaster to send lumber because of their "great want and emergency for this lumber . . . I am burying the dead without coffins."[25] Writing a few days later, Colonel Persons explains to a superior, "I had made every effort to secure such tools or implements as we then stood in need of. I had sent my quartermaster time and again, but to no avail, as the things we so much needed could not then be had. I wrote throughout the State and tried by proxy to supply the prison, all to no purpose."[26] In July of 1864, a desperate official writes, "I am so seriously in need of funds that I do not know what I shall do. For God's sake send me $100,000 for prisoners of war and $75,000 for pay of officers and troops stationed here . . . if you only knew what trouble I was in here for the want of funds I know you would do your very best to send me at once above amounts."[27]

Officials at Andersonville failed to supply two of the most crucial pieces of infrastructure: housing and a sanitation system. The initial plan was to house prisoners in barracks within the stockade. However, the difficulty of acquiring lumber, nails, and tools forced officials to look for alternatives, and they decided to purchase tents for the prisoners (and for the Confederate guards who also lacked accommodation).[28] Unfortunately, even this plan failed as officials could not find enough tents.[29] Officials never did build barracks at the camp.

Prisoners lived in tents and shanties, and some prisoners lacked shelter entirely.[30] As one observer reported, "At present their shelters consist of such as they can make of the boughs of trees, poles, &c., covered with dirt."[31] In May, one prison inspector reports that "The prisoners I found entirely without shelter, except the sick, and the number furnished them is entirely inadequate and of the most miserable kind."[32] In August, one inspector reports, "nor has it been possible, from the overcrowded state of the inclosure, to arrange the camp with any system. Each man has been permitted to protect himself as best he can, stretching his blanket, or whatever he may have, above him on such sticks as he can procure, thatches of pine or whatever his ingenuity may suggest and his cleverness supply."[33]

In addition to the lack of housing, the stockade had no functioning sewage system.[34] There was a creek flowing through the camp that officials planned to use for several purposes, but with too little preparation and a swell of prisoners entering the prison, the creek quickly became contaminated. Although never realized, the initial plan was to create a system of dams. The first dam would create a reservoir for clean drinking water, which could be released to create a middle area for bathing, and a second dam could then be opened that would allow all of the water to flush out the third area, which would be used as a latrine.[35] Instead, insects, cooking grease, and human waste quickly contaminated the creek, so prisoners could not safely use it for drinking or bathing.[36] It was so filthy, in fact, that prisoners would later throw thieves into it as punishment.

The lack of resources and preparation might have been manageable if the prison held only a small number of men, but instead when the prison opened, trainloads of hundreds of captives arrived daily.[37] There are no records of the daily prisoner populations for February and March of 1864. However, in early April, when records are available, the prison already held about 7,000 men (see Figure 4.1).[38] By May 1, Andersonville had surpassed its intended capacity of 10,000 men. By the end of June, it held more than 25,000 prisoners.[39] The population peaked in mid-August with

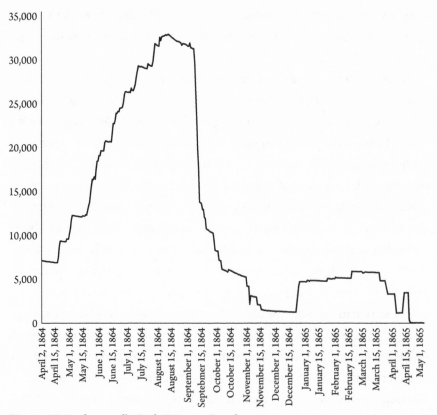

Figure 4.1 Andersonville Daily Prisoner Population
Source: Lundquist, John. (2004). Andersonville Prison Headcount Rosters. United States National Park Service.

nearly 33,000 men—more than three times the intended capacity.[40] In June 1864, in one of many such letters, General Winder pleads with his superiors to find a place for the prisoners, explaining, "Do earnestly urge upon the Secretary the necessity of immediately establishing another prison. Want of provisions is a serious matter, and there are too many prisoners for one point."[41]

The overcrowding caused great concern to officials. To suppress insurrection, Confederate officers aimed cannons at the enclosure. Prisoners also had less incentive to revolt because they believed that they would soon be exchanged for captured Confederate prisoners in the North. Officials stoked these beliefs to deter trouble, and prisoners' hopeful anticipation of an exchange discouraged uprisings. Prisoner exchanges were immensely political, with varied concerns ranging from whether it would lead to an endless war to how Confederates treated captured black Northern troops. Confederate officials also housed Northern military officers in different facilities, so they could not serve as leaders of a rebellion.

In September, in response to the evident problems of overcrowding and high fatality, officials started shipping prisoners to other camps. Between September 7 and 13, officials sent about 2,300 prisoners per day to other prisons, with many going to camps in Charleston and Savannah.[42] As a result, by late September, the prison population was within the intended capacity of the stockade. While life in Andersonville remained difficult, the lack of overcrowding was a welcome relief, and camp medical personnel attributed improvements in prisoner health directly to the easing of overcrowding.[43]

Especially at its height, the prisoner population was too large for the area within the stockade. After accounting for the creek and swampy areas, the stockade enclosed only 13.39 acres of livable area.[44] That is about the size of ten American football fields. In July 1864, officials expanded one side of the stockade, providing another 8.78 acres of livable space.[45] While this might sound expansive, the large number of men in the stockade during the summer resulted in significant crowding. Prisoners had an average of only about 40 square feet of space each, smaller than many modern U.S. prison cells.[46]

The mortality rate was exceptionally high. Of the 45,000 prisoners held at Andersonville, nearly 13,000 died (about 30 percent).[47] This was substantially higher than in other Northern and Southern prisoner of war camps, which had mortality rates of 12 percent and 15 percent.[48] In the North, Elmira prison camp also had a high death rate, about 25 percent. Averaged over the entire lifespan of the Andersonville camp, about 400 men died each month—a rate of 13 men per day. The deadliest day was August 23, 1864, when 127 prisoners died.[49] Prisoners mostly perished from preventable causes, of which the most common were diarrhea, scurvy, dysentery, and gangrene.[50]

In April 1864, a camp surgeon explained that the abnormally high death rate was the result of several factors. Many prisoners arrived in a "debilitated condition" because they had come from serving time in another prisoner of war camp.[51] Because of the inability to acquire lumber, the hospital at the camp was too small to accommodate all of the sick prisoners.[52] The number of hospital staff members was also insufficient, and the camp surgeon, at one point, complained to superiors that the medical personnel was "utterly inadequate."[53] Finally, crowding facilitated the spread of infectious disease and the lack of shelter exposed men to bad weather.[54]

The likelihood that a prisoner perished was also influenced, in part, by how well he adapted to prison life. Men relied on numerous strategies to survive such harsh confinement. Some prisoners collaborated with their captors to gain access to additional food or better work assignments.[55] The black mortality rate was about half that of white prisoners because black prisoners were forced to work at the camp and received extra rations for doing so.[56] Some prisoners survived confinement because they were fortunate enough to be in good health or to have mental and psychological strengths to withstand the horrific camp conditions.

Networks of associates and friends were a source of mutual aid, emotional and psychological support, and assistance in fending off thieves and other predators. Prisoners who had ten or more friends when entering the camp were more likely to survive than those who did not.[57] A prisoner's pre-war occupation was also correlated with death rates: a professional or proprietor was nearly half as likely to die as a farmer.[58] Laborers fared even worse, dying at rates of 1.3 to 1.5 times greater than did farmers.

FAILURE OF OFFICIAL GOVERNANCE

In addition to insufficient resources and, at times, tremendous overcrowding, the Andersonville prison lacked competent administration. The guards were typically poorly trained men who were either too young, too old, or not physically able to fight on the front lines of the war.[59] In one correspondence, General Winder refers to them "as raw as troops can be."[60] Some guards deserted their posts, and officials had few punishments to deter others from doing so.[61] There were few replacements available and the prison was already understaffed. Within three months of opening, guards were reportedly so disgruntled with the living and working conditions that they threatened to riot.[62] While it was clearly worse for the prisoners, more than 200 guards perished at the camp due to the poor conditions.[63] Other than better access to firewood and cooking materials, the guards basically received the same food rations as the prisoners did, though many of them had the option of leaving the camp to acquire food in neighboring towns.[64]

On a typical day, there might be 300 men fit for guard duty.[65] In June 1864, Winder writes that his "force ought to be doubled" and later that "the force is entirely inadequate to guard 24,000 prisoners, daily increasing."[66] At the peak of overcrowding, there was only one guard for every 110 prisoners. The guards were also poorly equipped, with some of them lacking functioning weapons, uniforms, and shoes (both prisoners and guards contracted hookworm).[67] A guard's main job was to prevent escapes and uprisings. If a large-scale revolt occurred, Winder predicted, "Every house would be burned, violence to women, destruction of crops, carrying off negroes, horses, mules, and wagons. It is almost impossible to estimate the extent of such a disaster."[68] Guards also supervised prisoners who were let out of the stockade to collect wood and complete other work to support prison operations. Other guards spent countless hours perched in the "pigeon roosts" that surrounded the perimeter of the stockade.

Officials established a "dead line" fifteen feet from the interior perimeter of the stockade, beyond which prisoners were not allowed to trespass.[69] Rumors of the deadline—and the wanton killing of Northerners who ventured near it—spread quickly after the war's end. In reality, guards killed few men for crossing the deadline. They had little reason to shoot, and many guards actually expected to be punished for doing so.[70] Moreover, many of their weapons were of such low quality or in such poor condition that they did not fire accurately. Historians William Marvel and Roger Pickenpaugh both conclude that probably fewer than 20 prisoners were actually killed in the dead zone.[71]

One camp inspector reported, "The police and internal economy of the prison was left almost entirely in the hand of the prisoners themselves, the

duties of the Confederate soldiers acting as guards being limited to the occupation of the boxes or lookouts ranged around the stockade at regular
intervals, and to the manning of the batteries at the angles of the prison."[72]
Moreover, he goes on to write, "Even judicial matters pertaining to themselves, as the detection and punishment of such crimes as theft and murder,
appear to have been in a great measure abandoned to the prisoners."[73]

Adding to the administrative problems was the organization of officials
in charge of the prison under what Marvel calls a "complicated bureaucratic structure."[74] The camp had three separate commands. First, there was
a commander of the post, whose jurisdiction covered the area surrounding
the prison, from the town of Anderson to the stockade gates, but not the
stockade itself. A second command was in charge of the troops in the region. The third command, held by Captain Wirz, was over the stockade.
His position was independent of the other two, and according to Marvel,
he enjoyed "only enough authority to demand a daily guard detail from the
commander of the troops and to requisition the necessary provisions and
supplies from the post quartermaster."[75] He held great responsibilities, but
had limited control of, and access to, resources.

One prison inspector wrote that a post as challenging as Andersonville
should be filled by a man with a significant military rank and reputation who
could thus command authority. Captain Wirz lacked these qualifications.[76]
In May 1864, Wirz requested a promotion on the grounds that the "orders
which I have to give are very often not obeyed with the promptness the occasion requires, and I am of opinion that it emanates from the reluctance
of obeying an officer who holds the same rank as they do."[77] In late May, an
inspector reported to officials in Richmond that there was great confusion
"in regard to rank among officers, quarrels and contentions as to who ranks
and commands, all tending to disturb the good order, discipline and proper
conduct of the post and prison."[78] The inspector also reported that Wirz
was tremendously overworked and had too little support, explaining, "He
does the work of commandant, adjutant, clerk, and warden, and without
his presence at Camp Sumter at this time everything would be chaos and
confusion; in my opinion, at least two commissioned officers should be
assigned to duty to assist him."[79] Another prison inspector felt that no more

than 15,000 men could be housed there "because it is impossible for one man to exercise a proper supervision over them."[80]

Finally, as trainloads of prisoners arrived at the stockade, officials provided them no information about the camp's rules and regulations. One prisoner diary reports that "nothing of the rules and regulations of the prison were announced by the authorities" when he arrived.[81] A few days later, the prisoner writes, "I learned they never published their rules, every man learns at his peril, just as I did, or by hearsay."[82] In addition, officials did nothing to direct how the men should organize their tents and makeshift shelters.[83] Officials did not mark out streets or walkways to comprise rows and blocks. Prisoners set up shelter wherever they could.[84] According to historian Ovid Futch, the result was "a hodgepodge of structures that rendered policing the prison practically impossible after it became crowded."[85] He continues, "despite the fact that the post was undermanned it seems surprising that no one had the foresight or took the time to systematize the arrangement of prison dwellings. Even a rough plan would have made future work much easier and would have saved many lives."[86] If officials had designed a layout of streets and blocks, there would have been more "free circulation of air" and an environment that was easier to police.[87] As men made choices—often shortsighted because of the mistaken belief that prisoner exchanges would soon free them—poor overall organization in the camp emerged.

POVERTY AND DEPRIVATION

According to Marvel, prisoners at Andersonville suffered "undoubtedly the most unpleasant experience of the Civil War."[88] Poverty touched every aspect of their lives. The failure to create a workable sewage system meant that the camp quickly became contaminated with waste, with one inspector calling the sanitary conditions "as wretched as can be."[89] One surgeon reports, "At all times of the day and night a most noisome stench arises from the decomposing excrementitious matter deposited in the prison and hospital grounds."[90] Another writes, "I observed men urinating and evacuating their bowels at the very tent doors and around the little vessels in which they were cooking their food. Small pits, not more than a foot or two deep, nearly filled with soft offensive feces, were everywhere seen, and emitted under the hot sun a strong and disgusting odor."[91]

In one report, the chief surgeon of the camp explains, "When the stream is swollen by rains the low portion of this bottom land within the stockade and for some distance outside is overflowed with a solution of human excrement, which subsiding and exposed to the sun produces an intolerable stench, which if not corrected before the fall months will in all probability produce some epidemic form of disease, increasing the already frightful mortality."[92] One prisoner said it was a "pen not-fit-for hogs."[93] Describing the prisoners, the camp surgeon reported that "with but few exceptions they are very filthy as regards their person and clothing and do not seem to appreciate the great necessity of bathing."[94] It is unclear where the surgeon expected the captives to find clean water or bathing facilities, as one camp inspector noted, "No soap or clothing has ever been issued."[95] The ground, often drenched in summer rains, was thick with mud.[96] On the day he arrived at the camp, prisoner Eugene Forbes wrote in his diary that "some of the men are like skeletons, from chronic diarrhea" and "our clothes are becoming the color of coffee grounds remarkably fast."[97]

To cook, prisoners huddled around pinewood fires, which gave off a strong, black smoke and darkened the bodies of most prisoners.[98] One South Carolinian visitor wrote to his wife, "The dirt, filth, and stench in and around the Stockade is awful. I frequently see the Yankees picking from their bodies lice and fleas."[99] The Chief Surgeon of the Georgia Reserves recommended "the construction of as many bathing-pools within the prison as the stream would warrant, feeling assured, from the appearance of the prisoners, that their use would contribute materially to the health of the bathers."[100]

The air in the stockade smelled foul.[101] Forbes's diary reports, "the odor from the swamp and sinks [is] by no means pleasant."[102] Lice, maggots, flies, mosquitos, and fleas infested the stockade and pestered the half-dead and suffering prisoners.[103] The camp never quieted of the sound of thousands of men attempting to survive another day.[104] In one report on the camp, an inspector writes, "Portions of the encampment I found in very filthy condition, the proper drainage of the grounds has been very much neglected, and the police of the entire encampment, until very recently, has been very defective."[105] Another inspector reported, "The foul, fetid malaria and effluvia coming from the prison occasioned by filth and a pool of almost stagnant water acting in concert with same caused the diseases of the prison to spread fearfully, and carried home to the number there quartered a frightful mortality."[106]

Prisoners typically entered Andersonville with only the clothes on their backs. Given the harsh setting, these clothes quickly became dirty and worn.[107] Prisoners who were captured soon after joining the war had newer uniforms, but the men who were captured near the end of their service or had been transferred from a different prison entered the stockade already in desperate need. Some prisoners' clothes were so worn as to leave them practically naked.[108] Northrop's prisoner diary reports, "I saw men without a thread of clothing upon their dirty skeletons."[109] Forbes's diary likewise reports that an "insane man" was robbed of everything but his shirt, "leaving him almost without anything to cover his nakedness."[110] Eleven days later, Forbes reports, "A crazy man running around naked this morning, some scoundrel having stolen his clothing."[111]

Most days, prisoners received a small ration of food. It lacked substantial nutritional value and the men suffered from dietary deficiencies, a major killer in the prison.[112] The men were always eager for more food, and some were able to kill local birds and rats to add to their caloric intake.[113] A few prisoners fashioned clay ovens out of the ground and baked their own bread.[114] One prisoner explained, "Men actually starve to death here for want of food. We are now getting scant rations of beef, some of the wormiest types I ever did see, and one-quarter ration of corn bread, one spoonful of salt a day and not one fifth wood enough to cook with."[115] One prison inspector reports, "the absence of vegetable diet has produced scurvy to an alarming extent, especially among the old prisoners."[116]

In one of his many letters seeking assistance, Captain Wirz explains, "The bread which is issued to prisoners is of such an inferior quality, consisting fully of one-sixth husk, that it is almost unfit for use and increasing dysentery and other bowel complaints . . . There is a great deficiency of buckets.

Rations of rice, beans, vinegar, and molasses cannot be issued to prisoners for want of buckets, at least 8,000 men in the stockade being without anything of the sort."[117] Many men did not have cooking utensils or plates.[118] This posed a significant problem because officials often doled out raw food to prisoners, who were expected to cook it themselves.[119]

Finally, wood was needed as fuel for cooking fires. However, prisoners quickly depleted all of the wood inside the stockade. Some prisoners volunteered to carry out the dead so that they could scavenge for wood on their return.[120] However, officials intermittently suspended this privilege because they feared escapes. Without access to wood from outside of the stockade, prisoners had to dig for tree roots or hope that paroled workers shared pieces of wood found outside the stockade.[121]

FEW ECONOMIC OPPORTUNITIES

In Latin America, reliance on visits by family and friends and access to external economic activity alleviated some of the poverty that prisoners face. In Andersonville, by contrast, markets and outside assistance were virtually nonexistent. People in neighboring towns were not allowed to enter the stockade. Visitors who had a legitimate reason to be at the camp were prohibited from speaking with prisoners unless an officer was present.[122] Since the prisoners came from distant states—in enemy territory—their friends and family could not easily visit and offer aid. Northrop's diary reports that one prisoner's wife actually arrived at the camp with clothes and provisions for her captive husband, but camp officials turned her away.[123] Some prisoners wrote home and asked family to send care packages, but even when they were sent, they were usually not received until many months later.[124] This is a sharp contrast with the access to the outside observed in many Latin American prisons.

Prisoners who happened to have had money when they were captured were expected to turn it over to the camp's quartermaster (though many prisoners avoided doing so), and the prisoner could draw on his account when making purchases from the camp merchant.[125] The merchant sold a variety of nutritious foods, including cucumbers, watermelons, onions, potatoes, wheat, flour, coffee, sugar, salt, fowl, and seafood.[126] However, few prisoners actually had the money to subsist on this food for a considerable length of time.[127] The merchant charged extremely high prices, in part because of the exorbitant costs that he had to pay to local farmers and bakers.[128] As a result, money and other valuable items soon emptied from the stockade.[129] Once a prisoner exhausted his resources, he had few ways of earning additional income, so for most prisoners—impoverished and starving—market exchange was not a genuine source of aid.

Trading with guards was a violation of the prison's rules, though guards and prisoners sometimes did so.[130] At times, for example, Captain Wirz halted wood collection, "owing to too great an intimacy which sprung up between the prisoners and their guard, the exchanging of clothes, &c."[131] Prisoners sometimes crossed the deadline to trade with guards at night.[132] Some guards were able to bring food from neighboring towns to sell to prisoners.[133] Nevertheless, there were relatively few guards, and they themselves had limited means.

As in most incarceration settings, camp prohibitions on prisoner-to-prisoner trading could not squelch the activity. One prisoner describes economic activity in the prison, reporting that, "North Street [an area of the stockade] . . . teemed with part- and full-time peddlers hawking rough corn meal, pones, and an assortment of edibles."[134] Another man writes, "It reminds me of Chatham street, New York; it is quite crowded, and the cries of the pedlars are incessantly heard; 'Who wants the wood?' 'Where's the lucky man who will buy the tobacco?' 'Here goes a bully dresscoat, only $4'; 'Here's your good sarsaparilla beer, only ten cents per glass'; 'Who wants the eggs, only 25 cents a piece'; 'Come and get your mustard and soda'; 'Here's your potatoes and squashes.' "[135] The stockade was home to several barbers, dentists, and a doctor.[136] There were also watchmakers, tailors, and cobblers.

While some artisans and merchants fared well enough, the prisoner economy did little for most prisoners in offsetting the deprivations they faced. There were simply not enough of the needed supplies available inside of the stockade, and most prisoners could not afford the staggeringly high prices demanded by the merchant and other sellers. Unlike San Pedro prison, there were few opportunities for prisoners to engage in productive activity. Likewise, outsiders rarely entered the facility, and officials certainly did not allow them to trade openly with prisoners. Two common ways of trafficking contraband into prisons today—during visits with family and friends and work details outside of the prison—were not available to most men in Andersonville. These prisoners lived in an isolated economy, and economic activity never developed to a significant extent.

CONFLICT, VIOLENCE, AND THE RISE OF RAIDERS

The sheer desperation of life in the stockade aggravated conflict over even the simplest things. Men fought over extra food rations. Some men defrauded people in commercial dealings.[137] Prisoners rummaged through the clothes of the recently dead and kept what they liked.[138] At times, the right to a dead man's possessions was disputed. One prison inspector reports, "The dead are hauled out daily by the wagonload and buried without coffins, their hands in many instances being first mutilated with an ax in the removal of any finger rings they may have."[139] In some cases, the right to remove the dead man's body—desired as providing a brief respite from the stockade and an opportunity to forage for wood—led to "full-scale brawls over possession of corpses."[140] One captive remarked, "Privation and abuse have made me Selfish and more like a Devil than a man."[141]

A prison inspector reports:

In this collection of men from all parts of the civilized world every phase of human character was represented. The stronger preyed upon the weaker, and even the sick, who were unable to defend themselves, were robbed of their scanty supplies of food and clothing. Dark stories were afloat of men, both sick and well, who were murdered at night, strangled to death by their comrades, for scant supplies of clothing or money. I heard a sick and wounded Federal prisoner accuse his nurse, a fellow prisoner of the U.S. Army, of having stealthily, during his sleep, inoculated his wounded arm with gangrene, that he might destroy his life and fall heir to his clothing.[142]

Conflicts arose when prisoners informed on one another's escape plans. Some men dug tunnels to escape, the entrances of which they hid inside of tents or disguised as wells.[143] Given that prisoners lacked proper tools for digging, using instead sticks, knives, and canteen halves, it was a tremendous loss to have a tunnel's existence revealed to the guards.[144] A "tunnel traitor" would often have half his head shaved and the letter T branded into his forehead.[145] Prisoners sometimes beat informants.[146] One prisoner describes such an instance. He writes, "A lame man, for telling of a tunnel, was pounded almost to death last night, and this morning they were chasing him to administer more punishment, when he ran inside the dead line claiming protection of the guard. The guard didn't protect worth a cent, but shot him through the head. A general hurrahing took place, as the rebel had only saved our men the trouble of killing him."[147]

The prison often bordered on lawlessness, and neither officials nor prisoners could establish much security or order within the stockade. Theft among prisoners was commonplace. The masses of the sick and weak were easy prey. One prisoner who observed a robbery wrote in his diary, the victim "now lies near the runlet, his feet awfully swollen, and gradually sinking under disease. Our own men are worse to each other than the rebels are to us."[148] Theft among friends was not unheard of. In one case, several prisoners were asleep when, "one of them got up and was stealing bread from a haversack belonging to his more prosperous neighbor, and during the operation woke up the owner, who seized a knife and stabbed the poor fellow dead."[149] In another case of self-defense, Forbes's diary reports on "a 'raider' caught last night, and kept prisoner till daylight, when he was bucked and gagged, his head shaved and afterwards marched around the camp."[150] Prisoner diaries tell of numerous instances of these types of prisoner self-protection efforts.[151] Northrop's diary reports, simply, "Mob law is our only recourse."[152]

While thieving and banditry were at first unorganized, over time thieves became more organized and thefts more brazen.[153] Opportunistic prisoners discovered the benefits of working together.[154] As the camp population surged in the late spring and summer months of 1864, increasingly organized bands of criminals emerged.[155] There were several such groups in operation, and while the historical records tell us the names of some of the men involved, many of the participants remain unknown. Some observers believe there were as many as 400 to 500 members across the different raiding groups.[156] A more modest estimate suggests they had only 150 to 200 members among them.[157] At one point, Captain Wirz "chided [the prisoners] for allowing perhaps fifty bandits to rob and kill from a prison population of some twenty-six thousand."[158] Nevertheless, Marvel writes that these men "constituted a sufficient force to terrorize the milling masses."[159] Their crimes meant that they enjoyed a higher standard of living than most other prisoners did.[160] They were better fed, armed, stronger, well organized, accustomed to fighting, and allies in criminality.[161]

The Raiders initially attacked and stole from sick, sleeping, and weak prisoners. Forbes's diary reports on one instance where the Raiders startled a sleeping man awake by holding a knife to his neck and demanding his blanket and money.[162] Their success emboldened them, and the daring and frequency of their crimes increased.[163] They began attacking new prisoners upon arrival. Men just entering the stockade were prime targets and the Raiders sometimes pounced upon them at the very moment they entered the gate.[164] Unlike current residents of the prison—most of whom had already exchanged their valuables to survive—new arrivals often had fresh clothes, clean blankets, money, and jewelry.[165] They were also often overwhelmed with the sight and smell of the stockade, leaving them vulnerable to attack.[166] New arrivals usually knew nothing about the Raiders and were unprepared for the danger they faced. According to one prisoner's diary, new arrivals might mount a defense, but they typically failed. Occasionally, Futch reports, "a party of new comers stick together and whip the raiders, who afterward rally their forces and the affair ends with the robbers victorious."[167] Resistance sometimes ended with the Raiders slashing a victim's throat or crushing his skull.[168]

The Raiders terrorized the stockade, and over the summer months of 1864, violence increased and murders were "not infrequent."[169] One camp surgeon estimated that the Raiders had bludgeoned to death 75 men.[170] Northrop, writing in his diary just after his arrival, describes a frightful scene, reporting:

The cry of 'raiders' awoke us last night. We were told by old prisoners yesterday, about gangs of thieves composed of brutal men who steal everything that they can use or sell to Rebels; and in some cases they brutally beat and kill. These organizations have grown rapidly since arrival of new prisoners, and act in concert in their nefarious practice. They boldly take blankets from over men's heads, pieces of clothing, anything that can be carried away, standing over men with clubs threatening to kill if they move. They are led by desperate characters said to have been bounty jumpers. They bear the name of raiders. Going among men of our company I found they had not realized their danger; some had lost boots, knapsack with contents, blankets, provisions and other things. In some parts, we hear of pocket picking, assaults with clubs, steel knuckles and knives. This happens every night; in some places at day, especially after new arrivals.[171]

Lawlessness was on the rise as May ended and June began. Marvel describes an attack on some new arrivals. He writes, "the newcomers put up a good fight once they pitched in, but the raiders had armed themselves with cudgels and slung shot: their weapons, numbers, and the element of sur- prise carried the day. They retired sullenly, leaving several cracked heads, only after the nearest guard fired his piece."[172] In another incident, they robbed the cap and canteen of a man suffering a seizure in the middle of the day.[173] Another man lost his watch and nearly $100 after the Raiders knocked him down in broad daylight.[174] Futch reports, "Prison authorities made no attempt to interfere with them and the other prisoners had no organization for dealing with the problem."[175] What is striking about much of this violence is that it occurred in broad daylight and often in sight of prison officials.[176] The Raiders were no longer skulking around at night to steal from sleeping men.

Murders and robberies continued in the following days. In a diary entry dated June 28, Northrop writes, "Nights are dreaded for reason of mur- derous raiders getting bolder, robbing men by force as well as by stealth; pounding with clubs, cutting with knives, even in day time. It is dangerous to sleep; not a night passes but the camp is disturbed; cries of murder are heard; somebody is hurt and robbed."[177]

The rising violence and threat of the Raiders increased the benefits to prisoners of participating in collective action. Previously, due to the lack of economic opportunities, there were few reasons to invest in extralegal governance institutions. However, with the Raiders terrorizing the camp, there was now a significant reason to do so, and a vigilante group formed. An Illinois cavalryman named Leroy Key began to arrange an organized group for self-defense.[178] An earlier attempt to do so in April had failed, but the desperation of the situation now demanded a renewed response.[179] Key recruited and organized 13 companies of 30 men, each led by an elected captain.[180] They organized in secret to prevent alerting the Raiders to their plan. By June 28, Key believed that these companies were sufficiently organized to initiate an attack against the Raiders.[181]

The following day, the stockade reached a breaking point.[182] A prisoner named Dowd, who was likely new to the prison, was chatting with two prisoners about the possibility of purchasing a watch from them. He decided against it, but in doing so, he made the mistake of explaining that he was happy with the watch that he already had. This revealed to the men that Dowd had both money and a watch.[183] Later that day, an armed group of Raiders confronted Dowd in his tent.[184] He refused to give over his valuables and a fight ensued. The Raiders stole Dowd's watch and nearly $200 that he had hidden in a lining in his waistband.[185] After the savage beating, they left him lying on the ground with a face so badly damaged and bloody that rescuers initially believed he was dead, sparking a rumor in the camp that another murder had occurred.[186] Instead, Dowd struggled to his feet, and with a bloodied face, he ran to the gate to seek help from officials.[187]

The guard at the fence could see that Dowd had suffered a horrific attack, so he led Dowd to the headquarters that stood beyond the stockade fence.[188] After about an hour, Dowd reentered the stockade with a small detachment of guards.[189] The men walked through the camp as Dowd pointed out his assailants and other members of the Raiders. One of the bandits promised he would cut out Dowd's heart and throw it in his face.[190] Other guilty men began to hide.

On the day of the attack, Leroy Key, the vigilante organizer, had asked Wirz to approve an armed prisoner police force. Wirz was initially skeptical because he felt that thousands of men should have no trouble suppressing the far smaller number of Raiders. However, when Wirz saw Dowd's bloody face later that day, he was convinced that something had to be done. Wirz supplied Key's vigilante group with clubs, and he agreed that the group could punish the raiders, as long as they followed military judicial practices and that the punishments given would first be reviewed and approved by officials.[191]

With Wirz's support, Key's group of Regulators began a search of the stockade.[192] As they hunted down members of the Raiders, some of the men complied peacefully, while others did so only after receiving strikes from the Regulators' clubs. Some Raiders refused to submit, igniting ferocious brawls that left many Raiders with severe injuries.[193] With a significant number of the Raiders outside of the stockade, men who were previously victimized scoured the thieves' shelters in search of their stolen goods.[194]

The Regulators handed over members of the Raiders to prison officials at the gates. Estimates of how many of the raiders were initially captured range widely, from 50 to 300 men.[195] They were detained in a small holding cell outside of the main stockade. However, Wirz feared housing so many dangerous men in a single small enclosure, so he demanded many of them be released.[196] It was decided that some of the men were not guilty or that there was too little evidence to prosecute them.[197] Eventually, only 14 men remained.[198] The men who were released would be free from further official reprimand or punishment, but their fellow prisoners met them at the gate. They faced a gauntlet of vengeful men swinging clubs and fists on each side. Many of them received significant injuries, and at least one man died during the assault.[199] The Regulators continued to search into the night and the following morning for any other remaining leaders of the Raiders. Many had gone into hiding or buried themselves beneath tent floors to avoid capture.[200]

Forbes's diary records his appreciation for officials' assistance:

Capt. Wurtz deserves great credit for his prompt action in this
matter, and will probably be successful in checking the operations
of these thieving scoundrels . . . It is an act of justice on the part of
the Confederate authorities which the men have not expected, they
supposing that no notice would be taken of their complaints; but
the reverse has been the case, and we can now feel secure from the
attacks of daylight assassins or midnight murderers.[201]

The next day General Winder issued General Order No. 57. It states,

A gang of evil-disposed persons among the prisoners of war at
this post having banded themselves together for the purpose of
assaulting, murdering, and robbing their fellow prisoners and having
already committed all these deeds, it becomes necessary to adopt
measures to protect the lives and property of the prisoners against
the acts of these men, and, in order that this may be accomplished,
the well-disposed prisoners may and they are authorized to establish
a court among themselves for the trial and punishment of all such
offenders.[202]

In addition, the "whole proceedings will be properly kept in writing, all the
testimony fairly written out as nearly in the words of the witnesses as possible" and the "proceedings, findings, and sentence in each case will be sent
to the commanding officer for record, and if found in order and proper, the
sentence will be ordered for execution."[203]

Wirz drew lots for the names of 24 men (aiming to include those who
were newest to the prison to avoid bias) who would preside over the trial.[204]
The prisoners then drew by lot a jury of 12 men. They allocated other judicial responsibilities as well, including designating counsel for the Raiders
on trial, a judge, and a record keeper. As Marvel describes the proceedings: "the raiders were brought in singly to face their accusers. Witnesses
one after another recounted tales of robbery, beatings, and murder, most of

them no doubt exaggerated, although many a prisoner had probably died as a result of the drubbing these men gave him, or from the lack of clothing, shelter, food, or money they had taken from him."[205]

The jury found six of the men guilty of murder and sentenced them to death.[206] On July 10, they escorted the convicted men to gallows that had been constructed within the stockade.[207] During construction of the scaffolding, members of the Regulators had surrounded the platform in case any lurking members of the Raiders attempted to destroy it.[208] Likewise, during the execution, the Regulators carefully watched the gallows to prevent escape attempts. One man did break loose and ran off into the camp.[209] However, he was quickly captured and returned to the gallows. All six men were hanged and died.[210]

CONCLUSION

For most of its existence, neither prisoners nor officials governed the Andersonville prison camp to a significant degree. The only substantial governance activity arose when prisoners and officials worked together to capture and prosecute the Raiders. During this short period in late June, Andersonville was a co-governing regime. However, after they disbanded the Raiders, prisoners no longer invested in significant extralegal governance institutions, and the prison returned to being a minimal governance regime.

Why didn't prisoners at Andersonville develop extensive institutions to govern life in the stockade? First, official governance was not merely ineffective, it also actively prevented prisoners from responding on their own to the harshness of the setting. Prisoners had essentially no access to the outside world. They could not trade with family, friends, and other prison visitors. The camp was geographically remote and isolated. While officials provided little governance and few resources, they also tightly controlled the perimeter and access to the stockade, thereby preventing prisoners from finding ways to improve their condition. The freedom to engage in economic activity and trade with the outside world was a key relief valve for prisoners at San Pedro prison that those at Andersonville lacked. If they had that freedom, the governance theory would predict an increase in economic activity and the extralegal governance mechanisms to support it.

Officials also had an incentive to prevent prisoners from accumulating significant resources. They feared that prisoners—already massively outnumbering the guards—would rise up, overthrow the camp officials, and escape, possibly to prey on neighboring towns. There were also simply few natural resources available in the stockade to produce tradeable goods or to grow food. Prisoners quickly used up those that existed. Even if prisoners were free to trade with each other, they faced a hard resource constraint. The limited gains from trade meant that creating elaborate, centralized governance institutions was not worth the effort.

Finally, prisoners at Andersonville had a far less certain time horizon than people in other prison environments. Many of the men believed that prisoner exchanges with the North would soon resume. Rumors swirled constantly around the camp that the next week would bring relief and a return trip to the North.[211] Officials sometimes spread these rumors to deter escape plans or to justify providing smaller food rations.[212] With an uncertain time horizon, it made less sense for prisoners to create extralegal governance institutions. Organizing a vigilance committee would not be worth the effort if a prisoner thought he would be gone in a few days.

In sum, Andersonville is a case study of a minimal governance regime. Officials did not provide for prisoners or govern their community. Prisoners themselves suffered and perished in the face of these deprivations because they were isolated from market activity and faced an uncertain future. This case demonstrates that lack of official governance is not sufficient to generate extensive extralegal governance institutions. Prisoner need to believe it is possible and desirable to do so, and in this case, that would have required access to resources and a longer time horizon.

PART II

How Do Prisoners Govern?

5

Small Populations

Women's Prisons in California

The only nice thing in prison is that women can be good to one another, they can create a family structure and work together.

Former prisoner[1]

In the last three chapters, I have focused primarily on trying to under-stand the relationship between the quality of official governance and prisoners' reliance on extralegal governance. In the next three chapters, I turn to prison systems where the quality of official governance is nei-ther extremely high nor low: women's prisons in California, English men's prisons, and the gay and transgender housing unit in the Los Angeles county jail system. In each of these cases, the quality of official governance falls in a more moderate range. The resources and facilities are not as good as in Nordic systems, but they are far better than in many Latin American prisons. Holding official governance roughly constant across these cases provides the opportunity to compare additional aspects of the governance theory.

To consider the importance of a small prison population, this chapter analyzes the history of women's prisons in California, which have seen dramatic changes over the last 60 years. The number of women in California prisons has increased from about 800 in 1960 to a high of nearly 12,000 in 2007. During that time the correctional philosophy guiding prison operation switched from a focus on rehabilitation and moral betterment to an emphasis on security and control. The basic architecture of prisons has evolved in important ways, allowing for better lines of sight, more automation, and less hands-on tasks for correctional officers. More generally, the world outside of prison has changed in significant ways, and women now enjoy better economic, political, and social opportunities than they did in the past.

Nevertheless, despite these changes, the social organization in women's prisons remains strikingly similar to what it was in the 1960s.[2] Criminologist Barbara Owen observes that between the 1960s and 1990s, the culture of women's prisons in California has remained relatively stable.[3] Writing in 2005, sociologists Candace Kruttschnitt and Rosemary Gartner likewise confirm the stability of social order in women's prisons.[4] One of their research subjects, who had served more than 15 years in prison, reports, "the faces have changed, the words have changed, the clothes have changed. But the way women do time has not changed that much."[5]

This stability is even more striking when compared with the dramatic changes in the social order of Californian men's prisons over the same period, which transformed from having no organized prison gangs to being dominated by ethnically segregated gangs that wield a tremendous influence on the everyday life of prisoners. Women's prisons are radically different. There is little to no evidence that female prisoners have ever created ethnically segregated gangs as men have.[6] Commenting in the late 2000s, one former prisoner explains, "The men, they are all about gang banging. We're not into it."[7] Another woman elaborates, "There's more of a formal system with the men; they assume their roles and they know their positions. With women, it's not like that."[8]

One possible explanation for why women do not form more centralized institutions, such as prison gangs, would be that they do not affiliate with street gangs. However, this is not so: a relatively large proportion of street gang members are female. Estimates suggest that females make up from one-third to nearly half of all street gang members.[9] In addition to gangs comprised of both men and women, there are also all-female street gangs.[10] Nevertheless, incarcerated women do not form prison gangs, and even women with street gang affiliations do not replicate or recreate gangs while incarcerated.[11]

It might also be that women are simply less likely than men are to resort to gang violence and racial discrimination because of gender or social factors. However, the available evidence on prison violence actually finds that women are "*at least* as violent and often more prone to violence than men are."[12] For example, a large study of Texas prisons found that for assaults with a weapon, men and women are involved at similar rates; for altercations not involving a weapon, women are involved at higher rates than male prisoners are.[13] A large study of North Carolina prisoners found that men and women commit violent offenses while incarcerated at nearly similar rates.[14] Based on comprehensive data from England and Wales, female prisoners assault each other twice as often as men do, and they fight one and a half times more often.[15] These findings are especially surprising given that outside of prison men commit violent crimes at vastly higher rates than do women. For instance, one Federal Bureau of Investigation report found that males accounted for 80 percent of arrests for violent crimes.[16] While we do not have a definitive answer to explain gender differences in prison violence, these data demonstrate that even if genetic or social differences might matter, the dynamics of prison life can still have a significant effect on women's behavior in prison.

This chapter investigates why there is so much stability in the way that women organize themselves when there is so much change elsewhere. I argue that because officials have always kept the women's prison populations relatively low, prisoners have never had a reason to stop relying on decentralized governance mechanisms. As Figure 5.1 shows, in California, the total female prison population has always been drastically smaller than the male population. In such small populations, female prisoners do not need the costly, centralized structures that facilitate a community responsibility system. They can collect information and enforce norms at low cost. Likewise, most states only have one or two women's prisons, and California currently operates only three facilities for women.[17] Women are thus concentrated in a few locations, making it easier to learn other people's reputations.

To assess this claim, I analyze the social organization of women's prisons in California as it is described in several landmark studies. The first investigation offers a snapshot of women's prisons in the early 1960s and comes from seminal research by sociologists David Ward and Gene Kassebaum, *Women's Prison: Sex and Social Structure* (1965). Their book is well known both for being an early study of women's prisons and for its focus on homosexual activity. Ward and Kassebaum interviewed prisoners about the

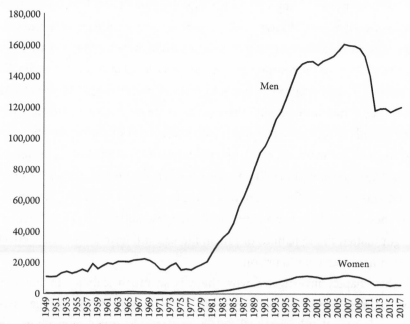

Figure 5.1 Male and Female Prison Populations in California, 1949–2017
Source: California Department of Corrections and Rehabilitation's Annual Reports.

prisoner community at the California Institution for Women: the first women's prison in California and still in operation today. The prison population at the time of their study had been growing in previous years, but it was still small, about 700 prisoners. Prisoners were housed in cottages that held between 60 and 75 women each, and prisoners typically lived alone in single rooms.[18]

The second study that I draw on is Barbara Owen's book, *In the Mix: Struggle and Survival in a Women's Prison* (1998). She studied prison life in the Central California Women's Facility in the 1990s. Central California Women's Facility opened in 1990 and is one of only three women's prisons in operation in California today. Central California Women's Facility is unique among the prisons discussed here because, at one point in time, it held as many as 4,000 women.[19] While this is a large population compared to most women's facilities (and more in line with men's prisons), the prison itself during the time of the study was segregated into significantly smaller housing units. Three general population housing units, for example, held roughly 500 prisoners each, and the reception center was designed to hold 356 prisoners.[20]

Because the housing units were separated, the prison population that a person would interact with was far smaller than the total prison population might suggest. Moreover, consistent with the claim that larger populations are less well governed by decentralized mechanisms, the prison yard— where prisoners from all housing units could intermingle—was the most chaotic and troublesome area.[21] Prisoners "in the mix" were those who actively participated in the drugs and drama of the prison yard, and it is where conflict was most likely to occur. Because of this, women tended to avoid it. Fewer than 5 percent of women went to the yard during their free time, so they effectively lived in far smaller communities.[22]

The third study of women's prisons comes from innovative work by Candace Kruttschnitt and Rosemary Gartner, *Marking Time in the Golden State: Women's Imprisonment in California* (2005).[23] This is a fascinating study because it replicates Ward and Kassebaum's (1965) research in the same prison thirty years later. They reproduced many of the same surveys and interview instruments. They also carried out research at a new prison that had opened in 1995, the Valley State Prison for Women (which has since been converted to a men's prison). By replicating the research design used in the 1960s, Kruttschnitt and Gartner provide a unique historical comparison of the social order in women's prisons across time (1960s versus 2000s) and across prisons at one point in time (in the 2000s).

The final main source comes from criminologist Rebecca Trammell, who has written a series of articles and a book, *Enforcing the Convict Code: Violence and Prison Culture* (2012).[24] Unlike the previous studies discussed, Trammell's works are not based primarily on in-prison interviews, observation, and surveys. Instead, she interviews former prisoners who served time in California and were willing to speak with her about their experiences. Despite the difference in research approach, her findings about the existing social order are consistent with the other studies. This offers a useful robustness check on previous findings. If her subjects provided radically different descriptions of prison life, then we might be more suspicious that earlier findings are biased because of the pressure of talking about prison while still incarcerated. Since that is not the case, Trammell's research provides a useful source of triangulation that should increase our confidence that these studies accurately describe the social order of women's prisons.

While I will occasionally reference other studies of women's prisons, it is useful for methodological reasons to focus mainly on the California studies.[25] Doing so provides an advantage because these cases hold constant many important factors. They are all state prisons, instead of county jails or federal facilities. They control for state-specific factors that will be more similar than would be the case in comparison of very different states such as California and West Virginia.[26] For example, unlike West Virginia, California is a large state, with a large and diverse population, and a large economy. Because these are state prisons rather than federal facilities, they draw prisoners from a single state (albeit a large one) rather than the entire country. Finally, for the studies from the 1990s onward, women's prisons are operated by the same corrections department and under the authority of the same state regulations that governed men's prisons.

DECENTRALIZED GOVERNANCE IN CALIFORNIAN WOMEN'S PRISONS

The major finding across studies of women's prisons in California is that they are, what I would describe as, self-governing prison regimes with decentralized extralegal governance institutions. In each of these studies, women describe a system of norms that resembles the "convict code" that men followed in California prisons prior to the 1960s.[27] It has been carried over from men's facilities with some significant modifications, but the basic content and enforcement mechanisms are similar.[28] The convict code plays such an important role in governing prisoner interactions that one scholar refers it as the "Magna Carta of prison life" in women's facilities.[29]

There is significant consensus in the literature that the women's system of norms has several key components, including to mind your own business, stay to yourself, have only a few friends, take care of each other, do not trust others, and do not inform on other prisoners.[30] The vast majority of female prisoners surveyed in the 1960s and 1990s believed that it was best to "mind one's own business" and "have little to do with other prisoners."[31] Between 77 and 84 percent of women believe that "when inmates stick together, it's easier to do time.[32]

One way to see whether these norms are important in practice is to see if prisoners behave as if they were. In fact, we do see behavior that is consistent with what we would expect from prisoners who identify and approve of this norm-based system. In both earlier and later eras, it was common for prisoners to communicate norms and practices to new arrivals, especially those who had not been previously incarcerated. In 2005, surveys in two California prisons found that virtually all women had been taught the importance of not informing about illicit activities taking place.[33] A prisoner at the Central California Women's Facility in the 1990s explains that she was taught the code when she first arrived. She says, "I did not know these things when I first started doing time. When I first started doing time, we had people who would take care of us. We had older people who had been in the system a while, who took you under their wing and we listened."[34] Another woman explains why she feels it is important to mentor new, young prisoners. She says, "these are girls we're talking about. They have no idea how to act in prison, and no one told them how to behave or how to stay out of trouble. I knew of so many street girls in prison; they'd been on the street for years before they went in. I figure it was my duty to help them. I have daughters, and I would hope that someone would take care of my little ones if they ever went away."[35] Another woman explains, "Who is going to help us in prison? No one, that's who. We would get with the new girls, show them the ropes."[36] New, and especially young, arrivals are seen as needing instruction, and they are often given it. If there were no norms of good behavior or if prisoners did not see value in them, then women would not take the time to give that instruction.

Adherence to the norms partly determines a prisoner's social standing. As in men's prisons, women distinguished between prisoners who were "convicts" in good standing with the code and mere "inmates" who were not. For example, one women says that a specific prisoner "is respected because she is a convict. She is not an inmate. She does what she can for us. Not because the cops tell her to. If she has something she can change for us in general, she will do it. Without even asking. If we go to her and ask for something, and she can do it, it is done . . . Because she is a convict."[37] Another woman explains, "It is how you carry yourself. A lot of women carry themselves like a bunch of wimps. There are a lot of inmates here, but you have to realize that there are a lot of convicts here too. I don't understand what an inmate is because I have never been an inmate. I have always been a straight-up convict."[38] One woman notes that a person does not get respect automatically. She says, "But I still have to earn respect. I just don't get automatic respect because I am forty-seven years old. I have to act like I am forty-seven years old. And act like I have some sense. If you act like an ignorant youngster, you get treated like an ignorant youngster."[39] These quotes illustrate the typical finding that women both observe and judge others based on their actions and that, as in men's prisons in an earlier era, female prisoners take pride in adhering to the convict code.[40]

Just because prisoners agree about what constitutes good behavior, it does not guarantee that prisoners abide by it. Women's allegiance to the convict code tends to depend on their age, length of sentence, commitment to prison culture, and how invested they are in rehabilitation.[41] Ward and Kassebaum's seminal study rejected the idea that some variant of the convict code existed within women's prisons because of many women's failure to comply with it. They found that it was common for women to inform on other prisoners, estimating that between 50 percent and 90 percent of prisoners were "snitches."[42] They go so far as to say that this was a defining feature of the prison.[43] However, there is reason to doubt Ward and Kassebaum's conclusion about the absence of a system of norms. First, subsequent analysis of their own data yields a different conclusion. After reexamining their survey results, one study found that a majority of prisoners "strongly endorse" five of the six questions designed to identify belief in the code.[44] There is a very high level of agreement about what the norms are. Second, other studies have found that women and men report adherence to the code in similar proportion. For instance, a careful comparison of confined men and women's belief in the code reveals less than universal agreement or adherence in both groups and no statistically significant difference between men and women.[45] There might not have been universal agreement or adherence to the convict code among women, but this has never been true among men either.

As in men's prisons, women relied on several mechanisms to encourage conformity to the code. Ostracism was a frequent response to violations. One woman at Central California Women's Facility notes that when there is a conflict with someone, "You won't speak when you are in the room. If you are not going to fight, you just don't speak. You act like she is not even there. That is how we do it."[46] Another woman says, "My cellie yelled at me once cuz she thought I took her stuff; I just ignored her. She was only interested in getting attention. If you ignored her, it drove her nuts. She would yell about something, and I'd give her the silent treatment and pretty soon, she was acting like an adult again."[47]

Gossip also discourages bad behavior. One woman explains, "You think that what people say about you cannot hurt you. But it can. In confined spaces like this, someone puts you down, it can bring you to tears in a heartbeat. Everything can hurt you here. And that is sad, because on the streets you can take just about everything and walk away. But you can't walk away in here. You have to take it and listen to what they have to say about you, even if it is not true."[48] Another woman says, "Women will fight with words; these words hurt more than the fist. We will lie and make others hate you. I saw women say horrible things in prison."[49] One woman explains that, "Women who are younger may fight more, you know, use their fists, but mostly women just tell each other off."[50] Some of these punishments might seem trivial, but in the small community of women's prisons, disrespect, gossip, and ostracism carry great weight. Isolation within an already highly isolated environment is a painful punishment.[51]

Women also enforce norms and resolve disputes with violence and threats of violence. One woman says, "Convicts are the ones that are real tough, down to earth. Like if someone steals something, they're not going to let it go by. They're, you know, there's going to be a fight." However, another woman explains that violence is usually not too severe. She notes, "Women fight but not serious stuff; we didn't ever want to really, you know, hurt each other or kill each other. We never wanted to do serious damage. Women will scar each other and stuff, leave someone's face scarred but not kill or stab each other."[52] One woman says, "It's more about catfights and throwing words around. They yell back and forth at each other. Not a lot of violence, no stabbings. The worst you're going to get probably is punching, fist to fist. Hand combat. You don't see women making shanks."[53]

In short, from the 1960s through the 2000s, female prisoners in California have relied on decentralized extralegal institutions based on the convict code. The normative content of the code is similar to the code that male prisoners relied on prior to the 1960s. Female prisoners know the content of the norms and often educate new prisoners about it. Women identified their own social status, and other people's status, by their adherence to the norms. As in men's prisons, women sometimes violated the code, but they recognized that others would view this negatively. Female prisoners used decentralized mechanisms that were very similar to those used by male prisoners, including gossip, ostracism, and limited threats of violence. Women do not rely on organized prisoner groups to write rules and regulations, monitor for rule violations, or to mete out punishments. They do not rely on a mutual responsibility system. An individual's own reputation was most important. There is no one in charge of organizing these extralegal mechanisms. This is important because it provides evidence that confirms one of the main empirical implications of the governance theory: small prison populations are more likely to rely on decentralized mechanisms. Women's prison populations have never reached the numbers seen in men's prisons, and they have never turned to the centralized extralegal institutions that dominate men's prisons. Instead, female prisoners have always used a similar set of norms as men used when their populations were far smaller and reputations could be learned at low cost. The governance theory helps explain why there was so much change in men's prisons and so little change in women's prisons.

PRISON FAMILIES

While the convict code is an important part of women's prison experiences, one difference with men's prisons is that women sometimes create "prison families" (also called pseudo-families and play families).[54] These fictive kinships are based on a nuclear family structure, with each woman taking on the role of "dad," "mom," or "kid."[55] Families can also branch out and intersect with other prison families. The result is that some women who are dads, moms, and kids are also uncles, aunts, nieces, and cousins to others. One woman explains, "The family is when you come to prison, and you get close to someone, if it is a stud-broad, that's your dad or your brother—I got a lot of them here. If it's a femme, then that is your sister. Someone who is just a new commitment, you try to school them into doing things right, that is your pup."[56] Another woman elaborates on the interconnectedness of these relationships. She explains, "Well, let's see, I have a mom, I have a dad, a brother, a sister, a sister-in-law. I have a little nephew, I have aunties, I have cousins."[57]

Women who identify as the mom often see themselves as primarily offering care and protection. For example, one women explains, "prison is scary place and the young girls are sometimes scared out of their mind and they don't know what to expect so we take them into our family. I had two prison kids, they were small and very sweet and I was their mom, they called me mom. In fact, I think I was the closest thing they had to a real mom."[58] One prisoner observes, "she is Mom because she always picks me up off the ground when everybody else knocks me down and walks all over me—she has always picked me up and dusted me off and said okay."[59]

Those prisoners who identify as the dad often take on a more disciplinarian role. One woman explains, "They called me dad in prison and I took care of my girls, some of these young girls have no respect for the rules or have a low-class background and stuff. I had to be the authority in their life. They never had anyone sit them down and tell them how to act."[60] Another woman remarks, "They called me 'dad' in prison cuz I was like a father figure for these girls. Lots of girls do not know how to show respect because they grew up in the system and now they're fucked up. I had to sit them down and say, 'Knock that shit off'; they'd listen to me and learn to clean up their act."[61] She goes on to report that "I knocked this girl around once; she was one of my kids, and she kept saying shit to the guards . . . You have to get serious with them right away or they bring a lot of shit onto themselves. They learn the right way, or they end up in trouble. I'm doing them a favor."[62]

Prison families provide a sense of community, mutual support, security, and sometimes intimacy.[63] One woman finds that "the only nice thing in prison is that women can be good to one another, they can create a family structure and work together."[64] Another woman remarks, "You end up mothering the weaker ones. You know you can tell when someone needs help and so yeah, you take care of those people. The mother comes out in you 'cuz there's a lot of mothers in prison. Men are more strict, more regimented. Women are more caring."[65] One woman says, "I have four kids. Most of the time they are young, or act like a kid. They can wear my clothes. They can get [from me] whatever they need—cigarettes or whatever. I protect them if I like them. I won't let anything happen to them."[66]

Family size varies, ranging from simple pairs to more than a dozen family members.[67] However, the size of families is not fixed over time. They grow and shrink as couples marry and divorce, adopt or disavow children, and as members are released from and return to prison.[68] In some facilities, prison families were also interracial and often spanned social classes.[69] Prison families can play a central role in facilities both in California and other states. At Central California Women's Facility, families were "a primary social unit in the organization of the prison culture."[70] In the 1960s, at the California Institution for Women, scholars observed widespread participation in homosexual relationships, which they described as the most relevant social unit in the prison.[71] At a reformatory in West Virginia, prison families were deemed the "most important structural unit of the inmate social system" and "the central dynamic factor."[72] In a study of a Virginia prison in 1972, sociologist Esther Heffernan observed that the prison family is "the basic economic unit in the inmate system of exchange."[73]

Nevertheless, not all women join a prison family. An early survey of the literature found six estimates of participation rates, with an average of 41.5 percent of prisoners participating in a family and a range from zero to 71 percent.[74] Participation varies with other observable characteristics, such as a prisoner's self-identification with a criminal lifestyle. A study in Virginia found that 31 percent of prisoners who are "squares" (that is, who adhere to conventional, non-criminal values) join families. Of those prisoners who take a pragmatic approach to prison, 48 percent joined families, while 58 percent of prisoners who embraced criminal- and prison-values joined families.[75] Participation also seems to vary by how long a woman has been incarcerated and the length of her sentence. For example, a study in Louisiana found that new prisoners joined families at high rates, regardless of whether they were doing long or short sentences, 72 percent and 77 percent respectively.[76] The study also found that of women who had already served a significant amount of time, only 31 percent of those serving long sentences joined such families. This is consistent with the argument that families play a role in initiating women into the community, stabilizing expectations about social life, and offering security to newly arrived prisoners. If these needs have been met after someone has spent a significant amount of time in prison, then women would have less desire to join or remain in a family.

CONCLUSION

Californian women's prisons provide a useful test of the governance theory. Their prison populations have always remained relatively small, and that has allowed norms to remain as one of the main governance mechanisms. As the qualitative evidence shows, female prisoners report that gossip and ostracism are powerful incentives to comply with accepted norms of behavior. In these ways, this social order resembles the men's social order prior to the 1960s, when the men's population was likewise relatively small. After the men's prison population began to increase in the 1960s, these norms broke down and men invested in more centralized governance mechanisms. While there was a substantial increase in the size of the women's population, the total number of female prisoners remains low. Consistent with the theory, they have never created similar groups, like prison gangs. The governance theory predicts that if the number of women incarcerated was similar to those in men's prisons, then they would begin creating more centralized extralegal governance institutions. The theory likewise predicts that if men's prisons experience a drastic fall in their population that they would return to the more decentralized mechanisms like those that female prisoners rely on.

Some scholars argue that we should think of women's prison families as being similar to men's prison gangs. Both forms of social organization arise in response to a similar need for mutual support and protection. For example, Owen explains, "The play family, with its interpersonal satisfactions, its web of mutual social and material obligations, and its ultimate sense of belonging, creates the sense of community and protection that the tips, cliques, and gang structure provide for male prisoners."[77] Others argue that these false distinctions result from biased gender norms. For example, sociologists Craig J. Forsyth and Rhonda D. Evans argue that "pseudo-families are indeed serving the same functions that gangs serve in male prisons and that the distinction that has been drawn between these two social groupings was constructed more from our stereotypical expectations of men and women . . . than from any real distinctions."[78]

While prison families perform some similar functions as prison gangs, it is crucial to recognize that there are fundamental differences between them that arise because of the smaller population of women's prisons. First, for female prisoners, the individual's reputation and social standing—rather than the group's reputation—is the central issue. Conflicts are typically short-lived and interpersonal, not permanent or group based.[79] For example, the actions of a prison family member do not automatically create obligations for other family members in the way that one gang member's actions create obligations for their fellow gang members. By contrast, in men's prisons, the entire gang is responsible if one of their members does not pay back a drug debt. This is not true of women's prisons.

Second, prison families lack the permanent membership that exists in men's prison gangs, which often require a lifetime commitment. Studies from both earlier and later periods find that membership in a family or relationship was often fleeting and short-lived.[80] People can be expelled from families. One woman explains, "If a kid crosses me, then they are out. Like just try to get involved with my woman, or do something against me, then you are out."[81] Prison families likewise lack clear-cut boundaries to distinguish membership, and affiliations are not mutually exclusive. One study describes membership in prison families as "overlapping" and as a "large network of loosely structured nuclear families."[82] The looseness of these structures undermines the ability for prisoners to easily identify a group to hold accountable. Within these shifting, overlapping, and intermixed family networks, it would be less clear who is responsible for some person's actions. However, since the prisoner community is relatively small, individual-based, decentralized mechanisms work. The intermingling that occurs within these families does not undermine the social order or the ability to hold individuals accountable for their actions.

Unlike men's prisons, female prisoners discriminate less against other prisoners based on their past criminal offense, and they do not develop explicit procedures for determining others' crimes and social standing. While the lack of privacy and the prominence of gossip means that this information is often available, prisoners do not systematically elicit it. One woman explains, "The worst offenders here are baby-killers. Child offenders. Child abusers. They don't tell us what they are in for. But we don't ask them. Mostly, you may know the person from the county and we may know what they are in for. But I prefer not to know why someone is here."[83] Prisoners at the Central California Women's Facility also identify an "informal prohibition" on asking a prisoner what they are serving time for.[84]

In contrast, male prisoners in California have explicit procedures to root out such information, including questionnaires for new arrivals, examining a prisoner's paperwork, accessing the prisoners' records, and phone calls to accomplices on the outside who search for information about a new prisoner in news stories, court records, and LexisNexis.[85] As a result, male prisoners know much more than women do about a new arrival's past. One reason for this might be that in a community responsibility system it is important to learn the history of a new prisoner because other people will be held responsible for his actions. Among women, however, a system based on an individual's standing means that other people are not responsible for someone's behavior. That makes it less important to know about other prisoners' pasts.

With less need for collection and circulation of personal information, there is also less need for organization, bureaucracy, and leadership among prisoners. In women's prisons, few people take on a leadership role like those that exist among men.[86] Male prisoners in California create explicit procedures for gaining well-defined leadership roles (often relying on either elections or consensus building). Leaders are in charge of negotiating with other groups, controlling their members, and setting rules of conduct. Female prisoners have not adopted any of these practices.

Finally, in California, female prisoners do not share the high degree of ethnic and racial segregation found in men's prisons, despite having the same level of ethnic diversity.[87] A woman notes, "Women don't get involved in race or gangs."[88] Owen reports that race "is not a primary element of prison social organization."[89] Both earlier and later studies show that within prison families, prisoners are ethnically and racially intermixed. Another study of Californian prisons notes, "we found little evidence to suggest that race is a major determinant of how they responded to prison."[90] One reason that men might segregate along racial lines is that a prisoner can easily know with which group an unknown prisoner affiliates. In large communities of strangers, this provides a significant advantage in facilitating social order. In women's prisons, the effectiveness of individual-based, decentralized mechanisms means that this is not needed.

In sum, women's prisons in California show a remarkable consistency in their social organization. They have never relied on more centralized extralegal governance institutions because officials have not incarcerated large numbers of female prisoners. Instead, female prisoners rely on norms to govern social and economic interactions, and they typically wield gossip and ostracism as powerful weapons to enforce order. A possible confounding factor is that gender differences, not the size of the prison population, drives these differences in men's and women's prison social order. To address this concern, the next chapter examines the men's prison system in England and Wales. Their prison system is similar to California's in important ways, but officials have also taken specific steps to incarcerate men in relatively small populations and near a prisoner's home. Consistent with the governance theory, prisoners rely on decentralized mechanisms that look similar to those found in both Californian women's prisons and men's prisons prior to the large growth in the prison population.

Social Networks

England

> The first things you ask someone new are where they're from, which jail they've come from, and what they're in for. Then you drop some names, and if they know them they're alright.
>
> Prisoner[1]

> With like 50 of us that's been on this wing for ages, we all know each other, it doesn't matter if you're black, white, Indian . . . you'd all be together.
>
> Prisoner[2]

T he prison system in England and Wales provides a useful case to examine because they have adopted many of the correctional practices found in California, but they differ on factors that the governance theory suggests are important. In general, both the United States and England are developed, Western countries with common law legal traditions, democratic institutions, and a commitment to the rule of law. More specifically, England has adopted many penal practices and criminal justice policies from the United States, including mandatory minimum sentences, three strikes laws, honesty in sentencing policy, zero tolerance policing, the drug war, a national drug czar, drug courts, juvenile curfews, private prisons, and electronic monitoring.[3] Although perhaps not to the same degree as in parts of the United States, England is also home to street gangs: London alone has an estimated 250.[4] On prison operations in particular, one group of criminologists argues that England has followed the United States "by virtually every measure except the death penalty."[5]

The formal operations and quality of official governance in the prison system of England and Wales are also far more similar to those in the California prison system than to those in Latin American and Nordic prisons. For instance, the ratio of prisoners to staff is 2.71 in England and Wales and 3.5 in California, while the ratio is 8.1 prisoners per staff member in Latin American prisons and 1 in Nordic systems. The California prison system has had a high occupancy rate, reaching a peak of 196 percent of design capacity in 2007.[6] However, a series of lawsuits and a ruling by the U.S. Supreme Court forced the prison system to reduce its prison population.[7] As a result, by 2015, the occupancy rates across these prison systems became more alike: prison occupancy is 112.3 percent of designed capacity in England and Wales and 135.6 percent in California (compared to 160 percent in Latin America and 93 percent in Nordic systems). Despite these similarities, there are several important ways in which prisons in England and Wales differ from Californian prisons, and these affect the types of extralegal governance institutions that prisoners rely on.

First, since the early 1980s, the total male prison population in England and Wales has been substantially smaller than that in California (see Figure 6.1). In 2016, the male prison population in English and Welsh prisons was about 81,500 prisoners. In California, it was nearly 119,000 prisoners. These differences are, in part, simply the result of differences in total resident populations, but there is also a significant difference

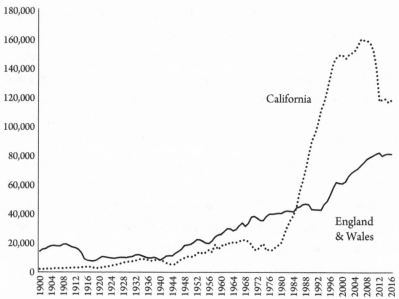

Figure 6.1 Male Prison Population in California and in England and Wales, 1900–2016

Sources: Sturge (2018). UK Prison Population Statistics. Briefing Paper: Number CBP-04334. California Department of Corrections and Rehabilitation's Annual Reports.

in prison use rates, which are much lower in England and Wales (146 prisoners per 100,000 residents) than in California (635 prisoners per 100,000 residents). At its peak prison population in 2007, with nearly 161,000 prisoners, California had about double the prison population of England and Wales.[8] The Californian prison system currently houses about 37,000 prisoners more than the English and Welsh system, which would have to grow by nearly 50 percent to match California's prison population. Likewise, starting in the 1980s, both prison systems saw an increase in their use of prisons, but at different rates of growth. California's male prison population grew about 477 percent between 1980 and 2016 and by an even more incredible 680 percent between 1980 and its peak in 2006. In England and Wales, by contrast, the male prison population doubled in size between 1980 and 2016. This is a significant increase, but it does not match the dramatic growth experienced in California.

A second major difference is that prison facilities in England and Wales are far smaller than those in California. In March 2017, the average size of the 108 male prison facilities in England and Wales was 754 prisoners.[9] In California, the average prison population is more than four times larger—about 3,500 prisoners per prison facility. There is also substantial variation in the size of facilities within systems. Figure 6.2 shows how many prisons each system has based on the number of prisoners housed in each facility. For example, in England and Wales, five prisons hold between zero and 250 prisoners, while the modal prison holds between 500 and 750 prisoners. In California, the modal prison holds between 3,501 and 3,750 prisoners. Californian prisons also have a larger range of prison sizes. In England and Wales, the smallest prison (HMP Werrington) held only 116 prisoners. The largest prison (HMP Oakwood), which held 2,090 prisoners, is smaller than the smallest men's prison in California (Pelican

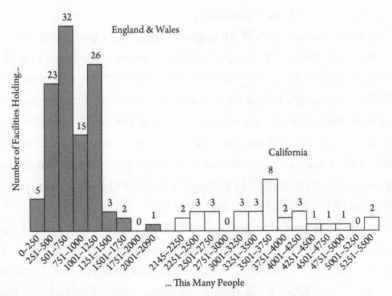

Figure 6.2 The Size of Prisons in California and in England and Wales
Source: Ministry of Justice (2017). HM Prison Population Data File, 31 March 2017, Table 1.8. California Department of Corrections and Rehabilitation (2016). Monthly Report of Population as of Midnight December 31, 2016.

Bay State Prison), which holds 2,145 prisoners, and is less than half the size of the largest prison in California (Substance Abuse Treatment Facility and State Prison), which holds more than 5,000 prisoners.[10]

In the discussion of Nordic prisons, I presented research arguing that smaller prisons tend to be operated more effectively. A 2009 study of English prisons by the Chief Inspector of Prisons provides additional evidence supporting this claim. They use data from inspections of 139 prisons in England and Wales to study how the size of the prison affects how safe and respected prisoners feel. After controlling for a number of factors, they found that prisoners were five times more likely to feel safe in prisons holding fewer than 400 prisoners, compared to prisons holding more than 800 prisoners.[11] The report explains, "large prisons with a population of over 800 prisoners were 79% less likely to perform well compared to a smaller prison holding 400 or fewer prisoners." Likewise, prisoners in facilities with fewer than 400 people were nearly two-and-a-half times as likely to feel that staff treated them with respect, compared to prisoners held in facilities with more than 800 prisoners.[12]

Third, the prison system in England and Wales also differs in how prisoners are allocated to prison facilities: a heavy emphasis is placed on sending prisoners to facilities that are close to their home communities. In 2009, 52 percent of prisoners lived within 50 miles of the prison where they were incarcerated.[13] By contrast, in 2004, the U.S. Bureau of Justice estimated that only 15.7 percent of prisoners were incarcerated within 50 miles of their pre-prison residence. A far larger percent of prisoners lived between 51 and 100 miles (21 percent of prisoners) and between 101 and 500 miles (53 percent of prisoners) away.[14]

Part of the reason why England and Wales are able to house so many prisoners close to their homes is that they have many more facilities: 123 compared to 35 in California (Figure 6.3). Moreover, the total land area in England and Wales is far smaller. In other words, England and Wales has about three and a half times as many facilities and they are spread throughout a geographic area that is about a third of the size of California. As a result, it is far easier to incarcerate a prisoner closer to his or her home.

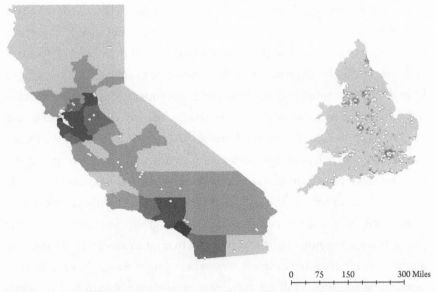

Figure 6.3 Map of Prison Locations in California and in England and Wales

In England, officials intentionally house prisoners close to their homes to improve rehabilitation by making family visits more convenient. In 1991, for example, the Woolf Report, an influential study on prison disruptions, argued that "prisons should be community prisons sited within reasonable proximity to the community with which the prisoners they hold have their closest links."[15] One consequence of this policy is that prisoners who are clustered in facilities close to their neighborhood are more likely to know other prisoners because of prior relationships and through social networks that existed before incarceration. Prisoners often associate along these lines, giving rise to "postcode pride" among many of them.[16] Both smaller prisons and pre-prison social networks mean that prisoners have a far easier time obtaining information about other prisoners and that low-cost mechanisms like shaming and ostracism are easier to implement and can carry a significant penalty for those subject to them. As a result, as the governance theory predicts, prisoners have less reason to invest in costly, centralized extralegal governance institutions. Despite taking on many criminal justice practices from the United States, prisons in England and Wales are relatively free of highly centralized extralegal institutions like prison gangs.

In the following, I examine three case studies of medium- and maximum-security prisons. I chose the first study because it compares two relatively small prison populations that vary in their level of security and style of official governance. This allows us to examine whether a more liberal versus a more strict approach to prison operations causes substantial differences in social order. I selected the second case because it was seen to be representative of medium-security prisons in England. In addition, I report the findings from a variety of other studies that suggest that the lack of centralized extralegal governance in these cases is not idiosyncratic or unique to these cases. I then conclude by discussing a possible example of a more centralized prisoner group, involving concerns about Islamic religious radicalization at a maximum-security prison. It is a prominent, but highly unusual, case where prisoners might have started developing more centralized extralegal institutions. As such, it is worth understanding what, if anything, is unique about this particular prison in recent years.

MAXIMUM-SECURITY PRISONS

In *Prisons and the Problem of Order*, criminologists Richard Sparks, Anthony Bottoms, and Will Hay study the management and social order at two maximum-security facilities (known as Category-A and Category-B facilities) in England.[17] Their goal was to describe the ordinary conditions of existence and to understand the social life at Albany and Long Lartin prisons.[18] Governors with reputations for encouraging strong relationships between prisoners and staff ran both prisons.[19] Long Lartin was known for operating a relatively liberal operation, whereas Albany was known as one of the most restricted ones.[20] Long Lartin housed 415 prisoners in total. Albany held 227 prisoners in the general population wings and 146 in the vulnerable population unit (which housed sex offenders and others susceptible to victimization).[21] If centralized extralegal governance institutions like prison gangs arise in the places that hold the most violent and dangerous men, then we should expect to observe them here.

However, in both prisons, the social order was a relatively decentralized community that emphasized adherence to a system of norms. To be a prisoner in good standing at Long Lartin was to be "sensible." This meant leading a quiet life, not being disruptive, gaining access to benefits, and doing one's own time. Prisoners described prison wings as being "very public places," so they could easily observe others' words and actions and decide whether someone was sensible or not.[22] Prisoners rarely formed groups with strict hierarchies. Instead, the community had a fluid pattern based on friendships, regional affiliations, and ethnicity.[23] Consistent with the governance theory, small populations allow information to flow easily and for decentralized mechanisms to work well.

There was some drug dealing in Long Lartin prison, but most prisoners were only involved in the periphery of the illicit market.[24] The underground economy was sometimes a source of conflict, especially when prisoners incurred debts for drugs or gambling that they could not pay back. One prisoner explains, "The trade is where the problem is at, people who get into debt and cannot pay."[25] Prisoners in the general population also disapproved of sex offenders, who they routinely threatened to harm and harass.[26] However, actual violence against them was not common.[27]

At Long Lartin, most prisoners and staff did not see gangs as a major issue. Prison staff at other facilities criticized the relatively liberal practices at Long Lartin because they believed they "had a tendency to allow free reign to 'gangsters.' "[28] One senior officer says, "an inmate once he's been at Albany shudders at the thought of going to Long Lartin. We know the protection rackets that are going on there. You can't stand on your own two feet there. There's power struggles, with little gangs, which doesn't occur here."[29] However, one prison officer reports that working at Long Lartin has been much better than he had expected. He thought it was going to be "a darn sight rougher than I found it to be. I was told it was—like— gangsters, and that it was going to be pretty rough and there was no communication between officers and the rest of them . . . but it seems a lot more friendly, and sociable, than I was expecting it to be."[30] Indeed, staff was in control, and it did not appear that any group constituted a "ruling class."[31]

Both prisoners and staff believe that self-described gangsters regulated their own activity because officials would not tolerate it if they accumulated significant influence. One such prisoner says, "You can't fight the system. You can't. It's no way. You might win a little fucking skirmish, but you don't win no fucking wars in the end."[32] Some prisoners did not acknowledge the self-proclaimed status of gangsters and did not defer to them. Prisoners at Long Lartin referred to some of them as "plastic gangsters" who overestimated or embellished their authority and influence.[33]

Albany prison was like Long Lartin in many of these same respects. One prisoner reports that the lack of gangs is partly the result of prison policy. He says, "There used to be gangs. Now there aren't, because of the way the prison is being run to a certain degree . . . As soon as a group of people get together in here, the tendency is to split them."[34] Proactive management disrupts groups that might otherwise have become more centralized gangs, and it is likely easier for officials to do so in smaller prisons.[35] Just as in Long Lartin, there was no "gangster class" or powerful group of prisoners in charge at Albany.[36]

Gang members did not dominate the drug trade at Albany, which was instead organized around user dealing.[37] The underground economy had a large number of small-time dealers who operated informally through networks of friends and associates.[38] Drug dealers held relatively small amounts of money or influence.[39] Drug operations were also ad hoc and relatively unprofessional.[40] Prisoners typically paid for drugs with in-kind payments.[41] As at Long Lartin, drug debts were a common source of conflict.[42] Racial and ethnic conflict appeared relatively unproblematic at Albany. Few prisoners reported problems of inter-ethnic hostility.[43] The only visible element of racism came from some of the older, white prisoners who complained about noisy and boisterous black prisoners in particular.[44]

In short, there was no dominant group of prisoners and no significant prison gang presence at either of these maximum-security prisons. Norms about being sensible were influential within the small prison populations where people's actions were highly visible to others. Prisoners did not write and distribute rules and regulations. The underground economy was limited, informal, and not highly structured. These findings are consistent with the governance theory's predictions that small prisons facilitate decentralized governance and do not require more centralized extralegal mechanisms.

MEDIUM-SECURITY PRISON

One possible objection to these cases is that because Albany and Long Lartin are maximum-security prisons, prisoners have too little freedom to interact so they have little need for extralegal governance. This should not be a significant concern because prisoners spent lots of time outside of their cells in those prisons. Nevertheless, we can address this concern by looking at a small, medium-security prison. In *The Prisoner Society: Power, Adaptation, and Social Life in an English Prison*, criminologist Ben Crewe studied Wellingborough, a medium-security (Category-C) prison, to dissect its social anatomy.[45] At the time of the study, medium-security prisons like this one held about a quarter of the total prison population, about 18,000 people. Wellingborough housed 516 prisoners within seven residential wings, which had capacities to hold 100, 90, 66, or 58 prisoners each.[46] Sixty-one percent of prisoners were serving sentences of between two and six years, and only 10 percent of prisoners were serving life sentences or sentences longer than 10 years.[47] The most common offenses were burglary, drug offenses, robbery, and violence against a person.[48] Prisoners often described it as an easy-going prison.[49] One prisoner described it as "a laid-back jail, nice and slow."[50]

Wellingborough did not have a distinctive reputation within the prison system. It was neither consistently over- or under-performing and had no major uprisings or serious control problems.[51] It was typical for medium-security prisons. Crewe chose it because it had "no obvious quirks or unusual characteristics" and since it was a medium-security prison, it was more normal than a maximum-security facility.[52]

Extralegal governance institutions at Wellingborough were relatively decentralized. Prisoners were respected if they were loyal, sincere, stoic, respected other people's space and property, did not cause problems, had good personal hygiene, and interacted skillfully with prison staff.[53] A major factor determining a person's standing was whether he was "weak."[54] Prisoners looked down upon, and sometimes bullied, weak prisoners who would not stand up for themselves. They built tests into everyday social interactions to identify weakness in other people.[55] As in Long Lartin and Albany, prisoners had little access to private space, so they could easily observe each other.[56] As a result, prisoners could also easily judge others' behavior and gossip about reputations. When a person's reputation was tarnished, it was hard to recover and good standing could be easily lost.[57]

Sex offenders, informants, and cell thieves were social pariahs.[58] Prisoners also viewed habitual heroin users as weak, untrustworthy, and likely to inform if they fell into an unmanageable amount of debt.[59] The split between those who did and did not use drugs was evident.[60] However, prisoners also distinguished somewhat between those who could manage their drug use and those who could not. One prisoner explains, "It depends on what type of smackhead you are. [Some are] just open about it, you can't fault them, as long as they keep themselves locked in their pad and pay their debts. Then you've got the ones who spend all their canteen buying brown, and then they ain't got shit, so they're begging and they try and bullshit you; dirty smackheads who don't give a fuck, they just want their smack."[61]

Prisoners likewise held nuanced views on what constituted informing. For example, some prisoners believed it was acceptable to tell officials if a prisoner bullied an especially weak prisoner or if they knew of a plan to commit a serious act of violence. However, even in the case of straightforward violations of norms against informing, the majority of prisoners were reluctant to physically punish the offender.[62] Instead, prisoners "simply shunned or grudgingly endured" suspected informants.[63] Prisoners did not approve of sex offenders, but perhaps out of fear of being transferred to a stricter prison, many men were hesitant to do more. One prisoner explains, "I don't like nonces, and I don't really want to associate with them. But it's not my business to go and do anything. As long as they don't bother talking to me or associate with me, I've not got a problem."[64] Ostracism was the penalty for these prisoners. In short, there was a system of norms about what constituted acceptable behavior. These norms contributed to a "precarious harmony of the wings."[65]

Abiding by norms determined one's status, but the social hierarchy was not perfectly rigid or well defined.[66] To some prisoners, there were only two broad groups of people, those who people "wouldn't mess with" and those with whom they would.[67] Other prisoners claimed that they did not see any hierarchy at all among prisoners.[68] One prisoner says, "I don't see anyone higher or lower. It's just a group of blokes doing time."[69] Another prisoner says "You're all the same. No-one's better than no-one else."[70] To most prisoners, there were clearly people at the bottom of the social hierarchy, such as sex offenders and drug users. But, the top end of the social hierarchy was less clearly articulated than the low end. For instance, while there were numerous terms for low-ranked prisoners, there were fewer distinctions made at the top.[71] Most prisoners acknowledged that some people had less power than others but many "dismissed the notion that there were men with significantly *more*. Nobody 'ran' the wings."[72] The dominant attitude was "prudent individualism" in a "culture of atomized self-interest."[73] Prisoners held people accountable for their choices, so prisoners—instead of gangs or a powerful individual—were expected to self-regulate their behavior.[74] The governance theory predicts this focus on individual standing would not be possible in large prison populations, and that instead prisoners would tend to create systems of community responsibility.

The underground economy at Wellingborough was active but limited.[75] A government report found that, during the period of study, 5.4 percent of mandatory drug tests were positive for controlled substances.[76] Nevertheless, it would be hard to overstate the importance of drugs in social life and culture of the prison. It was a cornerstone of public discussion and a major influence on social dynamics. Both members of staff and prisoners accepted that drugs were a common feature of day-to-day affairs. According to one prisoner, heroin had a "very, very, very powerful effect" in the prison.[77] The ability to traffic and distribute drugs was the primary source of influence, what prisoners referred to as "powder power."[78] The underground drug economy was competitive and operated by individual drug dealers rather than gangs.[79]

While prisoners tended to view Wellingborough as a relatively laid-back facility, the consensus was still that you could not trust most prisoners. Prisoners often remarked, "you don't make friends in prison."[80] Nevertheless, prisoners did form loose groups, sometimes known as "cliques." Prisoners differentiated between "proper friendships" and pragmatic acquaintances.[81] Most prisoners only had one to three genuine friends, and usually these friendships existed prior to incarceration.[82] Being part of a small group offered valuable benefits, including reducing social isolation, material hardship, and the risk of victimization.[83] For these reasons, affiliating with other people was a social necessity.[84] However, the problem was that prisoners might have difficulty knowing who was a trustworthy and reliable person with whom to associate. It could be tricky to verify a total stranger's claims about his crimes and history, so there was a significant risk for deception and strategic misrepresentation. As a result, locality was highly significant in determining norms and guiding who prisoners would associate with.[85]

The primary solution to this problem was extensive reliance upon pre-prison social networks. The primary and most reliable basis for associating with other prisoners was if prisoners shared a hometown.[86] When arriving at the prison, new prisoners "quickly found friends and acquaintances from their home communities, or built connections by discovering people and places in common."[87] Furthermore, these relationships were more important than most other affiliations.[88] The opportunity to find and forge these relationships is possible because the prison service prioritizes sending prisoners to facilities that are close to their home.[89] At Wellingborough, most prisoners came from either East Anglia or the Midlands, and only 10 percent of prisoners were foreign nationals.[90] As a result, locality was highly significant in determining norms and guiding who they associated with.[91]

Relying on pre-prison social networks had several benefits. It allowed prisoners to more credibly learn a new prisoner's reputation. One prisoner explains, "The first things you ask someone new are where they're from, which jail they've come from, and what they're in for. Then you drop some names, and if they know them they're alright."[92] Claims could be verified in phone calls to people in other prisons or on the outside, making it "highly risky to lie about one's background."[93] One prisoner notes, "I don't want to be hanging round with someone and then find out later that person's a rapist or that person's a nonce, or something like that. At least if I know the person's from Leicester, I'll feel comfortable, and I can find out if that person's all right. And if I hear through another friend that he's all right, I'll knock around with him. It's quite easy. Leicester is a small city, a close city, everyone knows everyone. Most estates in Leicester, I know someone from."[94] Another prisoner describes how easily information passes from the inside to the outside, explaining, "something can happen on a Tuesday, and by Wednesday afternoon it's all round Derby, everybody knows."[95]

Prisoners also believed that people from different locales had different ethics and dispositions, so that people from their hometown were more likely to share the same culture and worldview. One prisoner describes one of his friends in prison. He says, "There's one lad [from my hometown]. We know all the same working girls. We know all the same dealers. I've heard about him, he's heard about me. But we'd never bumped up [i.e., met] before. We were the only people that were alike in this jail, because we're from the same place. I don't mean the same place as in area, I mean the same place as in what we expect, our attitudes. Every area's got different cultures, different morals, different levels of drug use."[96] Prisoners had strong nostalgia and pride for their communities.[97]

The likelihood of future interactions with a hometown acquaintance disciplined behavior in prison. Friendships would extend past the time of confinement and offer social, economic, and criminal opportunities after release. One prisoner says, "if I stick up for him in here, in the long term, no doubt he will see me when I'm out on the street again, and I might have something for sale; and he might give me a better offer for it."[98] Prisoners could also punish people after release for choices they made in prison. One prisoner says, "If they grass [snitch] you up you're going to see them outside, aren't you."[99] These relationships also created obligations for prisoners to engage in illicit activity or violence that they might have wished to avoid.[100] One prisoner explains that he must be loyal first to friends from his hometown. He says, "I suppose that boils down to reputation as well. I can't be seen to be siding with him [or] my lads will go outside and say 'He stuck up for someone he don't know over me.' "[101]

Moreover, many prisoners come from not only the same region, but from the same towns and even the same housing estates, and the majority of prisoners could rely on these social networks.[102] These are tight-knit communities where "everyone knows everyone."[103] One prisoner offers a typical description: "The people who I hang around with when I'm out, from my estate, we've all known each other since we were kids. We've grown up together. And basically I treat them all like brothers."[104] Consistent with my argument, both small prison populations and the density of the social network means that a person's reputation is a crucial part of the social order. This makes decentralized mechanisms like gossip and ostracism easy and effective.

Affiliations based on one's hometown or estate provided a crucial social infrastructure, but unlike in California, these did not lead to the creation of large, powerful prison gangs. Instead, the basic social unit was the "clique."[105] Most prisoners associated with a group composed of four to 10 people.[106] These affiliations were based on a prisoner's hometown or estate, but also sometimes on religion, ethnicity, age, drug use, and other interests.[107] Cliques were fluid and overlapping.[108] Members of different groups openly socialized with each other during free time, while playing pool, listening to music, and working out.[109] About a fifth of prisoners did not affiliate with a clique.[110]

In addition to pre-prison social networks, another basis of affiliation was race and ethnicity.[111] However, these groups were not strictly racially segregated. Many minority and ethnic prisoners emphasized that it's a "bonding thing, not a segregation thing."[112] One prisoner says, "it's about culture and music and stuff . . . it's not really a big [race] thing."[113] About half of prisoners made no ethnic or racial distinction within cliques.[114] The governance theory predicts that race and ethnicity will become more salient in large populations of strangers. In such cases, community responsibility becomes more important, and for this to work, strangers need to know which group is responsible for any particular prisoner. In California, the color of one's skin provides a low-cost way to identify group affiliation. In Wellingborough, by contrast, the relative ease of learning a person's identity and standing suggests that prisoners do not need to focus on these characteristics.

No prisoner or group was in charge of the prison. One prisoner explains, "No one clique is going to be big enough to take the whole wing on."[115] Another suggests, "you might run things in two or three cells, and you might be running one thing, but you can't run everything."[116] Prison staff would also transfer prisoners to other facilities if they felt that too many of them were associating together or exerting too much influence.[117] Small housing units allowed officials to watch closely and discern such developments.

In short, prisoners incarcerated relatively close to home relied on pre-prison social networks to organize life on the wings. Combined with the relative effectiveness of decentralized governance in small prisons and small housing units, prisoners had little reason to invest in elaborate centralized structures like those found in California and Latin America. Moreover, even when prisoners harbored prejudiced and racist views, they tended to downplay or disguise these beliefs in the public arena of the prison.

LITTLE TO NO INVOLVEMENT IN PRISON GANGS

The three case studies just described show how decentralized extralegal governance institutions operated in both medium- and maximum-security prisons. These findings are consistent with the claim that in small prison populations prisoners rely on low-cost mechanisms. We can also look more specifically at the extent to which centralized groups—like prison gangs— operate within English prisons. Sociologist Coretta Phillips collected evidence about prison gang activity during the course of ethnographic research at the Rochester Young Offenders' Institution and Maidstone prison in Southeast England.[118] Both facilities hold about 600 prisoners. During three years of research, Phillips found no evidence of prison gangs. She explains, "there appears to be no recognizable equivalent of the organized U.S. gang in either Rochester or Maidstone prisons. Prisoners were unequivocal in denying the presence of organized gangs."[119] Her informants explain, "there's definitely not a gang scene going on."[120] Another prisoner reiterates that, "it's not really like there's a gang that runs the prison or some bullshit like that."[121] Another one asks, "where you heard of this gang thing?, I don't know nothing about that."[122]

As in Wellingborough, prisoners form loose associations, often with people they knew before incarceration and based on cultural, residential, or criminal networks.[123] One's neighborhood is the main driver on prisoner affiliations.[124] One prisoner describes how he viewed people coming into the prison from where he lived prior to incarceration. He says "if you're from someone's ends [neighbourhood] then, yeah, they are, they got a certain amount of liability to look out for you . . . you have to look out for each other."[125] For foreign-born prisoners, geographic affiliation based on country origin was even more important.[126]

Race and ethnicity were not especially salient to prisoners. One prisoner reports, "with like 50 of us that's been on this wing for ages, we all know each other, it doesn't matter if you're black, white, Indian . . . you'd all be together."[127] The small community in the prison and the publicness of living life on the wings means that people, according to this prisoner, "all know each other." This is not surprising given that they have been together "for ages." There is no need to rely on external markers, like race or ethnicity, to identify group affiliation. When prisoners know each other and can hold each other accountable, there is little need for mutual responsibility within a community responsibility system.

Another prisoner says, "Ethnicity is not really a big thing . . . nobody takes it as a main mark. It's more on the lines of who you are personally. Not your race as an individual."[128] Loose clusters of ethnicities exist, but they were not exclusive or conflictual.[129] Unlike gangs, these associations lack rigid and mutually exclusive membership. Many prisoners reported an absence of racism among prisoners.[130] The strict racial and ethnic segregation that exists in California's gang-controlled prisons is not found here. This is consistent with broader findings. In a recent review of the literature, two criminologists describe the lack of racial segregation as a "fundamental difference" between U.S. and English prisons.[131]

These loose prisoner affiliations lack the hallmark characteristics of California prison gangs. They do not require mutually exclusive, restrictive, and permanent membership. They do not exist into perpetuity or have a corporate entity. They are not centralized, top-down authority structures. These friendships are "loose collectives" with no internal organization.[132] Likewise, the main actors in the underground drug market were sole proprietors, not gangs.[133]

The absence of prison gangs is a common finding in research on England and Wales. For example, a study of Thameside prison found no evidence of gang-involved prisoners controlling life in the prison or dominating the underground economy.[134] There is nothing similar to the highly structured U.S. prison gangs.[135] Instead, geographic affiliations are natural guides about whom to trust.[136] One prisoner explains, "you've got some background with them . . . so you'll definitely be more open to talk and be friendly with them because you must have some sort of sense of each other."[137] Another prisoner explains, "I firstly like to be around people who are probably from where I'm from so the chance of me knowing them is high and everything or we have more in common and stuff like that."[138]

In another study, criminologists interviewed adult prisoners in England and street gang members outside of prison in Scotland, half of whom had been incarcerated previously.[139] Given that a large proportion of the sample were selected specifically because of a street gang affiliation, we might suspect that they would be more likely to view gangs as having a significant influence in prisons. However, that is not the case. The authors describe a "general lack of prison gang culture."[140] They instead found a large number of smaller, less powerful cliques.[141] One prisoner reports, "Prison gangs are non-existent."[142] In a related study, a prisoner observes, "In all the prisons I've been in, there's never been one where people are like, 'yeh, this prison's run by this gang.' And I've been in prisons all over the country."[143]

Not only do these studies indicate the absence of organized prison gangs, but also some research actually finds that street gang members tend to reduce their gang involvement while incarcerated.[144] In California, prisons are a place where street gang affiliations strengthen, where street gang members align with prison gangs, and where some prisoners strive to become "made members" of prison gangs. In England, street gang member-ship withers and is sometimes given up entirely.

One important caveat is that some people do refer to gangs in English prisons. However, they seem to do so in a way that is substantively different from gangs in Latin American or Californian prisons. First, past work sometimes offered an overly inclusive definition of what constitutes a prison gang. For example, one paper defines a prison gang "as a group of three or more prisoners whose negative behaviour has an adverse impact on the prison that holds them."[145] This definition would classify such a vast number of prisoners as gang members as to lose all usefulness. It implies that nearly all prisons in existence have had prison gangs. This is inconsistent with observations of staff members and prisoners who identify substantial variation in prison gang influence and activity across time and space.[146] The inability for this definition to distinguish loose, fleeting, and temporary associations from entrenched, race-based prison gangs obscures important differences. In addition, these studies identify gang membership by whether a prisoner violates the prison's official rules. It is a fallacy to argue that since prison gang members violate prison rules, anyone violating prison rules is part of a prison gang.

A second issue is that when English prisoners mention gangs, they do so often in reference either to street gang members who are incarcerated or to self-proclaimed "gangsters," not to distinct prison-based organizations.[147] English street gang members do go to prison and sometimes affiliate with prior associates while incarcerated. However, these affiliations lack the centralized elements and the governance functions that exist among California prison gangs, so their presence is consistent with the governance theory. In addition, they typically do not reconstitute the street gang entity in prison. Some research suggests that street gang members do not recruit new members or create new gangs in prison.[148] When street gangs are present in prison, one article concludes, "any gang rivalry is very much extrapolated into the prison system from the street."[149] By contrast, in many U.S. and Brazilian prisons, prison gangs project their power outward to street gangs. There is no expectation that all prisoners will affiliate with a gang or broader racial group in English prisons.[150] Sometimes prisoners have loose affiliations with a street gang, but it is far more common for prisoners to affiliate with other people based on their postcode.[151]

Even when street gang members go to prison, they rarely wield substantial influence and are not a crucial source of governance. According to one study, gang members did not exercise "authoritative power over prisoners generally."[152] Another study finds that prisoners in street gangs were unable to "control institutions" and that "the lives of all (or indeed most) prisoners were not defined by gang membership."[153] Furthermore, there is no evidence that street gang members in English prisons have written constitutions or codes of conduct that they distribute to new prisoners.[154] In short, even when prisoners refer to "gangs" in prison, there is far less centralization in the social order than what exists in prisons in other parts of the world. Given the small size of English prisons and the prominence of pre-existing social networks, this lack of centralization provides further support for the governance theory.

ARE PRISONERS RADICALIZING?

Despite the consistent finding that English prisoners rely on decentralized extralegal governance institutions, there are several reasons to be concerned that things might be changing. First, the quality of official governance seems to be falling in recent years. While there has been a small rise in the prison population since 2010, the prison system has lost nearly 3,800 officers (a 16 percent decline). In 2018, officials estimate that these departing staff members have a combined 70,000 years of experience, and staff with a total of 6,000 years of experience had left in the last year alone.[155] At that time, only a third of prison staff had less than three years of experience, while in 2010, only one in eight did.[156] Recent years have also seen a sharp increase in assaults against prison staff, prisoner-to-prisoner assaults, and prisoner self-harm.[157] The prison service has also discussed the possibility of building several "Titan" prisons, which would hold 2,500 prisoners and thus be significantly larger than most prisons in England and Wales.[158] Related to this, there has been a growing concern that prisoners are starting to radicalize in some maximum-security facilities. A 2008 *Telegraph* headline, for example,

reads "Extremist Muslim prison gang radicalizing inmates, says warders."
A 2014 *Daily Mail* headline states, "Britain's jails turning into breeding
ground for terrorists."

Yet, it is not clear that prisoners are radicalizing or forming prison gangs.
A number of studies have examined the role of radical Islam in prison, and
they did not find systematic problems. One study found that prisoners
perceived Muslims as being part of a "self-protective brotherhood," but
prisoners did not view these groups as prison gangs.[159] One Muslim prisoner says, "You get the Muslims that stick up for each other because it's
our religion; we need to look after our own."[160] But, standing up for other
members of one's faith community does not seem to rise to the level of gang
activity. More importantly, it does not constitute a significant degree of
centralization, so it is not inconsistent with the governance theory prediction for small prison populations and pre-prison social networks. Religion
is an obvious focal point around which to form relationships. A 2010 report
from the Chief Inspector of Prisons found these "concerns about intimi-
dation of non-Muslims, the emergence of gangs and conversions to Islam
were often linked, but were backed by little evidence."[161]

Fears about terrorism and radicalization raise several distinct issues,
some that relate to my argument and others that do not. In particular, the
governance theory is not a theory of radicalization or terrorism. It might
be that certain types of prisons are more likely to radicalize prisoners. For
example, leaders of ISIS reportedly first met in Camp Bucca, a detention
facility in Iraq, where a large number of extreme Sunnis were all housed together.[162] Officials had little control of the prison. Prisoners had free rein to
congregate, teach, preach, and network, and they could perhaps do so more
easily because of their confinement. Nevertheless, the governance theory is
not meant to explain what types of prisons facilitate religious radicalization.

Perhaps a more relevant concern is to what extent religion plays a role
in governing prisons. It might do so in several ways. More religious people
might have less conflict. If holier prisoners are less likely to fight and steal,
then they need less governance in general. Alternatively, it might be that religion is a different mechanism that prisoners use for governance. Both gangs
and religions can provide governance. In Brazil, Pentecostal Christianity

has a large and growing membership behind bars and the prison church regulates many aspects of prisoners' lives, including giving them the opportunity to take on new identities as reformed people.[163] It also operates in many of the same prisons as Brazilian prison gangs and for some of the same reasons.[164]

However, the extent and nature of Islam's involvement and influence in prison social order remains an empirical question. Two studies shed some light on this issue, though we still know relatively little. In 2018, Ryan Williams conducted ethnographic work among Muslim prisoners in two high-security English prisons.[165] Williams found that for many Muslim prisoners, making or renewing a religious commitment was an important part of their daily experience. Many of the Muslim prisoners strove to achieve some conception of the human good. The desire to "become good" was a recurrent theme in his interviews.[166] One prisoner says that members of staff often suspect that religious activities, such as cooking food for other prisoners, were actually criminal or gang-oriented activities. The prisoner says, "it's not part of some conspiracy hierarchy or gang culture."[167] Another prisoner likewise argues, "a lot of Muslim people . . . bake cakes and stuff, and when it's Eid they cook lots of food . . . and it's not just for Muslims, we invite non-Muslims as well, we say welcome, we've cooked some food, we've made some cakes, come and eat."[168] Prisoners did not appear to be using religion as a cover for gang activity, and there was no evidence that prisoners were compelled to join Islam.[169]

The most extensive study on this topic is a report for the UK Ministry of Justice, which investigates whether Muslim prisoners were radicalizing and whether these religious groups were actually covert gangs. Criminologists Alison Liebling, Helen Arnold, and Christina Straub interviewed staff and prisoners at Whitemoor prison, a maximum-security facility holding about 440 prisoners.[170] It is important to note that the site was chosen specifically because officials were concerned that prisoners were radicalizing or starting to form gangs, so it is not representative of English prisons, or even maximum-security prisons, generally.

The authors conducted their fieldwork over 14 months, and their evidence comes from observations, informal conversations, surveys, and interviews with prisoners and staff.[171] Ninety-seven percent of prisoners were serving sentences of 10 or more years, and officials identified 71 prisoners (16 percent of the population) as "known gang members."[172] Thirty-five percent of prisoners were Muslim. This was large relative to the system's total prison population, where only about 11 percent of prisoners are Muslim.[173]

The relationship between prisoners and staff at Whitemoor was distant and characterized as a "culture of distrust." In their survey on the quality of prison life, only 12 percent of prisoners agreed or strongly agreed with the statement, "I trust the officers in this prison."[174] Only 9 percent believed that "this prison is good at placing trust in prisoners."[175] The surveys and interviews also found that, in general, prisoners felt the prison was unsafe.[176] The lack of trust reduced the flow of information between prisoners and officials, making the prison harder to govern. These findings suggest that the quality of official governance was relatively poor.

It was not unusual for prisoners to convert to Islam during their sentences.[177] Prisoners did so for numerous reasons, including camaraderie, as a search for meaning and identity, and as an expression of protest against the government.[178] Despite popular concern about radicalization, there was only "indirect" and "very limited evidence" of it.[179] In addition, for prisoners who reportedly joined Islam for the benefits of "gang membership," both prisoners and staff used the term in ambiguous ways.[180] For example, one prisoners says "You can't have a fight with one Muslim without all of them getting involved."[181] Providing protection as described here has at least one characteristic of centralized governance mechanisms, but lacks many others.

Some members of staff were concerned that prisoners were coerced into joining Islam.[182] There was evidence that this happened in varying degrees. Some prisoners felt forced to convert because they believed the prison was not safe. For example, sex offenders and other vulnerable prisoners could join Islam and be safe from victimization.[183] One prisoner says, "It's like a protection racket. That's the way the Muslims operate, over a period of a few weeks they'll get these young lads into their confidence, comfortable, and it's basically like a protection racket, that's how it runs, 'we can offer you security, if ever anybody threatens you, we'll sort it,' but you've got to become a Muslim."[184] Interestingly, the prisoners in this context encourage sex offenders to join them, while in many prisons, gangs actively target the same types of prisoners for violence.

Some prisoners viewed "heavy recruitment" as coercive. Prisoners "reported being approached by Muslim prisoners who 'advertised' their faith in such an intense manner that they felt under pressure to comply. The most common narrative described persuading actions, a kind of 'heavy advertising.'"[185] An important issue is whether there were negative consequences for prisoners who declined to convert. Some prisoners argued that there were none.[186] However, some prisoners and members of staff report that there were instances in which prisoners were assaulted for refusing to convert, and they observed conversions that "looked like bullying in its purest form."[187] Nevertheless, the authors interviewed 12 prisoners who had converted to Islam, and only two of them had been coerced to any extent.[188]

Many prisoners felt that officials were too quick to interpret socializing or religious participation as membership in a gang or as radicalization.[189] For example, staff took any outward indication of membership in Islam as prima facie evidence of radicalization. One prisoner says, "When they [staff] see three people together in a cell, that's a gang already."[190] Another prisoner argued that helping someone in need would be misinterpreted as gang activity.[191] In one interview, they ask an officer what is the difference between a gang and a faith community. He responds, "There's not much. It's a sense of purpose, isn't it? They've got something there in common. They have their leaders and their soldiers."[192] These staff responses seem to define any group that offers protection as a gang.

There also appeared to be different factions among Muslim prisoners. Some Muslim prisoners focused on their faith, and others were allegedly more interested in using the religion as a way to wield power and influence.[193] Both non-Muslim prisoners and staff feared that the growing Muslim population would use its power against others.[194] However, the authors found it difficult to describe or find evidence of the type of power that some prisoners were thought to hold.[195] Some prisoners also found it difficult to distinguish between violence that was motivated by religion and violence that happens in prison more generally.

In sum, the prison's growing Muslim population has had a significant influence on the prison social order. Prison officials seem to be losing control of the prison, and some prisoners are joining Islam for protection. However, what remains unclear, based on the available evidence, is to what extent the community of Muslim prisoners is a centralized extralegal governance institution. The report does not identify an explicit hierarchy or internal organization. Presumably, religious writing influences their behavior and interactions with others, but it is unclear if this plays the same role as the written rules and regulations that prisoners use in, for example, some prisons in Brazil and Bolivia. It seems clear that the Muslim prisoner community provides protection, but that alone does not imply that it is a centralized, extralegal governance institution. It seems more likely that it is simply a natural response to seek out safety in the face of a fall in the quality of official governance.

CONCLUSION

This chapter has compared the social order that exists in men's prisons in California and England and Wales. The latter prison system has adopted a large number of criminal justice and correctional practices and policies directly from the United States. Yet, these two systems differ in ways that are important for the governance theory. Unlike California, England and Wales have a large number of small prisons that are sited close to offenders' home communities. This drastically lowers the cost of learning about people's reputations, meaning that decentralized extralegal governance institutions are both possible and desirable. Like Californian women's prisons, these facilities are relatively small, but differences in social order in these cases cannot be driven by gender differences. In addition, many English prisoners have the additional advantage of being able to rely on pre-existing social networks. Consistent with the governance theory, there is little evidence of any centralized extralegal institutions in most English prisons. Prisoners do not create written rules and regulations, form gangs with permanent membership, or create a community responsibility system. They also lack the racial and ethnic segregation that is both incredibly prominent in Californian men's prisons and crucial for facilitating group-based governance in a large population of strangers.

As in the previous chapters, the governance theory has several counterfactual predictions. If England and Wales consolidated their prison population into a small number of large prisons, then the theory predicts that centralized extralegal governance mechanisms would become more prominent and important. Small prisons are easier for officials to govern and decentralized mechanisms work better there. Likewise, if California dispersed its prison population into a larger number of small prisons sited near prisoners' homes, then the importance of centralized mechanisms would fall.

One challenge of comparative case studies is the difficulty of distinguishing how much each factor—size and social networks—matter. A useful additional case would be to study a large prison, like those found in California, but one that had social networks similar to those observed in England. That would allow us to test whether social networks can overcome the informational costs and problems associated with large prison populations. It might be that social networks make reputations a viable form of social control even in large populations. Unfortunately, I am not aware of a case that provides this test.

Observers studying the Muslim prisoner community in Whitemoor prison agree that it is unusual and not typical of most prisons in recent years. As such, it would be incorrect to extrapolate findings from this prison to prisons in England and Wales generally. However, it is valuable to study extreme cases like this one because they might differ in important ways from more typical cases. Whitemoor appears to differ in two important ways. First, the quality of official governance is relatively low, there is a culture of distrust between prisoners and staff, and both prisoners and staff feel unsafe in the facility. Given the sense of vulnerability, it is perhaps not surprising that prisoners seek out alternative sources of security. Compared to other prisons in England and Wales, the governance theory predicts it would be more likely to seek out a source of extralegal governance. The second major difference is that there is a disproportionately large number of Muslim prisoners at Whitemoor, which according to prisoner interviews, make them a focal source to turn to for protection. In addition, their willingness to accept sex offenders offers a unique path to safety in a dangerous environment.

Social Distance

Gay and Transgender Unit

> For some people, this is their home because a lot of their
> families have disowned them and shunned them, so we're
> their family.
>
> Prisoner at the Los Angeles County Jail[1]

The Los Angeles County Jail system is the largest in the United States. On any given day, it holds more than 17,000 prisoners.[2] Throughout the course of the year, an average of 166,000 people circulate through the county's eight facilities.[3] The population in state prisons is usually much larger than in county jails because they cover more territory and larger populations of people. However, the Los Angeles County Jail is so vast that it is larger than seven U.S. state prison systems.[4] It also has a checkered history marked by corruption, scandal, and violence. Recent lawsuits allege a high rate of officers using excessive force against prisoners and sometimes against citizens who have come to visit an incarcerated loved one.[5] Within the general population of the prison, organized gangs wield a tremendous amount of control and influence over the everyday life of prisoners.[6]

In all these ways, Los Angeles County Jail is quite unlike other county jail systems. This makes it a useful case to study because these factors have given rise to a peculiar housing area that might have never come into existence if not for the large size and perceived dangerousness of the prison. The Los Angeles County Jail has the only unit in the country operated exclusively to house male gay and transgender prisoners. Other precincts, such as San Francisco and previously New York, have provided some degree of segregation in sleeping and living arrangements for gay and transgender prisoners, but no jail or prison system has a similar, stand-alone housing area like the one found in the Men's Central Jail in Los Angeles.[7] The unique—and controversial—classification process that determines which prisoners can be housed in this unit means that it is a useful case. It is a small population of prisoners who share pre-prison social networks and have low social distance.

Several important studies offer insights into the housing unit.[8] The most systematic research comes from Sharon Dolovich, a professor of law at the University of California, Los Angeles, who has written several papers on the gay and transgender dorm.[9] Based on seven weeks of ethnographic work during the summer of 2007, her research draws on extensive observation of the daily operations of the facility and discussions with both prisoners and prison staff members. She surveyed roughly 10 percent of the gay and transgender unit's residents with a 176-question interview instrument, which generated more than 50 hours of conversations.[10] In addition to the formal interviews, she observed jail operations, had informal conversations with prisoners and staff, monitored intake classification interviews, and conducted in-depth interviews with the two key deputies involved in the dorm's operation.[11] A second important piece of research comes from Russell Robinson, a professor of law at the University of California, Berkeley. His research was less extensive than Dolovich's study, but it provides a useful complement to her work, in part because he has a far more critical view of the dorm than she does. Robinson based his research on interviews with lawyers (including those involved in the litigation that led to the creation of the dorms), advocates for prisoner's rights, people affiliated with the American Civil Liberties Union, government employees, and former prisoners.[12] He also spoke at length with one of the two main deputies involved in the operation of the dorm.[13]

These studies reach strikingly different conclusions about the desirability of the housing unit. Dolovich argues that the dorms provide a more humane environment that improves the lives and safety of vulnerable prisoners. Robinson, on the other hand, is far more skeptical about the operation and fears the consequences of state-based segregation based on a person's identity. Robinson argues that segregated housing harms gay and transgender prisoners in several ways, including by stereotyping them as victims, increasing exposure to HIV, ignoring other classes of vulnerable prisoners, overlooking bisexual prisoners, and forcing prisoners to come out.[14] Despite their disagreements over legal and normative issues, both scholars agree on relevant facts and descriptions of the prisoner community. These studies therefore provide a useful look into the life in the gay and transgender dorms in the late 2000s.

THE CLASSIFICATION PROCESS

Prison officials refer to the gay and transgender dorm as "K6G."[15] The housing unit has been in operation since 1985.[16] It is the result of a lawsuit brought in 1982 by the American Civil Liberties Union on behalf of male gay prisoners housed at the jail, alleging a violation of the 8th and 14th amendments. The lawsuit claimed that officials failed to protect gay prisoners from victimization by other prisoners in the general population.[17] The county settled the case without a trial, and they agreed to create a specific housing area for male gay and transgender prisoners that would keep them isolated and safe from prisoners in the general population housing units.[18]

There are three main dorms in K6G, and a fourth dorm is sometimes available if there is insufficient room in the other three.[19] The dorms hold a total of between 350 and 400 prisoners.[20] They consist of windowless rooms, full of bunk beds, housing between 128 and 140 people each.[21] Estimates suggest that transgender prisoners make up between 10 and 20 percent of the dorms' population.[22] Only a small fraction of prisoners in K6G is there for violent crimes.[23] Most are there on drug (31 percent of prisoners) and property offenses (32 percent of prisoners).[24]

The K6G dorms are located within the Men's Central jail, the large and somewhat antiquated centerpiece of the Los Angeles County jail system. Built in 1963, Men's Central is one of the oldest jails in the state and houses about 4,000 prisoners in both cellblocks and dormitories on any given day. While the goal of K6G is to segregate its residents from the general population, they sometimes intermingle, such as on visits to court. K6G dorm residents are easily distinguished from general population prisoners by the color of their prison clothing. In contrast to the dark blue uniforms that most prisoners in the general population wear, residents of K6G wear powder blue uniforms.[25]

Not all prisoners sent to the Los Angeles County jail have the option to live in K6G. Deputies administer a classification process to determine if a prisoner is, as Dolovich explains, "'really gay,' by which is meant that, when they are free, they seek out men and only men for sexual gratification, for romance, and for emotional intimacy."[26] All prisoners entering the jail must go through an intake interview to provide general information for determining where to house each person. One question that they ask is, "are you a homosexual?"[27] If a prisoner responds affirmatively, staff will move the prisoner to a waiting area that is visible to staff members to ensure the prisoner's safety. Prisoners must then wait for a second stage in the classification process (which often happens the following day) where they meet with two deputies in charge of determining which prisoners may be housed in K6G.[28]

Officials believe that determining whether a prisoner is transgender is a more straightforward process of visual inspection and because transgender prisoners "self-identify."[29] As a result, transgender prisoners often do not have a second classification interview. However, gay prisoners face an interview with the two deputies who are in charge of classification, both of whom have worked with this unit and with its population for more than two decades.[30] The deputies interview and classify between 10 and 25 prisoners per day.[31]

During the second interview, the two deputies have a conversation with the prisoner and ask a series of questions that they believe will help screen out prisoners who should not be housed in K6G, such as heterosexual or bisexual prisoners. Their main concern is that prisoners may wish to be housed in K6G only so that they can victimize its residents, as happened previously in a New York jail unit for gay prisoners.[32] In the New York case, the then-city corrections commissioner explained that the unit had to be closed because "What we ended up with was this housing unit where people were predatory and people were vulnerable. The very units that should be the most safe, in fact, had become the least safe."[33] Deputies in Los Angeles believe that some method of screening is necessary for K6G to remain safe. A second, less worrisome, reason why prisoners might seek to live in K6G is simply that they believe it to be less dangerous and less stressful than life in the general population housing areas.[34]

The questions deputies ask are intended to be easy for gay prisoners to answer and difficult for someone who is trying to pass as gay to answer. A senior deputy working with a formerly incarcerated gay activist who was affiliated with the American Civil Liberties Union (neither of whom is still involved) devised the process.[35] Deputies might ask for the names of local gay bars or clubs that the prisoner visits and what the cover charges are at these locations.[36] Deputies sometimes ask a prisoner, "How did your mother react when you came out?" to assess his reaction or to see if he can offer an authentic account.[37] They often ask about the names and birthdates of past boyfriends.[38] They sometimes ask for the meaning behind phrases that they believe are commonly known in the gay community.[39] Deputies ask personal questions, such as "tell me about your first sexual intercourse with a man."[40] Deputies are not running through a rote list of questions. There is no single correct answer.[41] Instead, the deputies' main interest is in getting a reaction and stimulating a conversation. Sometimes questions are simply useful prompts for prisoners to describe their situation. In others, basic questions are enough to prod prisoners to admit that they are not gay and are seeking to be housed in K6G for another reason.[42]

To better assess the credibility and honesty of prisoners' claims, the two deputies occasionally visit gay bars in West Los Angeles to become familiar with local clubs and to take pictures of the interior so that they can later ask prisoners to identify the club.[43] For prisoners living outside of Los Angeles, they might call locations reported to be gay bars to confirm the prisoner's story. In some instances, they will contact a prisoner's mother and indirectly inquire about her son's sexuality.[44]

These questions are not perfect screening mechanisms. During the wait between the first and second stage of the classification process, prisoners are sometimes coached by others on what type of questions will be asked and what are acceptable answers. Prisoners in K6G estimated that between 2 and 25 percent of K6G residents were not gay.[45] The questions and conversation are also based on an assumption about a specific lifestyle that is not universally lived within the gay community. It is potentially biased against non-white, working class, and poor prisoners.[46] However, in defense of the process, the major goal of these conversations is not to identify gay prisoners per se, but to identify prisoners who the deputies think that other prisoners in the general population would identify as gay and therefore targets for physical and sexual victimization.[47] To the extent that this is true, it might make these biased assumptions about prisoners' culture and lifestyle less problematic.

The result of these interviews is sometimes that deputies have to make a judgement call about whether a prisoner should be housed in K6G. In the unclear cases, the more senior of the two deputies will think about what his testimony would be in a situation where they turned away a prisoner who was subsequently assaulted. If he does not feel like he can provide a compelling defense for moving the prisoner to the general population, then the prisoner will be allowed into K6G.[48] Thus, even in cases where a prisoner appears to be dishonest, if there is no strong evidence against him, the deputies will typically allow the prisoner to reside in K6G.[49] This classification process thus creates a prison community with much lower social distance and denser social networks than is found in most other jails and prisons.

OFFICIAL GOVERNANCE

Life in K6G is quite different from life in the general population areas of the prison. The quality of official governance in K6G is better than in the parts of the prison where general population resides. This is partly because the housing of gay and transgender prisoners is seen to be a politically sensitive issue. The specific reason for creating the unit was to avoid a lawsuit from interested, outside observers; the American Civil Liberties Union continues to play an active role in monitoring the jail more generally. A second reason is that the deputies who have been in charge of programming in the unit tend to be more invested in the process than the typical jail deputy presiding over the general population. Prisoners tended to see the two deputies as dedicated.[50] Because prisoners trusted these deputies, they were far more comfortable communicating with them and seeking out help from them.[51] Prisoners in the general population, by contrast, often feel unable to appeal for help from deputies because other prisoners will view them as weak or as an informant. K6G prisoners are also safer because they are kept segregated from the general population prisoners (or when near them, are escorted) at basically all times—during intake, visiting times, trips to court, and movement around the facility.[52] Prisoners from the general population housing areas have few opportunities to harm them.

K6G prisoners enjoy higher-quality official governance because of the small population of the unit and the ability for deputies to get to know the prisoners. This is not feasible in the larger, general population. Dolovich explains, "There are officers who know everyone [in K6G] as individuals, and because people in the unit trust those officers to look out for their interests, they are willing to reach out to the officers when issues arise."[53] These relationships are cultivated partly because of the unfortunate fact that there is a high recidivism rate for its residents. Officials estimate that 90 to 95 percent of K6G prisoners will return at some point.[54] This revolving door means that deputies learn much more about the prisoners and develop relationships with them, in some cases over many years. Partly because of these connections, deputies can resolve problems with and between K6G prisoners in ways that demonstrate a high level of tactfulness and effectiveness.[55] Dolovich describes the two main deputies operating the unit, in particular, as fair, humane, and respectful.[56]

In addition, deputies in K6G do not have to contend with the entrenched power structures that exist in the general population, where the prison gangs enforce a strict, racially segregated regimen over nearly every aspect of daily life. K6G, by contrast, is wholly free of this. There are no "gang politics" in the gay and transgender dorms. Prisoners' use of telephones, toilets, and showers are not allocated based on a prisoner's ethnicity and gang affiliation.[57] Instead of rules about who gets to eat first during meals, prisoners in K6G get their food trays on a first-come, first-served basis. Prisoners of all races can sit and socialize together, share food, and physically embrace each other without fear of violent reprisal.[58] One prisoner describes social interactions in the unit, explaining, "You're allowed to be with whomever you want to, talk to whomever you want and do whatever you want to, basically, as long as you do it in a respectable way."[59] While there are some street gang members in K6G, the prisoners have little interest in or need for gangs to control the housing unit.[60] In the past, when gang members have attempted to replicate the structures that exist in the general population, K6G prisoners prevented them from doing so and have consistently rejected any attempts at doing so or of implementing racial segregation.[61] The result is that dorms are "remarkably free from the constant threat of gang-related violence."[62]

This appears to be a co-governance regime because officials incorporate prisoners into daily operations. There is a specific leadership position for prisoners in each dorm to promote the smooth running of the daily procedures at the facility. Within each dorm, prisoners elect a "House Mouth" who is responsible for facilitating communication between prisoners and officials.[63] This position has come to be known instead as the "House Mouse," apparently an endearing twist on the usually derogatory term "rat," an insult against someone who works with officials.[64] The House Mouse is the representative of the prisoners to the staff and of the staff to the prisoners. For example, the Mouse will let deputies know if there is a shortage of necessary supplies. Likewise, it is the Mouse's job to encourage prisoners to follow the rules of the housing unit, such as being in place and quiet during prisoner counts.[65] A former prisoner in K6G explains that the House Mouse is a "very powerful position [because] it is the liaison between the deputies and the dorms."[66] The quality of the relationship between the House Mouse and officials is crucial because, according to the former prisoner, it determines "the quality of life you had in the dorms."[67]

Prisoners organize events within the dorm, such as "Family Night" on Fridays, which might include singing songs, a fashion show (with dresses made by tailoring prison-issued clothing or bedsheets), playing games, pageants, or speed dating among the prisoners.[68] One former K6G resident explains, "The community comes alive, they look after one another . . . It's not just about violence. They're inventive."[69] Many prisoners develop intimate relationships with other prisoners. One study that surveyed K6G prisoners about sexual activity over the previous 30 days found that two-thirds of prisoners had engaged in oral sex and a little more than half of respondents had engaged in anal sex while incarcerated there.[70] The survey found that 10 percent of gay respondents and 28 percent of transgender respondents reported that they had sex in exchange for money, protection, food, or other goods.[71]

As in the women's prisons discussed earlier, some people in K6G also form fictive kinships.[72] One prisoner explains, "sometimes we have a mother and a father figure. And then you have sisters and brothers. Most of my sisters that I call my sisters or my brothers, we are friends on the street."[73] One prisoner explains, "we try to be there . . . for each other . . . No matter if we hate each other in the street, but, in here, it's just one big family."[74] Another says, "[She's] my gay jailhouse niece. So, the respect is there. I have a lot of . . . sisters, nephews . . . I have three gay kids that I call my kids . . . And they're very respectful where I am concerned . . . When I come to jail, no matter which of the three dorms I go into, it's at least five or more in there that calls me Auntie."[75] One prisoner estimates that about 30 percent of K6G prisoners are in a family.[76]

Prisoners in K6G tend to have a laissez-faire view about how others can act, and social sanctions tend to be loose and informal. However, prisoners enforce some norms more strictly. For example, one K6G prisoner preferred to shift between presenting as a female and presenting as a male. Prisoners exerted significant social pressure to make a permanent choice. According to Dolovich, the prisoner "felt at constant risk of being disciplined by those K6G residents who took it upon themselves to police the gender line. Hence, s/he found K6G 'both safe and unsafe,' a feeling that arose from the need to 'constantly monitor myself in my actions.' "[77]

SIZE, SOCIAL NETWORKS, AND SOCIAL DISTANCE

In addition to higher-quality governance from officials, K6G prisoners have several other advantages in providing order. First, the gay and transgender housing unit is small. With dorms holding fewer than 150 prisoners, it is significantly smaller than the rest of Men's Central jail, which holds more than 4,000 prisoners on any day. It is much easier in a small community to get to know other people. Prisoners know other people's reputations. This creates an incentive to avoid acting in ways that others will view badly.

Second, the prisoner community has relatively low social distance. Many of these prisoners feel it is a tight-knit community with a shared cultural and moral perspective. Many have faced the same challenges and discrimination in life. One prisoner at K6G explains, "For some people, this is their home because a lot of their families have disowned them and shunned them, so we're their family."[78] Prisoners articulate a sense of shared identity and worldview. Studies of transgender prisoners, more generally, have found that they are likely to sympathize with other transgender prisoners and that they feel more trust and more care for them than other prisoners.[79] In state prisons, transgender prisoners see themselves as not just part of a community, but also more intimately as a family.[80] One transgender prisoner explains, "The transgenders are all in one group. We get along. We're like community. We have to stick together in here."[81] Another transgender prisoner, who had previously reported being raped while in the general population housing area, explained that she felt safer being around other transgender prisoners "because there are so many family—so many transgenders there."[82] The prisoner elaborates, "I consider them family. I don't have much family on the streets. With lots of transgenders in here, it feels like one big family."[83] Another prisoner in the state system says, "It's very hard to be transgender in prison because you don't identify with the gender of the people you're incarcerated with. You're sexually vulnerable all the time. It's exhausting. Because you feel like you can't be yourself. Like most people, we just want to be ourselves and express ourselves."[84] To the extent that prisoners in K6G are more tightly knit, have more similar views about norms, and are easier to get along with each other, decentralized governance mechanisms are more effective.

Third, because K6G prisoners have such a high rate of recidivism, many prisoners know each other from previous periods of confinement. When a prisoner returns to the jail, he or she will typically be housed in K6G automatically and might already have an established reputation and know the personalities of those already incarcerated there. A survey of 24 prisoners sheds light on their social networks.[85] Fifteen prisoners, upon entering K6G for the first time, reported knowing another prisoner there. Thirteen reported spending time with other K6G prisoners outside of jail. One prisoner explains that when a new prisoner arrives, "everybody is at the front door, who is it, who is it? Is it somebody I know? And then when they walk in and some of them, they're all getting hugs like it's a big old family reunion."[86] Another explains, "in here, you come back to people that you know out there in the streets, and it's like coming back to your own people, to your own family."[87] One prisoner reports, "Some come in there and it's like Christmas to them ... I'm not from here, and I've noticed a lot of them come in here, they all know each other. They know each other from being incarcerated so many times, and from going into [K6G]. So, it's like, hey, they come in and they all cry because they haven't seen each other in a long time, or they cry when they go home."[88] As a result, when a prisoner returns to K6G they are often not frightened or anxious, but even anticipate that they will be met by "many familiar and even friendly faces when they get to the dorms."[89] For many, the unit is a "comfortable and even welcoming community for many of its residents."[90]

CONCLUSION

Given the higher quality of official governance, and that the conditions are amenable to the effective use of decentralized extralegal mechanisms, how does life in K6G fare when compared to the general population? One obvious criterion to examine is whether prisoners in K6G are safer than prisoners in the general population. The evidence on this question presents an interesting picture. First, one survey finds that prisoners in K6G feel strongly that they are safe in the unit.[91] When asked if a K6G prisoner felt "very safe," "safe," "unsafe," or "very unsafe," 30 out of 32 respondents answered "safe" or "very safe."[92] There is also the indirect evidence that some prisoners attempt to sneak into K6G because they feel it is safer or more relaxed than the general population.[93] In K6G, prisoners do not tend to fear each other, but are actually more likely to see jail deputies as a source of disrespect and potential harm.[94]

However, the evidence that K6G prisoners feel safe tells us less than it would ideally. Several issues limit our ability to make inferences from this sample. First, if we interpret people attempting to sneak into K6G as evidence for its greater safety, hundreds of prisoners everyday do not attempt to do so.[95] If people attempting to sneak into K6G is evidence for its safety, then people not attempting to do so would seem to offer evidence that K6G is viewed as less safe than the general population. The second limitation is that because the survey samples the opinions of prisoners in K6G, it is unable to observe the opinions of prisoners who did not view K6G as more desirable.[96]

As mentioned, another interesting difference with the general population housing units is that K6G is free of gang politics.[97] One deputy at the jail explains the absence of gang control, saying, "In K6G it's different, they don't run those politics."[98] The gay and transgender dorm is also not racially segregated, a hallmark of gang control in California's correctional facilities.[99] Prisoners in K6G do not rely on centralized governance institutions, like prison gangs, because they do not need to. Prisoners feel safe, so they do not need to turn to gangs for protection.[100] Small prison communities do not require the bureaucracy and organizational apparatus that characterize gang-controlled areas in the rest of the jail. The classification process leads K6G to have relatively low social distance, and prisoners share life experiences, worldviews, and interests. This explanation is consistent with the observed importance of gangs in the general population (where there are large, diverse populations of strangers) and their absence in K6G (small, more similar populations who share social networks). It also explains why prison gangs are important in today's massive California prison population, but did not exist for more than a century, when prisons and prison populations were far smaller.

Another puzzling factor in assessing K6G is that it appears there is actually more fighting there than in the general population. Prisoners participate in one-on-one altercations more frequently than in the general population.[101] One resident of the dorm believes that much of the violence in K6G results from jealousy over relationships.[102] The general population, by contrast, appears "remarkably calm," but this masks the pressure that prisoners feel to follow gang rules.[103] In fact, gang leaders prohibit prisoners from having unauthorized fights. Instead, they have systems of strict, written rules that prisoners must follow, systems for resolving disputes, and approved fights are conducted in a controlled way. Gangs provide this governance because large-scale riots and serious acts of violence are destabilizing to the social order and draw officials' attention to the underground economy.[104]

In summary, the case of K6G provides a final, useful test of the governance theory of prison social order. It combines all three of the demographic characteristics discussed thus far. Women's prisons were small, and English prisons were small with social networks. The K6G housing unit has a small population, with social networks, and low social distance. The governance theory predicts that K6G residents can easily rely on decentralized governance mechanisms, which will work well. The evidence is consistent with this claim. The counterfactual prediction is that if the population in K6G increased to levels similar to those in the general population housing units, then prisoners would invest more in centralized extralegal governance institutions. In addition, it would be informative if we could observe several additional cases to better discern the relative importance of size, social networks, and social distance. In particular, it would be useful to observe housing units with different combinations of these three factors. For example, what would the social order look like in prisoner communities that have low social distance and pre-existing social networks, but very large populations? Likewise, what happens when prisoners have low social distance and small populations, but no pre-existing social networks? These cases would teach us more about the relative importance of size, social networks, and social distance.

PART III

Conclusion

8

Understanding Institutional Diversity

The power of a theory is exactly proportional to the diversity of situations it can explain.

Elinor Ostrom[1]

All prisons are similar in fundamental ways. They incarcerate people who are charged with or convicted of crimes. They tend to hold a disproportionately large number of people from disadvantaged and ethnic, racial, and other minority communities. Prisoners tend to be more violent, less patient, less trusting, and less educated than the population outside of prison. Most prisoners must live and interact with other prisoners; they have no voluntary exit option. When social scientists think about social dilemmas, these are some of the most important theoretical characteristics that determine the nature and outcome of the interaction. These similarities between prisons are not superficial but central. For these reasons, I argue that we can study prison social order from a comparative perspective, even across what initially appears to be disparate settings.

However, it is also obvious that prisons differ in many ways, and this is precisely why we should study them from a comparative perspective. Nevertheless, there is very little comparative analysis in existing studies of prison social order. The focus is overwhelmingly on single-site studies.[2] The methodological approaches used in this research tradition drive this emphasis. However, Nicola Lacey argues that it also leads scholars to focus on documenting fascinating local details and to ignore comparisons.[3] Case studies and ethnography are valuable partly because the researcher can develop deep knowledge of the case, leading to a high degree of within-case explanation. Subtle and nuanced interactions observed in ethnographic studies can help us understand, for example, why different housing units within the same prison can have different feelings of orderliness. An astute observer might find that differences arise because of the personality of a few prisoners or a member of staff.

Yet, the problem with this extreme attention to detail is that some, or possibly many, of the explanations discovered in a particular case will have little to no external validity.[4] The more unique the details unearthed in a prison, the fewer generalizable claims one can make. The approach I advocate here is different. It is not designed to maximize within-case explanatory power. The goal is instead to increase our cross-case explanatory power—to identify factors that explain differences in many diverse prisons. That requires stepping away from many of the details that fascinate us and focusing on more general, systematic influences that exist across cases. The theory that I advance here cannot predict all of the variation in extralegal institutions at all prisons, and its predictions are more probabilistic than deterministic. However, the gain from a comparative approach is the ability to say something about a far broader range of social orders.

The results of this theoretical effort are the empirical predictions discussed in chapter 1 and tested in chapters 2 through 7. To review, these propositions can be framed as four ways that officials' choices influence extralegal governance institutions. First, one of the most important choices that officials make is about the amount and quality of resources, administration, and governance provided to prisoners. When officials govern well, prisoners have little need to govern themselves. The case studies of

Nordic prisons found that officials provide significant capacity and high-quality governance and prisoners invest extremely little in their own extra-legal institutions. Likewise, when officials do not govern, prisoners often find it valuable to do so. The cases of Brazilian and Bolivian facilities show that, in the face of few official resources, prisoners create extensive and elaborate institutions, including housing associations, extensive market exchange, and a vibrant civil society. Finally, for most of the history of the Andersonville prisoner of war camp, neither prisoners nor officials governed. Neither group had resources, nor were there significant benefits from engaging in collective action. Taken together, both the aggregate-level data on prison systems and the detailed case studies of specific facilities are consistent with the empirical implications of the governance theory.

Second, when prison officials incarcerate relatively few people in smaller prisons, it is easier for prisoners to rely on decentralized governance mechanisms. To test this claim, I compare prison social order in men's and women's prisons in California. There the population of men's prisons has skyrocketed in recent decades, and prisoners have turned to centralized extralegal governance, while the women's prison population has always been relatively small. Consistent with the governance theory, from the 1960s to the present, Californian female prisoners have relied on a decentralized system of social control where individuals' reputations are crucial. One key part of this decentralized system is adherence to the convict code, and some women also participate in fictive kinships. Compared to men's prisons, they are also more willing to rely on help from officials. There is little hierarchy, ethnic segregation, mutual responsibility, or organized leadership, and no reliance on their own written rules and regulations. At the same time, Californian male prisoners responded to increasing populations by investing in centralized extralegal governance because they could not rely on decentralized reputation mechanisms. The case studies from England and Los Angeles further support the prediction that decentralized governance can work well in relatively small prison populations.

Third, when prisoners wish to produce extralegal governance institutions, officials' choices about prison location influences whether prisoners can rely on pre-existing social networks to govern their interactions.

I assess this claim by examining several case studies of English prisons and comparing them to the extralegal institutions found in Californian men's prisons. In England, prison officials incarcerate people close to their home communities. They also have relatively small prisons. The combination of these two factors means that English prisoners can more easily obtain information about other prisoners' reputations. As a result, they rely on decentralized extralegal governance institutions. The case studies discussed provide substantial evidence that pre-prison social networks are a crucial source of information about people's reputations. Moreover, the knowledge that these networks and reputations will persist after incarceration incentivizes good behavior during confinement. In California, by contrast, prisoners are housed in relatively few prisons that are extremely large and that tend to be far away from a prisoner's home community. As a result, within any particular prison, there are far more communities represented and large prison populations undermine the effectiveness of decentralized mechanisms.

Finally, I argue that the classification process that officials use to make housing choices determines the social distance—the extent to which people share appearances, beliefs, customs, practices, and other characteristics that define their identity—within the prisoner community.[5] I test this claim by examining an unusual housing unit for gay and transgender prisoners in the Los Angeles County Jail. The classification process that regulates access to this housing area selects for a specific demographic of people based on their lifestyle, appearance, history, and social network. The result is that prisoners are characterized by low social distance, so decentralized governance works well. By contrast, the larger and more diverse community in the general population housing area of the same jail relies on more centralized extralegal governance institutions.

One aspect that I have not discussed directly is the relative desirability of different prison systems. One reason for not doing so is that we lack much of the information that would seem necessary to make any substantive normative assessments. Nevertheless, a more complete comparative analysis of prisons would be richer if it could say something about the effectiveness of prisons. The multifaceted nature of prisons means no single metric can summarize prison effectiveness. There are several different approaches. John J. DiIulio focuses on order, amenity, and service. We can measure some aspects of this in objective ways, such as with reported rates of rapes, assaults, homicides, and riots.[6] Surveys can also measure the more subjective elements. For example, surveys can ask prisoners how safe, calm, and predictable the prison feels. Sociologist Charles Logan identifies eight dimensions of prison performance: security ("keep them in"), safety ("keep them safe"), order ("keep them in line"), care ("keep them healthy"), activity ("keep them busy"), justice ("do it with fairness"), conditions ("without undue suffering"), and management ("as efficiently as possible").[7] He identifies more than two hundred possible measures that could be obtained through official prison records and surveys that would provide information about the performance on these eight dimensions. However, in many prisons around the globe, official records will not be systematic or reliable enough to contribute to these measures.

In the face of poor bureaucratic capacity, it might be better to rely on prisoner surveys. The Measuring the Quality of Prison Life survey measures the "moral performance" of prisons.[8] The survey focuses on relational aspects rather than objective measures and outcomes. It asks prisoners to report how much they agree with statements along numerous dimensions of prison performance: including respect, humanity, staff-prisoner relationships, support, trust, fairness, order, safety, well-being, personal development, family contact, power, meaning, and decency.

Measuring prison performance is difficult, but these approaches suggest that it is possible. Given the rigorousness and growing popularity of the Quality of Prison Life survey, it seems like a focal survey instrument for researchers to coordinate on. However, given that the survey emphasizes staff-prisoner relationships, it might need modification for use in prisons with little staff presence. Jennifer Peirce's research in prisons in the Dominican Republic shows one productive way to modify and implement it in prisons with less official capacity.[9] If qualitative and ethnographic scholars were able to implement these surveys alongside their own research interests, it would open up a wider range of inquiry into the comparative study of prison social order. This would allow scholars to better classify prisons by regime type, explain why particular governance mechanisms emerge, and measure how this affects prison performance.

There are a few issues that fall outside of the scope of my analysis. First, I have not explained why prison officials provide the quality of official governance that they do. Many factors can affect officials' choices, including financial and political constraints, public opinion, reigning philosophies of punishment, and correctional officers' unions. Second, I have not explained why regimes become either co-governing or self-governing. In the cases of the Brazilian jail and the gay and transgender dorms, it seems that it was politically acceptable and productive for officials to work somewhat openly with prisoners. In other instances, officials might view giving authority or resources to prisoners as too risky. I suspect that many of the factors that influence the quality of official governance likewise affect this choice. Finally, I have not explained how prison officials make choices about the size, location, and classification of prisons. Officials often believe that large prisons enjoy economies of scale that lower the average costs per prisoner. The location of prisons is sometimes politically motivated. Some communities dislike the appearance of prisons or the traffic of people who visit them. Others lobby for prison construction because of the jobs that prisons bring. Each of these are important questions, but they fall too far outside of the scope of this book to address.

COMPARATIVE ANALYSIS

While this book offers a theoretical and empirical argument, it also advances a methodological one. Essentially, I believe prison scholars have much to learn from the methods used in comparative institutional analysis. Comparative scholars study how differences in institutions cause differences in outcomes. For example, a classic question in comparative politics is why some countries that transition from autocracy to democracy are more stable than others are. One common explanation is that it depends on whether the new democracy is based on either a parliamentary or a presidential system.[10] These studies leverage similarities across political systems (both democracies) that vary in important ways (parliamentary or presidential system) while controlling for other possible explanatory factors (such as national income). Prison scholars can likewise leverage similarities across prison systems (self-governing regimes) that vary in important ways (small or large prison population) while controlling for other possible explanatory factors (low or high social distance).

There is also a large and well-developed literature on the methods and methodology of comparative institutional analysis from which to draw.[11] Many of the great works in comparative politics and comparative historical sociology rely on the historical investigations and evidence of others.[12] In a similar way, I have argued that we can rely on the single-site prison research of other scholars to make comparisons across prisons.

A major constraint that has prevented earlier attempts at comparative analysis of extralegal prison institutions is that there were simply too few studies to draw on. However, now we have more—and more diverse— studies available. The ability to "scale up" the number of observations in this way has the potential to make this a collaborative (though decentralized) intellectual effort. In this book, I draw on existing studies. However, a more intentional and systematic effort by researchers could greatly accelerate our learning by making more studies relevant to a comparative project.[13] This methodological argument is both ambitious and modest. I am calling for prison scholars to incorporate a far greater comparative perspective into their analysis. However, it is a modest argument in the sense that this approach has a long tradition in other social sciences, including political science, sociology, and economics.

One way to advance this comparative perspective is to develop a typology for classifying prisons. In chapter 1, I offered four possible regime types: self-governance, co-governance, official governance, and minimal governance. These seem helpful, but they are certainly not definitive. Some scholars will find that their study site fits nicely into one of these categories. Others will not. For example, this book did not consider life in concentration camps or under the Soviet Gulag, and those regimes seem to differ in substantive ways from the four types that I propose.[14] Like many Latin American prisons, for instance, gulags were places of desperate poverty. However, unlike Latin American prisons, captives there were not free to respond to their extreme deprivation. Instead, they were forced to work long hours of back-breaking manual labor. This type of "oppressive governance regime" does not fit easily into any of the four types that I discuss. If scholars can converge on a useful classification scheme, then comparative work becomes easier. It facilitates coding new cases and helps scholars to choose which cases to compare.

In this book, I identify several key governance mechanisms, including a trustee system, associations and committees, officials, prison gangs, fictive kinships, postcode affiliations, norms about sensibility, the convict code, and the House Mouse. There are likely many other ways that prisoners produce governance, such as religious groups, sports teams, and military and paramilitary organizations. The governance theory makes predictions about the degree to which these mechanisms are centralized, but not about the specific manifestation that emerges. It would be helpful to know more about the range and diversity of extralegal governance mechanisms.

The governance theory offers an explanation for whether extralegal institutions will be more or less important and whether they will be more or less centralized. Both existing studies and future work on prison governance can provide additional tests of these claims. To do so, scholars would examine the quality of official governance, prison size, social networks, and social distance to see if they correlate with the predicted scope and organization of extralegal institutions. In some cases, the prison social order will confirm the theory. As more out-of-sample cases fit the theory's predictions, it would increase support for the governance theory.

In some cases, new studies will disconfirm the theory's predictions. These cases might indicate that the theory is underdeveloped in some way. For example, it might be that housing prisoners close to their home communities is not especially helpful if the prison population is extremely large. Likewise, it might be that prisoners who are part of a paramilitary organization, like those that have been prominent in Northern Ireland's prisons, centralize even in the face of relatively small prison populations because the cost of doing so is low or because the centralization generates benefits outside of the prison or for non-governance related purposes.[15] Comparing across cases should help us untangle these messy relationships.

Ideally, when we discover new potential explanations in one case, we would be able to test its explanatory value in other cases as well. If past cases do not support the new explanation, then it raises the likelihood that the new variable is an idiosyncratic characteristic of the new case, rather than being systematically important. The ability to conduct such examinations depends partly on what information is available. Some key pieces of evidence might not have been collected at the time of past studies. For some types of evidence, it might be easy to collect relevant information for past cases, such as the year a prison was built or whether prison officers were unionized at the time of the study. Just as many people contribute to improving open-source software, other scholars could extend previous work completed by others. However, this will be more difficult when the initial study anonymizes the site of the prison. In general, the value of collecting comparable data across prisons is the ability to more easily test new variables across multiple cases.

BROADER LESSONS

Prisoners face many of the same problems that any society faces. How will violence and disorder be avoided? What institutions can facilitate order? Where will these institutions come from? Studying the diversity of institutions in prisons offers several broader lessons for understanding these questions. First, prisons provide a test of the common claim that self-enforcing exchange works best when populations are small and can easily use reputation mechanisms. The prison experience confirms this lesson. It also allows us to test a variant of that hypothesis. In many classic studies of self-enforcing exchange, such as the New York Diamond Dealers Club or the rural neighbors of Shasta County, participants could not rely on threats of, or the use of, serious violence.[16] This is not quite as true in prison. Prisoners are likely to have a more credible threat, and possibly more readiness, to use serious violence. If there is a larger proportion of "willing punishers" in the community, then there will be greater provision of the public good of enforcing norms. Nevertheless, cases discussed here show that these factors are insufficient to allow norms to scale up and govern large populations.

Second, prisons inform the debate on the viability and robustness of self-governance. For instance, many of the earliest stock exchanges operated as clubs, and they enforced agreements for a variety of financial options that governments outlawed.[17] Part of the reason why these exchanges flourished is that the clubs could exclude people who they thought would be uncooperative or untrustworthy. Prisoners, by contrast, do not get to decide who will live among them. Prisons are also likely to house people who are more likely to break the rules or be disruptive. Nevertheless, many prisoners engage in collective action. Studying prisons also provides a test of a second challenge to this literature, which is that self-enforcing exchange only works because people can rely on state courts in the event that extralegal mechanisms fail.[18] Prison social order shows us that this is not necessarily so. In prisons like San Pedro, trade flourishes despite residents' inability to rely on official governance as a fall-back option. This provides further evidence that the "shadow of the state" is not necessary to make self-enforcing exchange possible. In each of these ways, these cases show that self-governance institutions can be remarkably robust.

A third lesson is that prisons provide a useful test of how and why social distance influences social organization. The case studies here confirm that low social distance helps decentralized governance to work better. However, people vary in many ways, and it is not clear on which margin social distance matters. In the case of the gay and transgender dorm, certain lifestyle and lived experiences were focal. In the English prisons, the culture of one's postcode or housing estate played a significant role. This suggests that studies of social distance should focus on subjective perceptions and interpretations of participants, more than simple objective measures, such as the commonly used measure of ethno-linguistic fractionalization. Related to this, social distance is neither fixed nor exogenous.[19] People can alter themselves on certain margins to reduce their social distance in a community. Past work identifies other ways in which people can reduce their social distance, such as through intermarriage, learning a language, and adopting the rituals and practices of another culture.[20] Making changes like these can also provide a signal of trustworthiness and assurance. These investments are more valuable to a person who has a long time horizon over which to recoup their costs. Investments in reducing social distance credibly signal a desire for long-run, cooperative relationships.

A fourth lesson is about the relationships between demographics and ethnicity. Ethnic identity plays a less important role in the prisons studied here than it does in Californian prisons today. In California, ethnicity is incredibly important, but that was not always the case. Prior to the 1960s, prisoners did not rely on racial segregation as they do now. Prisons in California have become more racially intolerant during a time that overt prejudice has become far less common in the free world. Many prisoners say they are not racist, have interracial friendships, and conduct business across racial lines. We can explain these apparently contradictory observations by the fact that men's prisons transitioned from a system of norms based on an individual's reputation to a community responsibility system based on a group's reputation. Prisoners need the latter to govern large populations of strangers. However, for it to work well, people need a way to identify the group affiliation of unfamiliar people. Skin color is one low-cost way of doing so. The theory and evidence suggests that ethnic identity and salience is endogenous to demographic characteristics, such as the size of the population. The lack of strong ethnic divisions in the prisons studied in this book further supports this claim and suggests a new mechanism by which ethnicity becomes salient.

Finally, the absence of a community responsibility system within small prisons speaks to broader issues about institutions, individual rights, and freedoms. In Californian men's prisons today, individual's rights and autonomy are suppressed to facilitate coordination between larger ethnically and racially divided groups. We often observe this pattern in other settings when large populations of people cannot rely on strong and effective states. Historically, people often lived, and some still live, as part of community responsibility systems based on clans, ethnicity, or religion.[21] Legal scholar Mark Weiner documents how this "ancient form of social organization" is found around the world and through history, such as in Medieval Iceland

and parts of modern Afghanistan, India, Pakistan, and Southern Somalia.[22] In these systems, the group's reputation becomes more relevant than the individual's reputation. This creates a powerful incentive for each group to police its own members to ensure that its reputation is and remains in good standing. As a result, there is tremendous in-group pressure that facilitates cooperative relationships between groups. However, this often gives rise to horrific practices, such as honor killings and restrictions on women's rights. In these cases, better government could increase individual's rights by freeing them from the local authoritarianism of mutual responsibility systems.[23]

APPENDIX
A Note on Methods

There have been two major impediments to explaining variation in extra-legal prison governance. The first problem is that the question is so broad that standard statistical models of causal inference are difficult to apply. Ideally, we could intentionally alter the quality of official governance and of the demographics of the prisoner community to test these empirical predictions. That would allow us to change one factor at a time, observe the correlations that emerge, and address concerns about confounding variables and reverse causality. Of course, treating prisoners in this way is neither possible nor ethical. Experimental and quasi-experimental methods are not impossible, but findings ways to implement them are limited enough in number and scope that it does not offer much analytical traction.[1]

My empirical approach is to compare prisons based on a most-similar-systems design.[2] Prisons around the world share a number of fundamental similarities, either by definition or practice. They incarcerate people who have been charged with or convicted of a crime and hold a dispro-portionately large number of people from disadvantaged socioeconomic backgrounds and from ethnic, racial, and other minority communities. Compared to the non-prison population, prisoners tend to discount the future more highly, have less education, and more violent histories. They have few exit options. An obvious objection is that there are many differences across countries too. If we do not control for important differences, then the results will be unreliable. For example, Brazil and Norway are remark-ably different countries, so there might be a confounding factor that actually explains differences in prison social order. It is important to be alert to such problems. However, there is also a risk of controlling for factors that we are actually trying to test. The fact that Brazil and Norway have, for instance, different cultures is part of the reason why the quality of their official governance institutions differ. Controlling for culture writ large would undermine the analysis.

Following past work in comparative institutional analysis, my goal is to show that the governance theory is consistent with the evidence in a geographically diverse and historical sample of relevant cases.[3] The case studies are not a test of the framework in a technical or statistical sense. Instead, I argue that these cases are consistent with the theory's empirical implications. I also provide extensive evidence in each case arguing that these are not merely correlations, but that the specific mechanisms in operation are those implied in the theoretical discussion.[4] The richness of the case studies provides a wealth of evidence about these mechanisms that is simply not available in studies relying only on thin quantitative measures. This evidence is especially appropriate in studies of institutions, which often put the causal mechanism, rather than the causal effect, at the heart of the analysis. The goal is to understand the mechanisms that generate and sustain an institutional outcome.[5] In these ways, my aim is not only to understand variation across cases, but also to describe the governance institutions found within these cases.[6]

The second major impediment to understanding the diversity of prisoner governance institutions is lack of data. It would be helpful if we could accurately and precisely measure the quality of governance produced by both officials and prisoners. Unfortunately, this is not feasible. The concept of governance is multifaceted and difficult to reduce to simple quantitative measures without losing crucial parts of its meaning.[7] Throughout the book, I include data on factors that seem like reasonable proxies for dimensions of governance, such as the ratio of prisoners to staff, occupancy levels, and the availability of food, water, and clothing. I also provide evidence on how effective these efforts seem to be. However, this is still far from ideal, and I lack comparable, reliable, and systematic data on many important aspects of life in prison across these cases. In addition, officials do not collect or will not provide data on many issues because of concerns with confidentiality and security. Even when official data are available, they cannot tell us much about the underground economy and extralegal activities. As a result, if we wish to understand why the informal life in prison varies so much, we must look elsewhere for evidence.

I draw on the qualitative and ethnographic literatures in anthropology, criminology, and sociology.[8] Although ethnographers hesitate to do comparative work across different sites, I argue that these studies offer an excellent opportunity to combine a comparative institutional perspective with rich, qualitative evidence.[9] A major advantage of the qualitative methods used in studies like these is the thick description of prisoners' social environment, interactions, and identities.[10] They provide rich evidence on the everyday life of prisoners in a way that allows us to understand why prisoners require governance and how they access it.[11]

One challenge facing someone who wishes for a comparative perspective is that these works are overwhelmingly based on studies in a single prison or country.[12] Part of the reason for the narrow focus in these studies is the substantial investment of time and resources needed to conduct them. Learning the historical, organizational, and operational details of a specific prison system takes time. Gaining access to the field can be complicated and time-consuming. A scholar must establish his or her place as an observer in the community, discern subtle social dynamics, build trust with prisoners and staff, learn how prisoners view the world, and collect, code, and analyze large amounts of qualitative evidence. In some cases, scholars must also learn a new language or travel to distant countries.

For all these reasons, any particular piece of qualitative or ethnographic research can give us a tremendous depth of knowledge but relatively little breadth.[13] Legal scholar Nicola Lacey notes the near absence of comparative analysis and argues that it is driven partly by the methods used. She writes, the "very detailed elaborations of the internal dynamics of penal arrangements—is equally inhospitable to comparative approaches... [and] has generally precluded systematic analysis of differences at national or regional levels."[14] This has led to a regrettable situation. Scholars have "become mesmerized by the fascinating details of local particularity" and therefore can say little from a comparative perspective.[15]

To address this concern, I use the growing literature of qualitative and ethnographic studies to understand institutional diversity. The goal is to leverage enough of these studies of the local prison environment to provide a comparative account. To do so, there must be enough theoretically relevant studies and they must be drawn from a sufficiently wide sample of global prisons. Until recently, this might have been a significant problem. In the early 2000s, prison scholars Jonathan Simon and Loïc Wacquant both decried the decline of ethnographic studies of prison life, which (especially in the United States) happened at the same time that our need to understand incarceration was of great urgency because of the dramatic rise in use.[16]

Nevertheless, since their writing, the number and variety of qualitative and ethnographic studies of prison social order have continued to accumulate. There has been a reemergence of this type of work in the United States, and scholars have studied numerous aspects of men's and women's prisons across the country. Despite their concerns (or perhaps partly because of them), in the nearly 20 years since they wrote, we know a great deal more now about what life is like in U.S. prisons. Prison research has also thrived in other countries. In the United Kingdom, there is a robust qualitative research tradition.[17] There is a growing literature on life in Latin American prisons.[18] Studies of Nordic prisons have similarly proliferated.[19] The "Global Prisons Research Network" is further evidence of the geographic reach of ethnographic work. It is an online community of scholars that promotes in-depth studies of prison practices in Africa, Asia, the Middle East, Latin America, and the former Soviet states. Members of the group study prisons in 45 different countries and nine regions (not including the United States). There are perhaps now more scholars using qualitative and ethnographic methods to study prison life in more countries than ever before. Throughout the book, I draw on this work as evidence in my comparative institutional analysis of prison social order.[20]

To avoid concerns about cherry-picking these cases, it is important that I justify my case selection. I selected cases based on variation in the explanatory variables in my theory and with purposive sampling (see Table A.1). Random sampling of cases is inappropriate when there is a relatively small sample because it offers no guarantee against a biased sample and might not offer sufficient variation.[21] Instead, it is better to select cases intentionally to allow for variation in the explanatory variables: whether the quality of official governance is low, moderate, or high, and whether prisoner demographics are large, have pre-prison social networks, or low social distance.

Some cases are informative because they take an extreme value for one of the explanatory variables. This is useful for several reasons. It helps us sidestep the difficulty in precisely measuring the quality of governance. For example, we might not be able to accurately or precisely measure when the

Table A.1: Overview of Cases

Variation in the Quality of Official Governance

Polinter (Brazil)
San Pedro (Bolivia) — Low-quality
Andersonville (Georgia, USA)

Oslo Prison (Norway) — High-quality
Kollen (Norway)

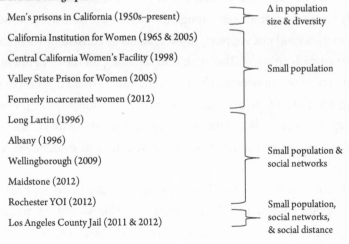

Variation in Demographics

Men's prisons in California (1950s–present) — Δ in population size & diversity

California Institution for Women (1965 & 2005)
Central California Women's Facility (1998)
Valley State Prison for Women (2005) — Small population
Formerly incarcerated women (2012)

Long Lartin (1996)
Albany (1996)
Wellingborough (2009) — Small population & social networks
Maidstone (2012)

Rochester YOI (2012) — Small population, social networks, & social distance
Los Angeles County Jail (2011 & 2012)

quality of official governance changes by a small amount. As a result, we cannot study how small changes affect the informal organization of prisoner society, which likewise might not change at all or might change only imperceptibly. However, by looking at an extreme case, such as the Bolivian case, we can see what governance mechanisms emerge when the quality of official governance is essentially zero. If the empirical implications are not met even in these extreme cases, then the theory is unlikely to be true. Analysis of extreme cases can never offer decisive confirmation of a theory, but it can provide strong evidence against it. Finally, we can draw on methodological arguments from the medical sciences about causal relationships to help understand these cases. In particular, even in the absence of randomization, the dose-response effect—where small doses have small effects, and larger doses have larger effects—is indicative of a causal relationship.[22] The extreme cases of prisons in Nordic and Latin American countries are analogous to incredibly large and small doses of the quality of official governance. In response, we see substantial variation in the importance of extralegal governance, and this is evidence in favor of the theory.

It is also important to use care in choosing which particular studies to draw on as evidence. Political scientist Ian Lustick warns, "If the selection of sources is performed unself-consciously and without adequate safeguards, then one must presume that there will be a tendency to elicit from the shelves of the library . . . those sources organized most consistently with the terms of the researcher's argument. Theories may therefore likely be corroborated even though the best or the bulk of relevant work by historians would not support, or even stand as consistent with, the theory under consideration."[23] This is akin to selecting on the dependent variable and is a type of confirmation bias. The literatures that I draw on as evidence bring a variety of theoretical, conceptual, and ideological presumptions and approaches to bear (including critical, constructivist, and positivist approaches), so researcher bias in the selection of evidence is a genuine concern.[24]

An obvious way to avoid this concern would be to replicate each of the original studies that I cite. However, this would be tremendously costly. Writing about the concern of selection bias in historical sociology, sociologist and political scientist Theda Skocpol argues that to re-do each historical study by engaging with the primary resources would be "disastrous."[25] It would require far too much time and training to become sufficiently expert to carry out one's own analysis. This is even truer in the case of resource-intense, ethnographic research in prisons around the globe.

Following Lustick's advice, I have adopted several strategies to avoid selection bias in my evidence.[26] First, I identify areas of overlap and agreement across scholars who may differ in their approach, discipline, or ideology. If most scholars agree with some core set of facts, even when they differ in their approaches or ideologies, then the reader can be confident that it is not merely an idiosyncratic finding or selection bias. Second, I discuss conflicting accounts when they arise. Where necessary, I explain why scholars disagree and why I find some research more persuasive than others. I likewise provide detail about the research design used in many of these studies so that the reader can assess their merits in a transparent way.[27] Finally, I have tried to be as clear as possible about what I believe are the most important alternative hypotheses and to what degree the evidence supports them. In short, being aware of the possibility of selection bias and adopting an open and critical assessment of sources reduces the likelihood of my seeking out only self-confirming sources.

NOTES

Chapter 1

1. Varella 1999, 118
2. Sykes 1958, xxx
3. Weiner 2014
4. Darwin 2003 [1859], 507. Following Michael Munger 2010, it is important to note that the selection mechanism for social institutions is quite different from the process of biological evolution. Neither should this analogy be construed to suggest that I think institutions are always globally efficient. More generally, see Elinor Ostrom 2005 for a masterful discussion on understanding institutional diversity.
5. Northrop 2013 [1904], 75
6. Shammas 2014, 107
7. Libell 2016
8. War of Rebellion, Series 2, Volume VIII, 599
9. Price 1973, 222
10. Price 1973, 221
11. Romero 2011
12. Romero 2011
13. Romero 2011
14. Inter-American Commission on Human Rights 2011, 29
15. Garces 2010, 462
16. Garces 2010, 478–479
17. Crewe 2009, 80–81; see also, Crewe and Laws 2016, 3; on the importance of exit options for promoting cooperation, see Orbell, Schwartz-Shea, and Simmons 1984; Vanberg and Congleton 1992; Schuessler 1989
18. Sykes 1958, xxxi
19. Coyle, Fair, Jacobson, and Walmsley 2016
20. Petersilia 2003, 3
21. Lessing and Denyer Willis 2019, 589
22. This book also contributes to academic debates on prison social order. See classic works, such as Clemmer 1940, Sykes 1958, Foucault 1977, Jacobs 1977, and DiIulio 1987. It also touches on broader debates on the role of punishment in society, such as Fleisher 1989; Garland 2001; Pratt, Brown, Brown, Wallsworth, and Morrison

2005; Tonry 2007; Lacey 2008; Lappi-Seppälä 2008; Nelken 2010; Christie 2017; Thompson 2017.

23. North 1990, 3; for a review of institutions, see Greif and Kingston 2011; on property rights in particular, see Barzel 1997; I mostly follow in the rational choice institutionalist tradition, but I do incorporate some elements of the historical and sociological institutionalists as well (Hall and Taylor 1996)
24. North 1990; Ostrom 1990; Greif 2006; Ostrom 2005; Acemoglu, Johnson, and Robinson 2005
25. Tullock 1967
26. Vogel 2018
27. See the literature on self-governance, such as Leeson 2007a; Leeson 2007c; Leeson 2014; Stringham 2015; Richman 2017
28. See, for example, Benson 1990, 1998; Cook 1986; Ayers and Levitt 1998
29. On the role of architecture and imprisonment, see Hancock and Jewkes 2011
30. Glaeser 1998, 3; Davis 1988; Lee and McCrary 2005; Beraldo, Caruso, and Turati 2013; Avio 1998, 145; DiIulio 1987, 177; prisons can also cause people to become more active offenders after release (Bayer, Hjalmarsson, and Pozen 2009; Drago, Galbiati, and Vertova 2011).
31. Leeson 2007b; Murtazashvili and Murtazashvili 2014
32. Kalinich and Stojkovic 1985; D'Amico 2008; Kaminski 2004 is a seminal analysis using game theory to understand prison social norms
33. Of course, corrupt officials can participate in the underground economy. However, when they do so, they too can no longer rely openly on legitimate governance sources.
34. Varella 1999, 141
35. Darke 2018
36. Crouch and Marquart 1989; DiIulio 1987, 111–113
37. Sykes 1958; Irwin and Cressey 1962; Irwin 1980
38. These four simple categories capture something vital in the particular cases that I study. However, it is likely that other cases might not fit easily into these categories and some will be hybrid cases. These categories are not meant to be mutually exclusive and exhaustive. A prison's regime type can also change over time. With these qualifications in mind, I hope these regime types can serve as a useful starting point for thinking about social order and make it easier to draw descriptive inferences about governance regimes in prisons around the world.
39. Landes and Posner 1975; on collective action problems more generally, see Olson 1971; Hardin 1982
40. Gambetta 1993; Varese 1994; 2001; 2011; see also important work on governance in Brazilian favelas and other Latin American regions by Arias 2006, 2017
41. See also Schelling 1971; Skaperdas 2001; Bandiera 2003; Varese 2010; Skarbek 2008; Skarbek 2011; Varese 2011; Shortland and Varese 2014; Skarbek 2016; Acemoglu, De Feo, and De Luca 2017; Buonanno, Durante, Prarolo, and Vanin 2015; Dimico, Isopi, and Olsson 2017; Wang 2017; Campana and Varese 2018; Shortland 2019.
42. Skarbek 2014; Skarbek 2016

43. Economists and political scientists likewise argue that state formation and centralization were driven partly by increases in the population (North 1987, 1990). On the relationship between states and organized crime, see Tilly 1985.
44. For important early work on the choice between markets and organizations, see Coase 1937 and Williamson 1985.
45. Bernstein 1992; Greif 1989; Landa 1981; Ellickson 1991; Schaeffer 2008
46. Leeson 2008; see also Akerlof 1997; Akerlof and Kranton 2010; in the context of self-enforcing exchange, see Landa 1981; Ellickson 1991; Bernstein 1992; Landa 1994; Schaeffer 2008
47. One proxy of social distance is measures of ethno-linguistic fractionalization; see, for example, Leeson 2008; Alesina and Spolaore 2003, 18–23
48. Alesina and Spolaore 1997; Easterly and Levine 1997; Alesina, Baqir, and Easterly 1999; Alesina and Spolaore 2003; Alesina and Ferrara 2005; Rugh and Trounstine 2011
49. Skarbek 2014
50. Trammell and Chenault 2009
51. Coyle, Fair, Jacobson, and Walmsley 2016

Chapter 2
1. Varella 1999, 163
2. Useem and Piehl 2008; Birkbeck 2011
3. Darke 2018, 30
4. Mariner 1998, 32
5. Birkbeck 2011
6. See Inter-American Commission on Human Rights 2011 for an extensive discussion of qualitative findings based on a survey of a sample of Latin American countries
7. Azaola and Bergman 2007, 105; on drinking water, see also Inter-American Commission on Human Rights 2011, 168–171; Wilkinson 1990
8. Ungar 2003, 913
9. Azaola and Bergman 2007, 106
10. Garces 2010, 478
11. Mariner 1998, 74
12. Mariner 1998, 81
13. Ungar 2003, 913
14. See Inter-American Commission on Human Rights 2011, 103–105
15. Cavallaro, Kopas, Lam, Mayhle, and Villagra de Biedermann 2008, 36–47
16. Cavallaro, Kopas, Lam, Mayhle, and Villagra de Biedermann 2008, 41
17. Azaola and Bergman 2007, 106
18. Wacquant 2003, 200
19. Wacquant 2003, 200–201
20. See, for example, Mariner 1998, 100
21. Mariner 1998, 100
22. Garces 2010, 480
23. Garces 2010, 480
24. Mariner 1998, 102

25. Darke and Karam 2016, 465
26. Darke 2013b, 275
27. Darke 2013b, 275
28. Wacquant 2008, 64
29. Mariner 1998, 105
30. Darke and Karam 2016, 466
31. Darke and Karam 2016, 467–468
32. Reuters 2012; see also Price 1973
33. Carter 2014, 490; see also similar discussions in Weegels 2017, Biondi 2017, Cerbini 2017, Antillano 2017
34. Birkbeck 2011, 315; see Crouch and Marquart 1989 on the declining role of informal "building tenders" in Texas
35. Brazilian prisoners are housed in several types of facilities: prisons (where they serve a sentence), jails and houses of detention (where they await trial and sentencing), and police precinct lockups (where they are first taken after arrest) (Mariner 1998, 15).
36. Darke 2013b, 276
37. Darke 2013b, 276
38. Darke 2013a, 18
39. Darke 2014, 58
40. Darke 2014, 62
41. Darke 2013b, 277
42. Darke 2013b, 277
43. Darke 2014, 57
44. Darke 2014, 57
45. Darke 2014, 60
46. Darke 2013b, 276
47. Varella 1999, 109
48. Varella 1999, 112
49. Varella 1999, 112
50. Varella 1999, 112
51. Varella 1999, 114
52. Darke 2013b, 277; Darke 2014, 64
53. Darke 2014, 64
54. Darke 2014, 65
55. Darke 2013a, 18–19
56. Darke 2013a, 19
57. Darke 2013a, 18
58. Darke 2013a, 19
59. Darke 2013a, 19
60. Darke 2013a, 19
61. Darke 2013b, 280
62. Darke 2014, 65
63. Darke 2013a, 19

64. Darke 2014, 63
65. Darke 2013a, 18
66. Darke 2013a, 19
67. Skarbek 2010
68. Schneider, Buehn, and Montenegro 2010, 20; on the informal economy in La Paz, see Hummel 2017
69. Inter-American Commission on Human Rights 2007, 49; Estefania 2009; Batansky 2014; Cerbini 2017
70. Young and McFadden 2003, 141
71. Baltimore et al. 2007, 23
72. Baltimore et al. 2007, 24
73. Young and McFadden 2003, 58; Mariner 1998, 86
74. Thanks to Rusty Young for providing this information.
75. Baltimore et al. 2007, 24
76. Inter-American Commission on Human Rights 2007, 54
77. Inter-American Commission on Human Rights 2007, 53, citing the Ministry of Government
78. Young and McFadden 2003, 60
79. Young and McFadden 2003, 80; Estefania 2009; Cerbini 2017, 32
80. Baltimore et al 2007; Inter-American Commission on Human Rights 2007, 52; other studies observe the same practice, see, Wacquant 2008, 64–65; Varella 1999, 34; Inter-American Commission on Human Rights 2011, 26
81. Young and McFadden 2003, 279
82. U.S. Department of State 2001; Baltimore et al. 2007, 23
83. Estefania 2009
84. U.S. Department of State 2001
85. Batansky 2014
86. Young and McFadden 2003, 134, 231
87. Baltimore et al. 2007, 24
88. Young and McFadden 2003, 81
89. Baltimore et al. 2007, 23
90. Young and McFadden 2003, 54
91. Young and McFadden 2003, 80
92. Young and McFadden 2003, 82
93. Young and McFadden 2003, 81
94. Young and McFadden 2003, 81
95. Young and McFadden 2003, 94
96. Young and McFadden 2003, 82
97. Estefania 2009
98. Young and McFadden 2003, 83
99. Baltimore et al 2007, 24
100. Varella 1999, 36
101. Young and McFadden 2003, 92
102. Young and McFadden 2003, 94; Baltimore et al. 2007, 24

103. Young and McFadden 2003, 96
104. Baltimore et al. 2007, 23
105. Baltimore et al. 2007, 24; Estefania 2009
106. Gassaway 2004
107. Young and McFadden 2003, 233
108. Batansky 2014
109. Young and McFadden 2003, 81
110. Young and McFadden 2003, 107
111. Young and McFadden 2003, 133–134
112. A similar system operates in Brazil, see Varella 1999, 55
113. Baltimore et al. 2007, 23; Estefania 2009
114. Estefania 2009
115. Young and McFadden 2003, 134
116. Young and McFadden 2003, 134
117. Burnett 2003; Young and McFadden 2003, 176–81
118. Young and McFadden 2003, 176–81
119. U.S. Department of State 2006
120. Young and McFadden 2003, 328
121. Estefania 2009
122. Young 2009
123. Llana 2007; Inter-American Commission on Human Rights 2007, 55; Shahriari 2014
124. Ceaser 1998
125. Baker 2009
126. Llana 2007
127. Olivero 1998, 104
128. Medrano 2013
129. Ceaser 1998
130. Ceaser 1998
131. Ceaser 1998
132. Ceaser 1998
133. Llana 2007
134. Young and McFadden 2003, 90–91, 333
135. Young 2009
136. Shahriari 2014
137. Shahriari 2014
138. Shahriari 2014
139. Shahriari 2014
140. Batansky 2014
141. Fujimura-Fanselow and Wickeri 2013, 884 fn383
142. Boettke, Coyne, and Leeson 2013
143. Mariner 1998, 55–62, 129; Inter-American Commission on Human Rights 2011, 107–111, 126–135; Wacquant 2003, 200–201
144. See Frey 2001 on functional, overlapping competitive jurisdictions
145. Birkbeck 2011

Chapter 3

1. Norwegian Correctional Service 2018
2. Pratt 2008a, Pratt 2008b. Pratt errs slightly in referring to "Scandinavian exceptionalism." Scandinavia refers to the countries Denmark, Norway, and Sweden, while his study looks at Finland, Norway, and Sweden. I will refer instead to the "Nordic" countries, which includes Scandinavia, plus Finland, Iceland, Greenland, and the Faeroe Islands.
3. Pratt and Eriksson 2011, 8. Within the debate on Nordic exceptionalism, scholars also debate the factors that cause possible differences in Nordic prisons and the role that Nordic values and the organization of Nordic welfare systems play in causing these differences (Scharff Smith and Ugelvik 2017, 22–23).
4. Mathiesen (1965) is a classic work on Nordic prisons. A history of the development of Sweden's prison system is offered in Nilsson 2003; three distinct approaches used historically in Scandinavian prisons are detailed in Pratt and Eriksson 2011; Snortum and Bødal 1985, Baer and Ravneberg 2008, and Ward 1972 compare prisons in one or several Nordic countries with those in the United States; see Green 2012, 69 and Scharff Smith 2012 on why Nordic prisons are so exceptional.
5. Pratt 2008a, 120; Mjåland 2014, 339
6. Johnsen and Granheim 2012, 200
7. Johnsen and Granheim 2012, 200, 205.
8. Johnsen and Granheim 2012, 203; on data for Iceland, see Baldursson 2000, 7. Nordic countries have a long history of smaller prisons. Writing in 1931, Viktor Almquist, the former Director-in-Chief of the Swedish Board of Prisons, reported that no Scandinavian facility held more than 500 men (Almquist 1931, 204).
9. Hammerlin and Mathiassen 2006, cited in Johnsen, Granheim, and Helgesen 2011, 519
10. Johnsen, Granheim, and Helgesen 2011, 519
11. Johnsen, Granheim, and Helgesen 2011, 519
12. Johnsen, Granheim, and Helgesen 2011, 523
13. Johnsen, Granheim, and Helgesen 2011, 524
14. O'Donnell 2005, 65; for a study of Spanish prisons that also found that there is more victimization in larger prisons, see Caravaca-Sánchez, Wolff, and Teasdale 2018.
15. Gambetta 2009, chapter 4
16. Johnsen, Granheim, and Helgesen 2011, 520
17. Johnsen, Granheim, and Helgesen 2011, 522; see also Johnsen and Granheim 2012, 205–208; Neumann 2012, 151
18. Ugelvik 2014b, 48–49. Note, however, that Nordic countries are not the only ones to use "open" prisons.
19. Pratt 2008a, 122; for a discussion of the history and philosophy of open prisons in Denmark, see Fransen 2017
20. Reiter, Sexton, and Sumner 2016
21. Pratt 2008a, 122
22. Pratt 2008a, 122
23. Pratt 2008a, 122; Shammas 2014, 106
24. Pratt 2008a, 122; Sutter 2012; on Denmark, see also Scharff Smith 2012, 39

25. Larson 2013
26. Ugelvik 2014b, 48–49; Neumann 2012, 147
27. Mathiesen 2012, 18
28. Pratt 2008a, 121
29. Pratt 2008a, 121
30. Pratt 2008a, 120–121
31. Pratt 2008a, 120–121; see also Bruhn, Lindberg, and Nylander 2012, 217
32. Bruhn, Lindberg, and Nylander 2012, 217
33. Pratt 2008a, 120
34. Ortiz 2015; California Department of Corrections and Rehabilitation 2017
35. DiIulio 1987, 101–102
36. Pratt 2008a, 120–121
37. Norwegian Correctional Service 2018; this is related to the Nordic tradition and understanding of "normalization" that should exist in Nordic prisons, Engbo 2017.
38. Pratt 2008a, 120
39. Pratt 2008a, 122. However, other accounts are more skeptical. Some prisoners report that the food does not taste good, there is too little of it, or it is too closely tied to the region's culinary tradition (Ugelvik 2014b, 14, 132, 134–137, 144; Ugelvik 2011, 47, 50; see also Minke and Smoyer 2017, 364–366; Shammas 2014, 110, Minke and Smoyer 2017, 354).
40. Pratt 2008a, 121
41. Ugelvik 2014b, 28; Reiter, Sexton, and Sumer 2016; Sutter 2012
42. Ugelvik 2014b, 124
43. Pratt 2008a, 122; Mathiesen 2012, 24–25
44. Shammas 2014, 106; on women's facilities, see Neumann 2012, 146
45. Some of the claims of Nordic exceptionalism evoked a strong response from Nordic prison scholars. They argue that these claims are overstated, incomplete, or not representative of Nordic incarceration (Ugelvik and Dullum 2012; Shammas 2014; Barker 2013; Scharff Smith and Ugelvik 2017; Reiter, Sexton, and Sumner 2018). Incorporating more evidence attenuates some of the original claims, but none undermines the substantive conclusion that Nordic prisons provide a radically different quality of official governance than found in prisons in the Americas, especially the cases studied in Bolivia and Brazil.
46. The Danish prison system is apparently home to both biker gangs and gangs of immigrants. However, it is unclear to what extent these gangs play a role in governing prisons. The presence of gang members in a prison is not sufficient to conclude that they are a centralized form of extralegal governance.
47. Snortum and Bødal 1985, 575
48. Nielsen 2012, 138
49. Ugelvik 2014b, 22
50. Ugelvik 2014b, 1, 20
51. Ugelvik 2014b, 21
52. Ugelvik 2012, 122
53. Ugelvik 2014b, 21
54. Ugelvik 2014, 107

55. Ugelvik 2014b, 107–108
56. Ugelvik 2014b, 109, 213–218
57. Ugelvik 2014b, 108
58. Ugelvik 2014b, 107
59. Ugelvik 2014b, 107–108
60. Ugelvik 2014b, 111
61. Trammell and Chenault 2009; Ugelvik 2014a, 215, who also cites Hanoa 2008 (a Norwegian book) noting that violence is uncommon
62. Ugelvik 2014b, 217
63. Ugelvik 2014b, 215, 216
64. Ugelvik 2014b, 218
65. Ugelvik 2014b, 218–219
66. Ugelvik 2014b, 222–223
67. Mjåland 2015, 782; on prisoners' views on prison drug treatment, see Frank, Dahl, Holm, and Kolind 2015.
68. Kolind, Holm, Duff, and Frank 2016, 136
69. Kolind, Holm, Duff, and Frank 2016, 138; in England, see Crewe 2005, 462
70. See, for example, Young and McFadden 2003, 81; Varella 1999, 55
71. Radford 1945, 193
72. Mjåland 2014, 343
73. Mjåland 2014, 344
74. Mjåland 2014, 344
75. Mjåland 2014, 345
76. Mjåland 2014, 343
77. Mjåland 2014, 342–343
78. Mjåland 2014, 343
79. Mjåland 2014, 345
80. Hayek 1945; DeCanio 2014; Meadowcroft 2005
81. Firms, to use a classic example, exist because it is less costly to organize production internally rather than rely on the market (Coase 1937; Williamson 1985).
82. Mjåland 2015, 783
83. Mjåland 2014, 341
84. Mjåland 2014, 345
85. Mjåland 2014, 341
86. Mjåland 2014, 341; Mjåland 2015, 785
87. Mjåland 2014, 341
88. Mjåland 2014, 341–342
89. Mjåland 2014, 346–347
90. Mjåland 2015, 783; Mjåland 2014, 339
91. Mjåland 2014, 340
92. Mjåland 2014, 339–340
93. Mjåland 2015, 786
94. Mjåland 2015, 786
95. Gerring 2017, 80
96. Ortiz-Ospina and Roser 2018

97. Johnson 2017
98. Crabtree 2010

Chapter 4
1. Futch 1999 [1968], 45
2. Marvel 1994, 190
3. Davis 2010, 53
4. Futch 1999 [1968], 2; Davis 2010, 9; Lundquist 2004, 5
5. On its scholarly place within the literature, see Gray 2011, ix, xiv–xv
6. McElroy 1913; Ransom 1881
7. Northrop 2013 [1904]; Forbes 1865
8. Costa and Kahn 2007, 1468
9. Gray 2011, x
10. Costa and Kahn 2007, 1468; Davis 2010, 16
11. The town's name was changed to Andersonville by the Post Office in 1856, but locals referred to it as Anderson for many years thereafter (Marvel 1994, 253–254, footnote 23).
12. Futch 1999 [1968], 3; Marvel 1994, 15
13. Davis 2010, 17
14. Davis 2010, 17
15. Lundquist 2004, 5
16. Davis 2010, 53
17. Futch 1999 [1968], 12; War of the Rebellion, Series 2, Volume VII, 832
18. Davis 2010, 25; Pickenpaugh 2013, 120
19. Futch 1999 [1968], 4; War of the Rebellion, Series 2, Volume VII, 541; War of the Rebellion, Series 2, Volume VIII, 596
20. Futch 1999 [1968], 5; War of the Rebellion, Series 2, Volume VII, 119; Davis 2010, 26
21. Futch 1999 [1968], 9, 15; Marvel 1994, 17–19; War of the Rebellion, Series 2, Volume VII, 63, 89
22. Davis 2010, 53; War of the Rebellion, Series 2, Volume VIII, 350
23. Marvel 1994, 25
24. War of the Rebellion, Series 2, Volume VII, 63
25. War of the Rebellion, Series 2, Volume VII, 40
26. War of the Rebellion, Series 2, Volume VII, 63. Andersonville officials often pleaded with others in the Confederate army for additional resources to reduce the suffering (War of the Rebellion, Series 2, Volume VII, 222, 410–411; 624, 625).
27. War of the Rebellion, Series 2, Volume VII, 473
28. Futch 1999 [1968], 11; see also Pickenpaugh 2013, 138
29. War of the Rebellion, Series 2, Volume VIII, 732
30. War of the Rebellion, Series 2, Volume VII, 168, 541–542; Futch 1999 [1968], 31; War of the Rebellion, Series 2, Volume VIII, 597; Pickenpaugh 2013,122
31. War of the Rebellion, Series 2, Volume VII, 120
32. War of the Rebellion, Series 2, Volume VII, 168
33. War of the Rebellion, Series 2, Volume VII, 547

34. Futch 1999 [1968], 19
35. Marvel 1994, 45–46; War of the Rebellion, Series 2, Volume VII, 547; Pickenpaugh 2013, 123–124
36. Davis 2010, 58; Northrop 2013 [1904], 64; Pickenpaugh 2013, 139
37. Davis 2010, 25–26
38. Lundquist 2004, 13
39. Futch 1999 [1968], 31
40. Marvel 1994, 180; Davis 2010, 25
41. War of the Rebellion, Series 2, Volume VII, 392, see also 411
42. War of the Rebellion, Series 2, Volume VII, 773; Lundquist 2004, 10, 12
43. War of the Rebellion, Series 2, Volume VII, 923
44. Lundquist 2004, 3
45. Lundquist 2004, 3
46. Lundquist 2004, 4; see also Futch 1999 [1968], 44
47. National Park Service 2015
48. Davis 2010, 16
49. Futch 1999 [1968], 44
50. Costa and Kahn 2007, 1468; see also War of the Rebellion, Series 2, Volume VII, 547; Pickenpaugh 2013, 145–150; also War of the Rebellion, Series 2, Volume VIII, 602, and the medical reports on the health of prisoners on pages 590–632
51. War of the Rebellion, Series 2, Volume VII, 89
52. War of the Rebellion, Series 2, Volume VII, 89
53. War of the Rebellion, Series 2, Volume VII, 417
54. War of the Rebellion, Series 2, Volume VII, 89; see also War of the Rebellion, Series 2, Volume VII, 386; see also Northrop 2013 [1904], 110–113
55. Futch 1999 [1968], 52
56. Marvel 1994, 155
57. Costa and Kahn 2007, 1475
58. Costa and Kahn 2007, 1476
59. Futch 1999 [1968], 20; Davis 2010, 27; War of the Rebellion, Series 2, Volume VII, 392
60. War of the Rebellion, Series 2, Volume VII, 396
61. Davis 2010, 30–31
62. Davis 2010, 29
63. Davis 2010, 29
64. War of the Rebellion, Series 2, Volume VII, 392; Pickenpaugh 2013, 140
65. Davis 2010, 27
66. War of the Rebellion, Series 2, Volume VII, 378, 386
67. Davis 2010, 28
68. War of the Rebellion, Series 2, Volume VII, 411
69. Marvel 1994, 38
70. Davis 2010, 26
71. Marvel 1994, 172; Pickenpaugh 2013, 153–154
72. War of the Rebellion, Series 2, Volume VIII, 597
73. War of the Rebellion, Series 2, Volume VIII, 597

74. Marvel 1994, 21
75. Marvel 1994, 21
76. War of the Rebellion, Series 2, Volume VII, 168
77. War of the Rebellion, Series 2, Volume VII, 170
78. War of the Rebellion, Series 2, Volume VII, 168
79. War of the Rebellion, Series 2, Volume VII, 168
80. War of the Rebellion, Series 2, Volume VII, 548
81. Northrop 2013 [1904], 58
82. Northrop 2013 [1904], 66
83. Futch 1999 [1968], 18
84. War of the Rebellion, Series 2, Volume VIII, 597
85. Futch 1999 [1968], 18
86. Futch 1999 [1968], 18
87. Futch 1999 [1968], 20
88. Marvel 1994, ix
89. War of the Rebellion, Series 2, Volume VII, 547
90. War of the Rebellion, Series 2, Volume VII, 831
91. War of the Rebellion, Series 2, Volume VIII, 599
92. War of the Rebellion, Series 2, Volume VII, 558–559
93. Pickenpaugh 2013, 119
94. War of the Rebellion, Series 2, Volume VII, 558
95. War of the Rebellion, Series 2, Volume VII, 548; Pickenpaugh 2013, 123
96. Northrop 2013 [1904], 71; War of the Rebellion, Series 2, Volume VII, 583–584; Pickenpaugh 2013, 138
97. Forbes 1865, 11, 15
98. Futch 1999 [1968], 23; Marvel 1994, 71; Forbes 1865, 11, 15; Pickenpaugh 2013, 123
99. Futch 1999 [1968], 45
100. War of the Rebellion, Series 2, Volume VII, 121
101. Futch 1999 [1968], 38; on the sensory environments of Civil War prisoner of war camps see Kutzler 2019
102. Forbes 1865, 12
103. Davis 2010, 58; Pickenpaugh 2013, 134
104. Marvel 1994, 138; see also Kutzler 2014
105. War of the Rebellion, Series 2, Volume VII, 167
106. War of the Rebellion, Series 2, Volume VII, 63
107. Davis 2010, 58; War of the Rebellion, Series 2, Volume VII, 558
108. Futch 1999 [1968], 32; Forbes 1865, 15
109. Northrop 2013 [1904], 58
110. Forbes 1865, 19
111. Forbes 1865, 23
112. Futch 1999 [1968], 32
113. Davis 2010, 54
114. Marvel 1994, 11
115. Futch 1999 [1968], 37; see also Pickenpaugh 2013, 141–142

116. War of the Rebellion, Series 2, Volume VII, 558
117. War of the Rebellion, Series 2, Volume VII, 207
118. Futch 1999 [1968], 19
119. War of the Rebellion, Series 2, Volume VII, 548; Northrop 2013 [1904], 71; Pickenpaugh 2013, 141
120. Marvel 1994, 58; Northrop 2013 [1904], 108
121. Marvel 1994, 58; see also War of the Rebellion, Series 2, Volume VII, 757; Forbes 1865, 20. Prison officials disagreed with the prison inspector about the availability of wood, but based on the available evidence, the inspector's account seems reliable (War of the Rebellion, Series 2, Volume VII, 757–759).
122. Futch 1999 [1968], 21
123. Northrop 2013 [1904], 101
124. Marvel 1994, 81
125. Futch 1999 [1968], 22
126. Marvel 1994, 108
127. Futch 1999 [1968], 33
128. Marvel 1994, 108; Northrop 2013 [1904], 78
129. Futch 1999 [1968], 34
130. War of the Rebellion, Series 2, Volume 7, 393, 437; Futch 1999 [1968], 34; Forbes 1865, 12
131. Futch 1999 [1968], 22
132. Marvel 1994, 50
133. Marvel 1994, 48
134. Marvel 1994, 108; see also Pickenpaugh 2013, 142–144
135. Forbes 1865, 23; see also Marvel 1994, 110; Northrop 2013 [1904], 65–66; Forbes 1865, 13
136. Marvel 1994, 111
137. Futch 1999 [1968], 34
138. Futch 1999 [1968], 40
139. War of the Rebellion, Series 2, Volume VII, 547
140. Futch 1999 [1968], 40
141. Marvel 1994, 190
142. War of the Rebellion, Series 2, Volume VIII, 597
143. Marvel 1994, 90; Pickenpaugh 2013, 151–153
144. Futch 1999 [1968], 50
145. Futch 1999 [1968], 53; Northrop 2013 [1904], 92; Forbes 1865, 31; Pickenpaugh 2013, 154
146. Futch 1999 [1968], 53; Davis 2010, 70; Marvel 1994, 65–66
147. Futch 1999 [1968], 53
148. Forbes 1865, 22
149. Futch 1999 [1968], 41
150. Forbes 1865, 12
151. See, for example, Marvel 1994, 68–69, 95; Northrop 2013 [1904], 64; Forbes 1865, 17, 22, 24, 27; Pickenpaugh 2013, 128
152. Northrop 2013 [1904], 64

153. Marvel 1994, 68–69
154. Marvel 1994, 68
155. Marvel 1994, 95
156. Futch 1999 [1968], 63; Marvel 1994, 96
157. Marvel 1994, 96
158. Davis 2010, 97
159. Marvel 1994, 96
160. Futch 1999 [1968], 63
161. Futch 1999 [1968], 67
162. Forbes 1865, 18
163. Futch 1999 [1968], 65; Pickenpaugh 2013, 127
164. Futch 1999 [1968], 66
165. Futch 1999 [1968], 65
166. Marvel 1994, 71
167. Futch 1999 [1968], 66
168. Futch 1999 [1968], 66–67
169. Futch 1999 [1968], 42
170. Davis 2010, 96
171. Northrop 2013 [1904], 60–61
172. Marvel 1994, 69
173. Marvel 1994, 95–96
174. Marvel 1994, 96
175. Futch 1999 [1968], 65
176. Marvel 1994, 68–69, 95; Pickenpaugh 2013, 128
177. Northrop 2013 [1904], 79
178. Marvel 1994, 96; Northrop 2013 [1904], 80–81
179. Futch 1999 [1968], 68
180. Davis 2010, 96; Marvel 1994, 96
181. Marvel 1994, 96
182. Futch 1999 [1968], 68; Davis 2010, 96; Northrop 2013 [1904], 80; Pickenpaugh 2013, 129
183. Futch 1999 [1968], 68; Forbes 1865, 25
184. Marvel 1994, 97; Futch 1999 [1968], 69
185. Marvel 1994, 97; Forbes 1865, 25
186. Marvel 1994, 97
187. Futch 1999 [1968], 69; Northrop 2013 [1904], 80
188. Marvel 1994, 97
189. Marvel 1994, 97; Northrop 2013 [1904], 80
190. Marvel 1994, 97
191. Marvel 1994, 97–98
192. Futch 1999 [1968], 71; Forbes 1865, 25–26
193. Marvel 1994, 98; Futch 1999 [1968], 69; Northrop 2013 [1904], 80–81
194. Futch 1999 [1968], 70; Forbes 1865, 26
195. Marvel 1994, 98; Futch 1999 [1968], 69; Davis 2010, 97; Northrop 2013 [1904], 81; Forbes 1865, 25; Pickenpaugh 2013, 129

196. Northrop 2013 [1904], 82

197. Marvel 1994, 98; Futch 1999 [1968], 70. It appears that some innocent men were falsely swept up as Raiders at the behest of "malicious companions bent on settling a personal grudge" (Marvel 1994, 99).

198. Davis 2010, 97; Pickenpaugh 2013, 129

199. Marvel 1994, 98; Futch 1999 [1968], 70; Davis 2010, 97; Northrop 2013 [1904], 82

200. Marvel 1994, 99

201. Forbes 1865, 25–26

202. War of the Rebellion, Series 2, Volume VII, 426

203. War of the Rebellion, Series 2, Volume VII, 426; see also Pickenpaugh 2013, 129

204. Marvel 1994, 99; Forbes 1865, 26

205. Marvel 1994, 99–100

206. Futch 1999 [1968], 71; War of the Rebellion, Series 2, Volume VII, 547; War of the Rebellion, Series 2, Volume VIII, 597

207. Futch 1999 [1968], 72–74; Marvel 1994, 141

208. Northrop 2013 [1904], 88

209. Marvel 1994, 143; Northrop 2013 [1904], 88–89; Forbes 1865, 29; Pickenpaugh 2013, 130

210. War of the Rebellion, Series 2, Volume VII, 547; Northrop 2013 [1904], 90

211. Marvel 1994, 92; Forbes 1865, 14, 18, 19, 24, 27, 28, 29

212. Forbes 1865, 14

Chapter 5

1. Trammell 2009, 275

2. There are several excellent historical and comparative accounts of women's imprisonment, focusing on the United States and Canada (Pollock 2002, chapter 2 and 207–213), the United States and England (Kruttschnitt and Gartner 2003), California (Bloom, Chesney-Lind, and Owen 1994), England (Bosworth 1996), France (Bosworth 2000), and California, England, and the Netherlands (Kruttschnitt, Slotboom, Dirkzwager, and Bijleveld 2013). In addition, Bosworth (2000), Fox (1984), and Pollock (2002, 48–53) analyze imprisonment from a feminist perspective.

3. Owen 1998, 4, 7

4. Kruttschnitt and Gartner 2005

5. Kruttschnitt and Gartner 2005, 85. California women's prisons also appear to organize life in many of the same ways as English women's prisons, where prison populations are also low (Cheliotis and Liebling 2006; Owen 1998; Kraeger and Kruttschnitt 2018). However, there are some differences, such as in views about race and mental health (Kruttschnitt and Hussemann 2008; Kruttschnitt and Vuolo 2007).

6. Owen 1998, 19, 157; see also Kruttschnitt and Gartner 2005, 71, 91; Kreager and Kruttschnitt 2018

7. Trammell 2012, 55

8. Trammell 2012, 56–57

9. Panfil and Peterson 2018, 209; see also Moore 1991; Miller 2001; Mendoza-Denton 2008; Vigil 2008
10. Peterson, Carson, and Fowler 2018, 954
11. See, for example, Trammell 2012, 54–55; Rierden 1997, 52
12. Gambetta 2009, 93; on the role of intimate relationships and violence, see Trammell, Wulf-Ludden, and Mowder 2015; for a comprehensive review of the literature and estimates of the correlates of violence in women's prisons, see Teasdale, Daigle, Hawk, and Daquin 2016
13. Tischler and Marquart 1989, 511
14. Craddock 1996, 69
15. Gambetta 2009, 93. It might also be that women are written up more often than men are for minor altercations.
16. Uniform Crime Report 2012, Table 42
17. Pollock 2002, 9
18. Ward and Kassebaum 1965, 7; see also Ward and Kassebaum 1964; Snortum and Bødal 1985, 583
19. Owen 1998, viii
20. Owen 1998, 29, also 86
21. Owen 1998, 86
22. Owen 1998, 181
23. See also Gartner and Kruttschnitt 2004
24. Trammell 2009, 2011, 2012
25. For example, sociologist Rose Giallombardo's (1966) seminal study of a Federal Reformatory for Women in West Virginia finds a prison social order that resembles that seen in California in the 1960s. Consistent with my argument, the environment and prisoner demographics in that facility were similar to those in California.
26. On subnational analysis, see Snyder 2001
27. See, for instance, Irwin 1980
28. Owen 1998, 175; Banks 2003, 49
29. Pollock 2002, 125
30. Owen 1998, 176; Kruttschnitt and Gartner 2005, 89, also 135; Owen 1998, 177; Girshick 1999, chapter 5; similar evidence is found in women's prisons in other states; in Virginia, see Heffernan 1972, chapter 7, in West Virginia, see Giallombardo 1966, 166
31. Kruttschnitt and Gartner 2005, 112
32. Kruttschnitt and Gartner 2005, 110. While there is some variation across samples, the authors conclude that this is only a matter of degree and does not lead to different qualitative results or substantive conclusions. They argue that there has been no major transformation across these periods or prisons (Kruttschnitt and Gartner 2005, 113).
33. Kruttschnitt and Gartner 2005, 90
34. Owen 1998, 174
35. Trammell 2012, 35
36. Trammell 2012, 36
37. Owen 1998, 171

38. Owen 1998, 177; see also Kruttschnitt and Gartner 2005, 134; Mahan 1984, 362
39. Owen 1998, 174
40. Owen 1998, 171
41. Owen 1998, 175
42. Ward and Kassebaum 1965, 32–33; for similar claims regarding Virginia, see Heffernan 1972, 121–122
43. Ward and Kassebaum 1965, 32
44. Zingraff and Zingraff 1980, 36
45. Tittle 1969. A study of a North Carolina women's facility in the 1970s found that between 45 and 65 percent of women subscribed to the Convict Code, depending on whether they were in the early, middle, or late time in their prison sentence (Jensen and Jones 1976, 593; see also Larson and Nelson 1984).
46. Owen 1998, 94
47. Trammell 2012, 100; regarding ostracism in a New Mexico women's prison, see also Mahan 1984, 360
48. Owen 1998, 172
49. Trammell 2009, 277
50. Trammell 2012, 100
51. See also Heffernan 1972, 78; Giallombardo 1966, 110–114; Kruttschnitt and Gartner 2005, 134
52. Trammell 2012, 97
53. Trammell 2012, 97
54. Heffernan 1972; Giallombardo 1966; Foster 1975; Forsyth and Evans 2003, 18; Banks 2003, 50–52; Girshick 1999, 90; Pogrebin and Dodge 2001, Pollock 2002, 138–140; Kolb and Palys 2018
55. Owen 1998, 134
56. Owen 1998, 134
57. Owen 1998, 135
58. Trammell 2009, 274
59. Owen 1998, 135; see also Giallombardo 1966, 168
60. Trammell 2009, 275
61. Trammell 2012, 34–35
62. Trammell 2012, 34–35; see also Giallombardo 1966, 165
63. Sex is sometimes an important part of prison families. Studies of prison sexuality, in general, find large variation in estimates of participation in intimate relationships, typically ranging from 30 percent to 70 percent of women (Girshick 1999, 86–89). See, for some of the earliest studies on the topic, Ford 1929, Otis 1913, and Selling 1931; for estimates of participation rates in homosexual relationships, see Leger 1987; Heffernan 1972, 92; Propper 1978; Holyoak 1972; Jones 1993, 87; Tittle 1969, 498; Pardue, Arrigo, and Murphy 2011, 284; Koscheski and Hensley 2001, 274; Propper 1982, 131; for useful discussions, Genders and Players 1990, 49; Pardue, Arrigo, and Murphy 2011; Severance 2004.

While victimization sometimes occurs, a significant proportion of intimate prison relationships are voluntary and positive experiences (Pardue, Arrigo, and Murphy 2011, 292; Hensley, Castle, and Tewksbury 2003, 83; Stemple, Flores, and Meyer 2017, 5). Past studies vary in estimating how frequent victimization is within women's prisons. Pardue, Arrigo, and Murphy (2011, 292) found that 4.5 percent of their respondents had been sexually victimized. Hensley, Castle, and Tewksbury (2003, 83) found that 11 percent of women reported incidents of sexual coercion. Stemple, Flores, and Meyer (2017, 306) report on research that "found that women state prisoners were more than three times as likely to experience sexual victimization perpetrated by women inmates (13.7%) than were men to be victimized by male inmates (4.2%)."

64. Trammell 2009, 275
65. Trammell 2009, 274
66. Owen 1998, 136; see also Heffernan 1972, 90–92; Girshick 1999, 90; Giallombardo 1966, 169
67. Giallombardo 1966, 175; Jones 1993, 84
68. Giallombardo 1966, 175, 172
69. See, for example, Giallombardo 1966, 159, 181; Ford 1929
70. Owen 1998, 120
71. Ward and Kassebaum 1965, 78
72. Giallombardo 1966, 158
73. Heffernan 1972, 91, also chapter 5
74. Foster 1975, 74; see also early studies, such as van Wormer 1981, 188; Fox 1984, 26; Heffernan 1972, 90; Jones 1993, 86; Greer 2000; Propper 1982, 133; Propper 1978; Mawby 1982, 33; Mahan 1984, 378; Giallombardo 1966, 175
75. Heffernan 1972, 102
76. MacKenzie, Robinson, and Campbell 1989, 233
77. Owen 1998, 8
78. Forsyth and Evans 2003, 15, also 21
79. Kruttschnitt and Gartner 2005, 91; see also Pollock 2002, 129
80. Owen 1998, 134
81. Owen 1998, 136
82. Giallombardo 1966, 164
83. Owen 1998, 112
84. Owen 1998, 112; see also Trammell and Chenault 2009; Owen 1998, 93–94, 111; Faith 2011, 240; Mahan 1984, 362–363
85. Skarbek 2014, 87–90
86. Pollock 2002, 131; Moyer 1980; Giallombardo 1966, 156–157, 173; Trammell 2012, 56–57
87. Pollock 2002, 129–130; Banks 2003, 52; Greer 2000, 462; Kruttschnitt and Gartner 2005, 107–108; Trammell 2012, 53; Kruttschnitt, Gartner, and Miller 2000, 695; Owen 1998, 152–155
88. Owen 1998, 152
89. Owen 1998, 152
90. Kruttschnitt, Gartner, and Miller 2000, 695

Chapter 6
1. Crewe 2009, 317
2. Phillips 2008, 316–317

3. Newburn 2002; Jones and Newburn 2007
4. Densley 2013, 8
5. Kruttschnitt, Slotboom, Dirkzwager, and Bijleveld 2013, 20
6. California Department of Corrections and Rehabilitation 2007
7. Simon 2014
8. California Department of Corrections and Rehabilitation 2007
9. Ministry of Justice 2017, Table 1.8
10. While there is no overlap in the two systems' prison population sizes, note that that in this figure, the bins would overlap but they are separated for clarity of exposition.
11. HM Chief Inspector of Prisons 2009, 14
12. HM Chief Inspector of Prisons 2009, 15
13. HM Chief Inspector of Prisons 2009, 13
14. Rabuy and Kopf 2015
15. Woolf 1991, 17; see also Crewe 2009, 30; Petersilia 2003, 41–46; Bales and Mears 2008
16. Phillips 2008, 322
17. Sparks, Bottoms, and Hay 1996; for descriptions of security categories, see Wood and Adler 2001, 175
18. Sparks, Bottoms, and Hay 1996, 30, 113
19. Sparks, Bottoms, and Hay 1996, 102
20. Sparks, Bottoms, and Hay 1996, 99
21. Sparks, Bottoms, and Hay 1996, 114–115
22. Sparks, Bottoms, and Hay 1996, 177
23. Sparks, Bottoms, and Hay 1996, 178
24. Sparks, Bottoms, and Hay 1996, 184
25. Sparks, Bottoms, and Hay 1996, 185
26. Sparks, Bottoms, and Hay 1996, 179–180
27. Sparks, Bottoms, and Hay 1996, 179
28. Sparks, Bottoms, and Hay 1996, 130
29. Sparks, Bottoms, and Hay 1996, 148
30. Sparks, Bottoms, and Hay 1996, 133
31. Sparks, Bottoms, and Hay 1996, 177
32. Sparks, Bottoms, and Hay 1996, 178
33. Sparks, Bottoms, and Hay 1996, 178
34. Sparks, Bottoms, and Hay 1996, 189
35. Sparks, Bottoms, and Hay 1996, 189
36. Sparks, Bottoms, and Hay 1996, 199
37. Sparks, Bottoms, and Hay 1996, 201
38. Sparks, Bottoms, and Hay 1996, 201
39. Sparks, Bottoms, and Hay 1996, 201
40. Sparks, Bottoms, and Hay 1996, 201–202
41. Sparks, Bottoms, and Hay 1996, 201
42. Sparks, Bottoms, and Hay 1996, 200
43. Sparks, Bottoms, and Hay 1996, 197
44. Sparks, Bottoms, and Hay 1996, 18

45. Crewe 2009, 3
46. Crewe 2009, 3
47. Crewe 2009, 32
48. Crewe 2009, 32–33
49. Crewe 2009, 53
50. Crewe 2009, 269
51. Crewe 2009, 49, 70
52. Crewe 2009, 464
53. Crewe 2009, 250
54. Crewe 2009, 283
55. Crewe 2009, 283
56. Crewe 2009, 303
57. Crewe 2009, 307–308
58. Crewe 2009, 250
59. Crewe 2009, 252–253
60. Crewe 2009, 352
61. Crewe 2009, 254
62. Crewe 2009, 400
63. Crewe 2009, 400
64. Crewe 2009, 400
65. Crewe 2009, 243
66. Crewe 2009, 258
67. Crewe 2009, 257
68. Crewe 2009, 263
69. Crewe 2009, 275
70. Crewe 2009, 275
71. Crewe 2009, 257
72. Crewe 2009, 257
73. Crewe 2009, 229, 281, 315
74. Crewe 2009, 237
75. Crewe 2009, 369
76. Crewe 2009, 44
77. Crewe 2009, 370
78. Crewe 2009, 264
79. Crewe 2009, 375; Crewe 2006, 361
80. Crewe 2009, 301
81. Crewe 2009, 305
82. Crewe 2009, 305
83. Crewe 2009, 259, 304
84. Crewe 2009, 304
85. Crewe 2009, 307–308
86. Crewe 2009, 320, also 319
87. Crewe 2009, 320
88. Crewe 2009, 324
89. Crewe 2009, 30

90. Crewe 2009, 33
91. Crewe 2009, 319
92. Crewe 2009, 317
93. Crewe 2009, 317, also 320
94. Crewe 2009, 320–321
95. Crewe 2009, 321
96. Crewe 2009, 319
97. Crewe 2009, 318
98. Crewe 2009, 321
99. Crewe 2009, 322
100. Crewe 2009, 322, also 326
101. Crewe 2009, 325
102. Crewe 2009, 317
103. Crewe 2009, 317
104. Crewe 2009, 318
105. Crewe 2009, 350
106. Crewe 2009, 350
107. Crewe 2009, 350
108. Crewe 2009, 350
109. Crewe 2009, 351
110. Crewe 2009, 350
111. Crewe 2009, 327
112. Crewe 2009, 328
113. Crewe 2009, 328
114. Crewe 2009, 353. While prisoners tended not to emphasize racial antagonisms in public interactions, in private, some prisoners expressed prejudiced views (Crewe 2009, 354–358).
115. Crewe 2009, 263
116. Crewe 2009, 263
117. Crewe 2009, 263
118. Phillips 2012
119. Phillips 2012, 56
120. Phillips 2012, 56
121. Phillips 2012, 56
122. Phillips 2012, 56
123. Phillips 2008, 322; Phillips 2012, 57; Crewe 2009; similar to early studies of California, Irwin 1980, 58–60
124. Phillips 2008, 323
125. Phillips 2008, 323
126. Phillips 2008, 324
127. Phillips 2008, 316–317
128. Phillips 2008, 317
129. Phillips 2008, 318
130. Phillips 2008, 320–321
131. Kreager and Kruttscnitt 2018

132. Phillips 2012, 51
133. Phillips 2012
134. Setty, Sturrock, and Simes 2014, 6
135. Setty, Sturrock, and Simes 2014, 9
136. Setty, Sturrock, and Simes 2014, 26
137. Setty, Sturrock, and Simes 2014, 26
138. Setty, Sturrock, and Simes 2014, 26
139. McLean, Maitra, and Holligan 2017, 441
140. McLean, Maitra, and Holligan 2017, 449
141. McLean, Maitra, and Holligan 2017, 448
142. McLean, Maitra, and Holligan 2017, 442
143. Maitra 2015, 225
144. McLean, Maitra, and Holligan 2017
145. Wood 2006, 605–606; see also Wood and Adler 2001; Wood, Moir, and James 2009
146. Hunt, Riegel, Morales, and Waldorf 1993
147. Sparks, Bottoms, and Hay 1996, 178; McLean, Maitra, and Holligan 2017
148. Maitra 2013, 29–30; Setty, Sturrock, and Simes 2014, 5, 26
149. McLean, Maitra, and Holligan 2017, 441
150. See, for example, Maitra 2013, 40
151. Maitra 2013, 35; Maitra 2015
152. McLean, Maitra, and Holligan 2017, 442
153. Maitra 2013, 45, 29–30
154. Maitra 2013, 31
155. Savage 2018
156. Savage 2018
157. Grierson 2018
158. Grimwood 2016
159. Phillips 2008, 319
160. Phillips 2008, 319–320
161. HM Chief Inspector of Prisons 2010, 29
162. Parks 2015
163. Johnson 2017
164. Johnson and Densley 2018; see also, Brenneman 2012
165. Williams 2018
166. Williams 2018, 737
167. Williams 2018, 740
168. Williams 2018, 740
169. Williams 2018, 743
170. Liebling, Arnold, and Straub 2011, 9
171. Liebling, Arnold, and Straub 2011, 4
172. Liebling, Arnold, and Straub 2011, 9
173. Liebling, Arnold, and Straub 2011, 59
174. Liebling, Arnold, and Straub 2011, 122
175. Liebling, Arnold, and Straub 2011, 122

176. Liebling, Arnold, and Straub 2011, 102, 107, 114
177. Liebling, Arnold, and Straub 2011, 58
178. Liebling, Arnold, and Straub 2011, 58–72
179. Liebling, Arnold, and Straub 2011, 92, also 94
180. Liebling, Arnold, and Straub 2011, 58, 67
181. Liebling, Arnold, and Straub 2011, 109
182. Liebling, Arnold, and Straub 2011, 58
183. Liebling, Arnold, and Straub 2011, 69
184. Liebling, Arnold, and Straub 2011, 69
185. Liebling, Arnold, and Straub 2011, 73
186. Liebling, Arnold, and Straub 2011, 74
187. Liebling, Arnold, and Straub 2011, 75
188. Liebling, Arnold, and Straub 2011, 77
189. Liebling, Arnold, and Straub 2011, 30
190. Liebling, Arnold, and Straub 2011, 67
191. Liebling, Arnold, and Straub 2011, 68
192. Liebling, Arnold, and Straub 2011, 67
193. Liebling, Arnold, and Straub 2011, iv
194. Liebling, Arnold, and Straub 2011, 88
195. Liebling, Arnold, and Straub 2011, 100

Chapter 7

1. Ucar 2014
2. McDonnell 2017, 2
3. Dolovich 2011, 19
4. Kaeble and Glaze 2016, 12
5. Rosas and Goodwin v Baca 2012; Romero 2014
6. Skarbek 2011
7. Dolovich 2012, 1101–1102.
8. See Andreoli 2004; Ucar 2014; 2015
9. Dolovich 2011; 2012
10. Dolovich 2011, 5
11. Dolovich 2011, 92
12. Robinson 2011, 1319
13. Robinson 2011, 1319, footnote 40
14. See Robinson 2011, especially, 1309, 1312, 1335, 1328–1330
15. This is part of a standard reference scheme the jail system uses to classify types of prisoner housing. For example, K1 are prisoners with a law enforcement affiliation (who might be subject to violence from other prisoners). K10 prisoners are housed in administrative segregation because they are a danger to themselves or others. K6T prisoners are charged with contempt of court (McDonnell 2015, 11). The gay and transgender dorms were previously known as K11, but the installation of a new computer system prevented the use of codes higher than K10, so officials changed it to K6G (Dolovich 2011, 4, footnote 15; Lara 2010, 591).
16. Dolovich 2011, 21

17. Robinson 2011, 1320
18. Dolovich 2011, 22; Robinson 2011, 1319
19. Lara 2010, 591–592
20. Dolovich 2011, 23; Dolovich 2012, 980
21. Harawa, Sweat, George, and Sylla 2010, 2
22. Dolovich 2011, 24; Harawa, Sweat, George, and Sylla 2010, 5
23. Ucar 2014
24. Ucar 2014
25. Ucar 2014
26. Dolovich 2011, 26
27. Dolovich 2011, 28
28. Dolovich 2011, 30. Technically, prisoners are automatically classified as K6G after the first interview. The interview by the two deputies determines whether a prisoner is reclassified to the general population housing area.
29. Dolovich 2011, 26. Robinson (2011) outlines several significant concerns about this procedure and the assumptions it is based on. More generally, Sexton, Jenness, and Sumner (2010) provides an excellent overview and study of transgender prisoners in the California state prison system. While the literature on transgender and prison is relatively small, much of it focuses on transgender prisoners in men's prisons (Sexton, Jenness, and Sumner 2010; Lara 2010; Emmer, Lowe, and Marshall 2011; Jenness and Fenstermaker 2015; Sexton and Jenness 2016). One exception is Sumner and Sexton (2015), who investigate transgender prisoners in women's prisons.
30. Dolovich 2011, 30
31. Dolovich 2011, 30; Robinson 2011, 1324. These deputies are both heterosexual, white, middle-aged men (Robinson 2011, 1324). Because of the prominent role these deputies have played in the unit's operation and the extensive rehabilitative programs that they have introduced, many members of the LGBT community, former prisoners in K6G, and current prisoners view these deputies positively, and in some cases, apparently, quite fondly (for example, Dolovich 2011, 30, footnote 165; Dolovich 2011, 89, footnote 396; Andreoli 2004).
32. Dolovich 2011, 32; Von Zielbauer 2005
33. Von Zielbauer 2005
34. Dolovich 2011, 40–42
35. Robinson 2011, 1324
36. Ucar 2014; Dolovich 2011, 34, 37; Robinson 2011, 1311
37. Robinson 2011, 1326
38. Dolovich 2011, 38–39, footnote 194
39. Robinson 2011, 1326
40. Robinson 2011, 1326
41. Dolovich 2011, 34
42. Dolovich 2012, 990
43. Dolovich 2011, 37, footnote 190; Robinson 2011, 1325
44. Dolovich 2011, 34; Robinson 2011, 1311, 1327
45. Dolovich 2011, 43. Deputies intend to prevent prisoners who have sex with women from living in K6G, but they are not completely successful in doing so. One study

found that 25 percent of prisoners surveyed in K6G reported having sex with at least one woman in the 6 months prior to incarceration (Harawa, Sweat, George, and Sylla 2010, 5).

46. Robinson 2011, 1335
47. Dolovich 2011, 35
48. Dolovich 2011, 34
49. Dolovich 2011, 39
50. Ucar 2014
51. Ucar 2014
52. Dolovich 2012, 1033
53. Ucar 2014
54. Dolovich 2011, 30, 31, footnote 167
55. Dolovich 2012, 1039. More serious infractions in K6G can be punished by moving the prisoner to a disciplinary cell in another part of the jail (Dolovich 2011, 23).
56. Dolovich 2012, 1038
57. Dolovich 2011, 52–53
58. Dolovich 2011, 52–53
59. Ucar 2014
60. Dolovich 2011, 52–53
61. Dolovich 2012, 971
62. Dolovich 2011, 53
63. Dolovich 2012, 1041 footnote 310
64. Ucar 2014
65. Ucar 2014
66. Ucar 2014
67. Ucar 2014
68. Ucar 2014
69. Ucar 2014
70. Harawa, Sweat, George, and Sylla 2010, 5
71. Harawa, Sweat, George, and Sylla 2010, 6
72. Dolovich 2012, 1014–1015
73. Dolovich 2012, 1049
74. Dolovich 2012, 1048–1049
75. Dolovich 2012, 1049
76. Dolovich 2012, 1050
77. Dolovich 2011, 45, footnote 222
78. Ucar 2014
79. Jenness and Fenstermaker 2016; Sexton and Jenness 2016
80. Sexton and Jenness 2016, 560
81. Sexton and Jenness 2016, 560
82. Sexton and Jenness 2016, 560
83. Sexton and Jenness 2016, 560
84. Sexton and Jenness 2016, 560
85. Dolovich 2012, 1047
86. Dolovich 2012, 1048

87. Dolovich 2012, 1048
88. Dolovich 2012, 1048
89. Dolovich 2012, 1047
90. Dolovich 2012, 1047
91. Dolovich 2011, 44–48
92. Dolovich 2011, 44
93. Dolovich 2011, 48
94. Dolovich 2011, 44–45 and footnote 220
95. Dolovich 2011, 93; see also Robinson 2011, 1361 footnote 302
96. A bias of which Dolovich is aware (Dolovich 2011, 48).
97. Dolovich 2012, 966; also Dolovich 2011, 48–54
98. Ucar 2014
99. Dolovich 2011, 63
100. Dolovich 2012, 1025
101. Dolovich 2011, 43
102. Ucar 2014
103. Dolovich 2011, 52
104. Skarbek 2014

Chapter 8

1. Ostrom 1990, 24
2. Crewe 2009, 9; for important exceptions, see DiIulio 1987; Sparks, Bottoms, and Hay 1996; Cavadino and Dignan 2005; Kruttschnitt and Gartner 2005; Crewe 2015; Butler, Slade, and Dias 2018
3. Lacey 2011
4. Gerring 2017, 239
5. Leeson 2008; see also Akerlof 1997; Akerlof and Kranton 2010; in the context of self-enforcing exchange, see Ellickson 1991; Bernstein 1992; Landa 1994; Schaeffer 2008
6. DiIulio 1987, 50
7. Logan 1993
8. Liebling, Hulley, and Crewe 2012
9. Peirce 2019; see also Sanhueza, Brander, and Fuenzalida 2018
10. For an overview of this debate and empirical evidence, see Cheibub 2007
11. See, for instance, Ostrom 1990, 2005; Mahoney and Rueschemeyer 2003; Gerring 2017; Giraudy, Moncada, and Snyder 2019; important contributions documenting the history of the field and method can be found in Munck and Snyder 2007
12. See, for example, Moore 1966 (1991); Skocpol 1979; Levi 1988; Lijphart 2012; see also Giraudy, Moncada, and Snyder 2019 for a valuable collection of subnational comparisons
13. Arias 2009
14. Solzhenitsyn 1973; Applebaum 2003; Shalamov 2018
15. Butler, Slade, and Dias 2018
16. Ellickson 1991; Bernstein 1992; Richman 2017

17. Stringham 2015, chapters 4 and 5; though, the success of self-governance often depends on the proximity of the state (Grossman 2019).
18. Ogilvie 2011, chapter 7
19. Leeson 2008; Akerlof and Kranton 2010
20. Leeson 2008
21. Fearon and Laitin 1996; Greif 2006; Weiner 2013
22. Weiner 2013
23. Acemoglu and Robinson 2019, Chapter 1

Appendix

1. See, for a critique of focusing too much on causal inference, Ruhm 2019; for a discussion of the difficulty of using case studies to examine large, diffuse causes, such as inequality, class alliances, and racism, Gerring 2017, 243; see also, on big structures, large processes, and huge comparisons, Tilly 1984
2. Przeworski and Teune 1970
3. See, for example, Levi 1988; Boone 2014
4. King, Keohane, and Verba 1994, 24, 218, 223; also Bennett and Elman 2006; on causal process observations, see Collier 2011; Brady, Collier, and Seawright 2010, 24.
5. Munger 2010; Ostrom 2005; Poteete, Janssen, and Ostrom 2010, 35; Bates, Avner Greif, Rosenthal, and Weingast 1998; Greif 2006, chapter 11
6. Collier 2011, 823
7. Fukuyama 2013; on thick concepts, see Coppedge 1999
8. "Ethnography" is a somewhat contested term. According to the textbook *Ethnography: Principles in Practice*, "'ethnography' does not have a standard, well-defined meaning" (Atkinson and Hammersley 2007, 2; see also Schatz 2009, 5; Geertz 2017, 3–33). Scholars disagree in what it means to do ethnography. To avoid confusion, I simply mean research that is focused on the everyday life of a particular community. This work is often interview- and observation-based. It tends to offer a thick description of local knowledge.
9. See, for the case in favor of comparative ethnography, Simmons and Smith 2019
10. This is the "intensive description" that is a necessary foundation for process tracing (Collier 2011, 824).
11. It is often important to incorporate informal institutions into comparative analysis (Helmke and Levitsky 2004). Ethnographies can be especially well-suited to doing so (Schatz 2009, 11). Kubik (2009, 32–35) argues that ethnography in political science is especially productive in assessing game-theoretic models; understanding the relationship between formal and informal institutions; and specifying the specific mechanisms that underlie institutions and institutional change and the nature of how markets are embedded. Each of these is a major focus of this book.
12. Crewe 2009, 9; for important exceptions, see DiIulio 1987; Sparks, Bottoms, and Hay 1996; Kruttschnitt and Gartner 2005; Butler, Slade, and Dias 2018
13. Crewe 2009, 3; Liebling 2004, 53
14. Lacey 2011, 215

15. Lacey 2011, 215; see also, on the need for comparisons in the study of punishment, Garland 2018, 14
16. Simon 2000; Wacquant 2002
17. Crewe 2009, Liebling 2004; Phillips 2012
18. Biondi 2016, 2017; Dias and Salla 2017; Darke 2018; Denyer Willis and Lessing 2019; Antillano 2015, 2017; Weegels 2017; Macaulay 2017; Cerbini 2017
19. Ugelvik and Dullum 2012; Scharff Smith and Ugelvik 2017
20. Schatz (2009) is a valuable collection of essays on the use of ethnographies in political science.
21. King, Keohane, and Verba 1994, 139–140; Seawright and Gerring 2008; Gerring 2017, 120–122; for a general treatment on case studies, see Gerring 2017
22. Glasziou, Chalmers, Rawlins, and McCulloch 2007; in the context of criminal violence, see also Lessing 2018, 24–25
23. Lustick 1996, 608; see also Gerring 2017, 170–176
24. Lustick 1996, 606. On the other hand, if the entire field shared an identical approach, we might be even more concerned that its results were biased. Thanks to Richard Snyder for the point.
25. Skocpol 1984, 382
26. Lustick 1996, 615–616
27. My evidentiary sources might also be biased because my work draws on English-language publications. This is a valid concern, but I have no reason to believe it is a major problem. People from many countries, speaking many languages, publish in English-language journals and books. Many scholars writing about places like Brazil or Norway are natives who publish in both English and non-English outlets (Biondi 2016; Mjåland 2014, 2015). Some of these English language works cite and discuss non-English publications, and they do not seem to suggest significant differences in research findings across languages (Ugelvik and Dullum 2012). I cannot prove a negative—that I have not missed important non-English language sources that differ in important ways from the English literature—but I hope to persuade the reader that my empirical account is accurate and compelling.

REFERENCES

Acemoglu, D., De Feo, G., & De Luca, G. (2017). *Weak states: Causes and consequences of the Sicilian mafia* (No. w24115). National Bureau of Economic Research.

Acemoglu, D., Johnson, S., and Robinson, J. (2005). Institutions as a fundamental cause of long-run growth. In P. Aghion & S. Durlauf (Eds.), *Handbook of Economic Growth* (pp. 385–472). Amsterdam: Elsevier.

Acemoglu, D., & Robinson, J. A. (2019). *The narrow corridor: States, societies, and the fate of liberty.* New York, NY: Penguin Press.

Akerlof, G. A. (1997). Social distance and social decisions. *Econometrica: Journal of the Econometric Society, 65*(5)1005–1027.

Akerlof, G. A., & Kranton, R. (2010). *Identity economics: How our identities shape our work, wages, and well-being.* Princeton, NJ: Princeton University Press.

Alesina, A., Baqir, R., & Easterly, W. (1999). Public goods and ethnic divisions. *The Quarterly Journal of Economics, 114*(4), 1243–1284.

Alesina, A., Devleeschauwer, A., Easterly, W., Kurlat, S., & Wacziarg, R. (2003). Fractionalization. *Journal of Economic Growth, 8*(2), 155–194.

Alesina, A., & Ferrara, E. L. (2005). Ethnic diversity and economic performance. *Journal of Economic Literature, 43*(3), 762–800.

Alesina, A., & Spolaore, E. (1997). On the number and size of nations. *The Quarterly Journal of Economics, 112*(4), 1027–1056.

Alesina, A., & Spolaore, E. (2003). *The size of nations.* Cambridge, MA: MIT Press.

Almquist, V. (1931). Scandinavian prisons. *The Annals of the American Academy of Political and Social Science, 157*(1), 197–207.

Andreoli, R. (2014, May 25). Angels for gay inmates. *Advocate.*

Antillano, A. (2015). When prisoners command: Informal control within the Venezuelan prison. *Espacio Abierto Cuaderno Venezolano de Sociología 24*(4), 16–39.

Antillano, A. (2017). When prisoners make the prison: Self-rule in Venezuelan prisons. *Prison Service Journal, 229,* 26–30.

Applebaum, A. (2003). *Gulag: A history of the Soviet camps.* London: Penguin.

Arias, E. D. (2006). *Drugs and democracy in Rio de Janeiro: Trafficking, social networks, and public security.* Chapel Hill: University of North Carolina Press.

Arias, E. D. (2009). Ethnography and the study of Latin American politics: An agenda for research. In E. Schatz (Ed.), *Political ethnography: What immersion contributes to the study of power* (p. 239). Chicago, IL: University of Chicago Press.

Arias, E. D. (2017). *Criminal enterprises and governance in Latin America and the Caribbean*. New York, NY: Cambridge University Press.

Atkinson, P., & Hammersley, M. (2007). *Ethnography: Principles in practice* (3rd ed.). New York, NY: Routledge.

Avio, K. L. (1998). The economics of prisons. *European Journal of Law and Economics 6*(2), 143–175.

Azaola, E., & Bergman, M. (2007). The Mexican prison system. In W. Cornelius & D. Shirk (Eds.), *Reforming the administration of justice in Mexico* (pp. 91–114). Notre Dame, IN: University of Notre Dame Press.

Ayres, I., & Levitt, S. D. (1998). Measuring positive externalities from unobservable victim precaution: An empirical analysis of Lojack. *The Quarterly Journal of Economics, 113*(1), 43–77.

Baer, L. D., & Ravneberg, B. (2008). The outside and inside in Norwegian and English prisons. *Geografiska Annaler: Series B, Human Geography, 90*(2), 205–216.

Baker, V. (2009, January 16). Prison break. *Guardian*.

Baldursson, E. (2000). Prisoners, prisons and punishment in small societies. *Journal of Scandinavian Studies in Criminology and Crime Prevention, 1*(1), 6–15.

Bales, W. D., & Mears, D. P. (2008). Inmate social ties and the transition to society: Does visitation reduce recidivism? *Journal of Research in Crime and Delinquency, 45*(3), 287–321.

Baltimore, B., van der Meer, A. B., Brennan, M., Burton, M., Castillo, M., Cavise, L., Tockman, L. (2007). *Report of delegation to Bolivia*. New York, NY: National Lawyers Guild.

Bandiera, O. (2003). Land reform, the market for protection, and the origins of the Sicilian mafia: Theory and evidence. *Journal of Law, Economics, and Organization, 19*(1), 218–244.

Banks, C. (2003). *Women in prison: A reference handbook*. Santa Barbara, CA: ABC-CLIO.

Barker, V. (2013). Nordic exceptionalism revisited: Explaining the paradox of a Janus-faced penal regime. *Theoretical Criminology, 17*(1), 5–25.

Barzel, Y. (1997). *Economic analysis of property rights*. New York, NY: Cambridge University Press.

Batansky, J. (2014, October 12). Cocaine, politicians and wives: Inside the world's most bizarre prison. *Daily Beast*.

Bates, R. H., Avner Greif, M. L., Rosenthal, J.-L., & Weingast, B. R. (1998). *Analytic narratives*. Princeton, NJ: Princeton University Press.

Bayer, P., Hjalmarsson, R., & Pozen, D. (2009). Building criminal capital behind bars: Peer effects in juvenile corrections. *The Quarterly Journal of Economics, 124*(1), 105–147.

Bennett, A., & Elman, C. (2006). Complex causal relations and case study methods: The example of path dependence. *Political Analysis, 14*(3), 250–267.

Benson, B. L. (1990). *The enterprise of law: Justice without the state*. San Francisco, CA: Pacific Research Institute for Public Policy.

Benson, B. L. (1998). *To serve and protect: Privatization and community in criminal justice*. New York, NY: NYU Press.

Beraldo, S., Caruso, R., & Turati, G. (2013). Life is now! Time preferences and crime: Aggregate evidence from the Italian regions. *Journal of Socio-Economics, 47*, 73–81.

Bernstein, L. (1992). Opting out of the legal system: Extralegal contractual relations in the diamond industry. *The Journal of Legal Studies, 21*(1), 115–157.

Biondi, K. (2016). *Sharing this walk: An ethnography of prison life and the PCC in Brazil.* Chapel Hill, NC: UNC Press Books.

Biondi, K. (2017). Movement between and beyond walls: Micropolitics of incitements and variations among São Paulo's prisoners' movement the "PCC" and the prison system. *Prison Service Journal, 229,* 19–25.

Birkbeck, C. (2011). Imprisonment and internment: Comparing penal institutions North and South. *Punishment & Society, 13*(3), 307–332.

Bloom, B., Chesney-Lind, M., & Owen, B. (1994, May). Women in California prisons: Hidden victims of the war on drugs. Center on Juvenile and Criminal Justice.

Boettke, P. J., Coyne, C. J., & Leeson, P. T. (2013). Comparative historical political economy. *Journal of Institutional Economics, 9*(3), 285–301.

Boone, C. (2014). *Property and political order in Africa: Land rights and the structure of politics.* New York, NY: Cambridge University Press.

Bosworth, M. (1996). Resistance and compliance in women's prisons: Towards a critique of legitimacy. *Critical Criminology, 7*(2), 5–19.

Bosworth, M. (2000). Confining femininity: A history of gender, power and imprisonment. *Theoretical Criminology, 4*(3), 265–284.

Brady, H. E., Collier, D., & Seawright, J. (2010). Refocusing the discussion on methodology. In H. E. Brady & D. Collier (Eds.), *Rethinking social inquiry: Diverse tools, shared standards* (2nd ed., pp. 15–31). Plymouth, UK: Rowman and Littlefield.

Brenneman, R. (2012). *Homies and hermanos: God and gangs in Central America.* New York, NY: Oxford University Press.

Bruhn, A., Lindberg, O., & Nylander, P. (2012). A harsher prison climate and a cultural heritage working against it: Subcultural divisions among Swedish prison officers. In T. Ugelivik & J. Dullum (Eds.), *Penal exceptionalism? Nordic prison policy and practice* (pp. 215–231). London, England: Routledge.

Buonanno, P., Durante, R., Prarolo, G., & Vanin, P. (2015). Poor institutions, rich mines: Resource curse in the origins of the Sicilian mafia. *The Economic Journal, 125*(586), 175–202.

Burnett, T. (2003, December 14). Kindergarten behind bars. *Toronto Sun.*

Butler, M., Slade, G., & Dias, C. N. (2018). Self-governing prisons: Prison gangs in an international perspective. *Trends in Organized Crime,* 1–16.

California Department of Corrections and Rehabilitation. (2007). *Historical trends, 1987–2007.* Offender Information Services Branch, Data Analysis Unit.

California Department of Corrections and Rehabilitation. (2016). *Monthly Report of Population as of Midnight December 31, 2016.* Data Analysis Unit.

California Department of Corrections and Rehabilitation. (2017). *OTPD 2017 Training Schedule and Course Information.* Office of Training and Professional Development.

Campana, P., & Varese, F. (2018). Organized crime in the United Kingdom: Illegal governance of markets and communities. *British Journal of Criminology* 58(6), 1381–1400.

Caravaca-Sánchez, F., Wolff, N., & Teasdale, B. (2018). Exploring associations between interpersonal violence and prison size in Spanish prisons. *Crime & Delinquency*, 65(14), 2019-2043.

Carter, J. H. (2014). Gothic sovereignty: Gangs and criminal community in a Honduran prison. *South Atlantic Quarterly*, 113(3), 475–502.

Cavadino, M., & Dignan, J. (2005). *Penal systems: A comparative approach.* London, England: Sage.

Cavallaro, J., Kopas, J., Lam, Y., Mayhle, T., and Villagra de Biedermann, S. (2008). *Security in Paraguay: Analysis and responses in comparative perspective.* Cambridge, MA: Harvard University Press.

Ceaser, M. (1998, December 17). In Bolivia, children often live with their fathers in prison. *Miami Herald.*

Cerbini, F. (2017). From the panopticon to the anti-panopticon: The "art of government" in the prison of San Pedro. *Prison Service Journal,* 229, 31–34.

Cheibub, J. A. (2007). *Presidentialism, parliamentarism, and democracy.* Cambridge, UK: Cambridge University Press.

Cheliotis, L. K., & Liebling, A. (2006). Race matters in British prisons: Towards a research agenda. *British Journal of Criminology,* 46(2), 286–317.

Christie, N. (2017). *Crime control as industry.* New York, NY: Routledge Classics.

Clemmer, D. (1940). *The prison community.* Boston, MA: Christopher Publishing.

Coase, R. H. (1937). The nature of the firm. *Economica,* 4(16), 386–405.

Collier, D. (2011). Understanding process tracing. *PS: Political Science & Politics,* 44(4), 823–830.

Cook, P. J. (1986). The demand and supply of criminal opportunities. *Crime and Justice,* 7: 1–27.

Coppedge, M. (1999). Thickening thin concepts and theories: Combining large N and small in comparative politics. *Comparative Politics,* 31(4), 465–476.

Costa, D. L., & Kahn, M. E. (2007). Surviving Andersonville: The benefits of social networks in POW camps. *The American Economic Review,* 97(4), 1467–1487.

Coyle, A., Fair, H., Jacobson, J., & Walmsley, R. (2016). *Imprisonment worldwide: The current situation and an alternative future.* Chicago, IL: Bristol University Press.

Crabtree, S. (2010). Religiosity highest in world's poorest nations. Gallup. https://news.gallup.com/poll/142727/religiosity-highest-world-poorest-nations.aspx

Craddock, A. (1996). A comparative study of male and female prison misconduct careers. *The Prison Journal,* 76(1), 60–80.

Crewe, B. (2005). Prisoner society in the era of hard drugs. *Punishment & Society,* 7(4), 457–481.

Crewe, B. (2006). Prison drug dealing and the ethnographic lens. *The Howard Journal of Crime and Justice,* 45(4), 347–368.

Crewe, B. (2009). *The prisoner society: Power, adaptation, and social life in an English prison.* New York, NY: Oxford University Press.

Crewe, B. (2015). Inside the belly of the beast: Understanding the experience of imprisonment. *International Journal for Crime, Justice and Social Democracy,* 4(1), 50–65.

Crewe, B., & Laws, B. (2016). Subcultural adaptation to incarceration. In J. Woolredge & P. Smith (Eds.), *The Oxford handbook on prisons and imprisonment* (pp. 125–142). New York, NY: Oxford University Press.

Crouch, B. M., & Marquart, J. (1989). *An appeal to justice: Litigated reform of Texas prisons.* Austin: University of Texas Press.

D'Amico, D. J. (2008). Tattoo prohibition behind bars: The case for repeal. *The Journal of Private Enterprise,* 23(2), 113–134.

Darke, S. (2013a). Entangled staff-inmate relations. *Prison Service Journal,* 207, 16–22.

Darke, S. (2013b). Inmate governance in Brazilian prisons. *The Howard Journal of Criminal Justice,* 52(3), 272–284.

Darke, S. (2014). Managing without guards in a Brazilian police lockup. *Focaal,* 68(1), 55–67.

Darke, S. (2018). *Conviviality and survival: Co-producing Brazilian prison order.* Cham, Switzerland: Springer.

Darke, S. , & Karam, M. L. (2016). Latin American prisons. In Y. Jewkes, B. Crewe, & J. Bennett (Eds.), *Handbook on prisons* (pp. 460–474). (2nd ed.). New York, NY: Routledge.

Darwin, C. (2003 [1859]). *The origin of species.* New York, NY: Signet Classics.

Davis, M. L. (1988). Time and punishment: An intertemporal model of crime. *Journal of Political Economy,* 96(2), 383–390.

Davis, R. S. (2010). *Andersonville civil war prison.* Charleston, SC: The History Press.

DeCanio, S. (2014). Democracy, the market, and the logic of social choice. *American Journal of Political Science,* 58(3), 637–652.

Densley, J. A. (2013). *How gangs work: An ethnography of youth violence.* New York, NY: Palgrave Macmillan.

Dias, C. N., & Salla, F. (2017). Formal and informal controls and punishment: The production of order in the prisons of São Paulo. *Prison Service Journal,* 229, 19–25.

DiIulio, J. J. (1987). *Governing prisons.* New York, NY: Simon & Schuster.

Dimico, A., Isopi, A., & Olsson, O. (2017). Origins of the Sicilian mafia: The market for lemons. *The Journal of Economic History,* 77(4), 1083–1115.

Dolovich, S. (2011). Strategic segregation in the modern prison. *American Criminal Law Review,* 48(1), 11–22.

Dolovich, S. (2012). Two models of the prison: Accidental humanity and hypermasculinity in the LA county jail. *The Journal of Criminal Law & Criminology,* 102(4), 965–1118.

Dooley, B. D., Seals, A., & Skarbek, D. (2014). The effect of prison gang membership on recidivism. *Journal of Criminal Justice,* 42(3), 267–275.

Drago, F., Galbiati, R., & Vertova, P. (2011). Prison conditions and recidivism. *American Law and Economics Review,* 13(1), 103–130.

Easterly, W., & Levine, R. (1997). Africa's growth tragedy: Policies and ethnic divisions. *The Quarterly Journal of Economics,* 112(4), 1203–1250.

Ellickson, R. C. (1991). *Order without law: How neighbors settle disputes.* Cambridge, MA: Harvard University Press.

Emmer, P., Lowe, A., & Marshall, R. B. (2011). *This is a prison, glitter is not allowed: Experiences of trans and gender variant people in Pennsylvania's prison systems.* Philadelphia, PA: Hearts on a Wire Collective.

Engbo, H. J. (2017). Normalisation in Nordic prisons: From a prison governor's perspective. In P. Scharff Smith & T. Ugelvik (Eds.), *Scandinavian penal history, culture and prison practice* (pp. 327–352). London: Palgrave Macmillan.

Estefania, R. (2009). Photo journal: Inside a Bolivian jail. BBC News. http://news.bbc.co.uk/2/shared/spl/hi/picture_gallery/06/americas_inside_a_bolivian_jail/html/1.stm

Faith, K. (2011). *Unruly women: The politics of confinement & resistance.* Chapel Hill, NC: Seven Stories Press.

Fearon, J. D., & Laitin, D. D. (1996). Explaining interethnic cooperation. *American Political Science Review, 90*(4), 715–735.

Fleisher, M. S. (1989). *Warehousing violence.* Newbury Park, CA: Sage.

Forbes, E. (1865). *Diary of a soldier and prisoner of war in the rebel prisons.* Trenton, NJ: Murphy & Bechtel, Printers.

Ford, C. A. (1929). Homosexual practices of institutionalized females. *The Journal of Abnormal and Social Psychology, 23*(4), 442.

Forsyth, C. J., & Evans, R. D. (2003). Reconsidering the pseudo-family/gang gender distinction in prison research. *Journal of Police and Criminal Psychology, 18*(1), 15–23.

Forsyth, C. J., Evans, R. D., & Foster, D. B. (2002). An analysis of inmate explanations for lesbian relationships in prison. *International Journal of Sociology of the Family, 30*(1), 67–77.

Foster, T. W. (1975). Make-believe families: A response of women and girls to the deprivations of imprisonment. *International Journal of Criminology & Penology, 3*(1), 71–78.

Foucault, M. (1977). *Discipline and punish: The birth of the prison.* New York, NY: Vintage.

Fox, J. G. (1984). Women's prison policy, prisoner activism, and the impact of the contemporary feminist movement: A case study. *Prison Journal, 64*(1), 15–36.

Frank, V. A., Dahl, H. V., Holm, K. E., & Kolind, T. (2015). Inmates' perspectives on prison drug treatment: A qualitative study from three prisons in Denmark. *Probation Journal, 62*(2), 156–171.

Fransen, P. (2017). The rise of open prisons and the breakthrough of the principle of normalisation from the 1930s until today. In P. Scharff Smith & T. Ugelvik (Eds.), *Scandinavian penal history, culture and prison practice: Embraced by the welfare state?* (pp. 81–102). London: Springer.

Frey, B. S. (2001). A utopia? Government without territorial monopoly. *Journal of Institutional and Theoretical Economics JITE, 157*(1), 162–175.

Fujimura-Fanselow, A., & Wickeri, E. (2013). We are left to rot: Arbitrary and excessive pretrial detention in Bolivia. *Fordham International Law Journal, 36*(4), 812.

Fukuyama, F. (2013). What is governance? *Governance, 26*(3), 347–368.

Futch, O. L. (1999 [1968]). *History of Andersonville prison*. Gainesville: University Press of Florida.

Gambetta, D. (1993). *The Sicilian mafia: The business of private protection*. Cambridge, MA: Harvard University Press.

Gambetta, D. (2009). *Codes of the underworld: How criminals communicate*. Princeton, NJ: Princeton University Press.

Garces, C. (2010). The cross politics of Ecuador's penal state. *Cultural Anthropology, 25*(3), 459–496.

Garland, D. (2001). *The culture of control: Crime and social order in contemporary society*. Oxford, England: Oxford University Press.

Garland, D. (2018). Theoretical advances and problems in the sociology of punishment. *Punishment & Society, 20*(1), 8–33.

Gartner, R., & Kruttschnitt, C. (2004). A brief history of doing time: The California Institution for Women in the 1960s and the 1990s. *Law & Society Review, 38*(2), 267–304.

Geertz, C. (2017). *The interpretation of cultures: Selected essays*. New York, NY: Basic Books.

Genders, E., & Player, E. (1990). Women lifers: Assessing the experience. *The Prison Journal, 80*(1), 46–57.

Gerring, J. (2017). *Case study research: Principles and practices* (2nd ed.). Cambridge, UK: Cambridge University Press.

Giallombardo, R. (1966). *Society of women: A study of a women's prison*. New York, NY: Wiley.

Giraudy, J., Moncada, E., & Snyder, R. (2019). *Inside countries: Subnational research in comparative perspective*. New York, NY: Cambridge University Press.

Girshick, L. B. (1999). *No safe haven: Stories of women in prison*. Boston, MA: Northeastern University Press.

Glaeser, E. L. (1998). Economic approach to crime and punishment. In P. Newman (Ed.), *New Palgrave dictionary of economics and the law* (Vol. 1, pp. 1–5). London, England: MacMillan.

Glasziou, P., Chalmers, I., Rawlins, M., & McCulloch, P. (2007). When are randomised trials unnecessary? Picking signal from noise. *BMJ, 334*(7589), 349–351.

Gray, M. P. (2011). Introduction: Advancing Andersonville. Ovid L. Futch as prison micro-monograph pioneer. In O. L. Futch (Ed.), *History of Andersonville Prison* (pp. iix–xxiv). Gainseville: University Press of Florida.

Green, D. A. (2012). Media, crime and Nordic exceptionalism: The limits of convergence. In T. Ugelivik & J. Dullum (Eds.), *Penal exceptionalism? Nordic prison policy and practice* (pp. 58–75). London, England: Routledge.

Greer, K. R. (2000). The changing nature of interpersonal relationships in a women's prison. *The Prison Journal, 80*(4), 442–468.

Greif, A. (1989). Reputation and coalitions in medieval trade: Evidence on the Maghribi traders. *The Journal of Economic History, 49*(4), 857–882.

Greif, A. (2006). *Institutions and the path to the modern economy: Lessons from medieval trade*. New York, NY: Cambridge University Press.

Greif, A., & Kingston, C. (2011). Institutions: Rules or equilibria? In N. Schofield & G. Caballero (Eds.), *Political economy of institutions, democracy and voting* (pp. 13–43). Berlin, Germany: Springer Berlin Heidelberg.

Grierson, J. (2018, April 26). Prison violence in England and Wales hits record levels. *Guardian.*

Grimwood, G. G. (2016, February 12). Building prisons in England and Wales: The bigger, the better? House of Commons, Briefing Paper #05646.

Grossman, S. (2019). The politics of order in informal markets: Evidence from Lagos. *World Politics, 72*(1), 47–79.

Hall, P. A., & Taylor, R. C. (1996). Political science and the three new institutionalisms. *Political Studies, 44*(5), 936–957.

Hancock, P., & Jewkes, Y. (2011). Architectures of incarceration: The spatial pains of imprisonment. *Punishment & Society, 13*(5), 611–629.

Hanoa, K. (2008). *Vold og trusler mellom innsatte: En intervjuundersøkelse.* Oslo, Norway: KRUS.

Harawa, N. T., Sweat, J., George, S., & Sylla, M. (2010). Sex and condom use in a large jail unit for men who have sex with men (MSM) and male-to-female transgenders. *Journal of Health Care for the Poor and Underserved, 21*(3), 1–17.

Hardin, R. (1982). *Collective action.* New York, NY: RFF Press.

Hayek, F. A. (1945). The use of knowledge in society. *The American Economic Review, 35*(4), 519–530.

Heffernan, E. (1972). *Making it in prison: The square, the cool, and the life.* New York, NY: Wiley-Interscience.

Helmke, G., & Levitsky, S. (2004). Informal institutions and comparative politics: A research agenda. *Perspectives on Politics, 2*(4), 725–740.

Hensley, C., Castle, T., & Tewksbury, R. (2003). Inmate-to-inmate sexual coercion in a prison for women. *Journal of Offender Rehabilitation, 37*(2), 77–87.

HM Chief Inspector of Prisons. (2009). The prison characteristics that predict prisons being assessed as performing "well." HM Inspectorate of Prisons.

HM Chief Inspector of Prisons. (2010, June). Muslim prisoners' experiences: A thematic review.

Holyoak, W. H. (1972). Playing out family conflicts in a female homosexual "family" group (Chick-Vot) among institutional juveniles: A case presentation. *Adolescence, 7*(26), 153.

Hummel, C. (2017). Disobedient market: Street vendors, enforcement, and state intervention in collective action. *Comparative Political Studies 50*(11), 1524–1555.

Hunt, G., Riegel, S, Morales, T., & Waldorf, D. (1993). Changes in prison culture: Prison gangs and the case of the "Pepsi generation." *Social Problems 40*(3), 398–409.

Inter-American Commission on Human Rights. (2007). Access to justice and social inclusion: The road towards strengthening democracy in Bolivia. Organization of American States.

Inter-American Commission on Human Rights. (2011). Report on the human rights of persons deprived of liberty in the Americas. Organization of American States.

Irwin, J. (1980). *Prisons in turmoil.* Boston, MA: Little, Brown.

Irwin, J., & Cressey, D. R. (1962). Thieves, convicts and the inmate culture. *Social Problems, 10*(2), 142–155.

Jacobs, J. B. (1978). *Stateville: The penitentiary in mass society*. Chicago, IL: University of Chicago Press.

Jenness, V. , & Fenstermaker, S. (2015). Agnes goes to prison: Gender authenticity, transgender inmates in prisons for men, and pursuit of "the real deal". In M. B. Zinn, P. Hondagneu-Sotelo, M. A. Messner, & A. M. Denissen (Eds.), *Gender through the prism of difference* (pp. 223–235). New York, NY: Oxford University Press.

Jenness, V., & Fenstermaker, S. (2016). Forty years after Brownmiller: Prisons for men, transgender inmates, and the rape of the feminine. *Gender & Society, 30*(1), 14–29.

Jensen, G. F., & Jones, D. (1976). Perspectives on inmate culture: A study of women in prison. *Social Forces, 54*(3), 590–603.

Johnson, A. (2017). *If I give my soul: Faith behind bars in Rio de Janeiro*. New York, NY: Oxford University Press.

Johnson, A., & Densley, J. (2018). Rio's New Social Order: How Religion Signals Disengagement from Prison Gangs. *Qualitative Sociology, 41*(2), 243–262.

Johnsen, B., & Granheim, P. K. (2012). Prison size and the quality of life in Norwegian closed prisons in late modernity. In T. Ugelivik & J. Dullum (Eds.), *Penal exceptionalism: Nordic prison policy and practice* (pp. 199–214). London, England: Routledge.

Johnsen, B., Granheim, P. K., & Helgesen, J. (2011). Exceptional prison conditions and the quality of prison life: Prison size and prison culture in Norwegian closed prisons. *European Journal of Criminology, 8*(6), 515–529.

Jones, R. S. (1993). Coping with separation: Adaptive responses of women prisoners. *Women & Criminal Justice, 5*(1), 71–97.

Jones, T., & Newburn, T. (2007). *Policy transfer and criminal justice: Exploring US influence over British crime control policy*. London, England: Open University Press.

Kaeble, D. , & Glaze, L. (2016). *Correctional populations in the United States, 2015*. U.S. Department of Justice, Office of Justice Programs, Bureau of Justice Statistics.

Kalinich, D. B., & Stojkovic, S. (1985). Contraband: The basis for legitimate power in a prison social system. *Criminal Justice and Behavior, 12*(4), 435–451.

Kaminski, M. M. (2004). *Games prisoners play: The tragicomic worlds of Polish prison*. Princeton, NJ: Princeton University Press.

King, G., Keohane, R. O., & Verba, S. (1994). *Designing social inquiry: Scientific inference in qualitative research*. Princeton, NJ: Princeton University Press.

Kolb, A., & Palys, T. (2018). Playing the part: Pseudo-families, wives, and the politics of relationships in women's prisons in California. *The Prison Journal*, 0032885518811809.

Kolind, T., Holm, K., Duff, C., & Frank, V. A. (2016). Three enactments of drugs in Danish prison drug treatment: Illegal drugs, medicine and constrainers. *Drugs: Education, Prevention and Policy, 23*(2), 135–143.

Koscheski, M., & Hensley, C. (2001). Inmate homosexual behavior in a southern female correctional facility. *American Journal of Criminal Justice, 25*(2), 269–277.

Kreager, D. A., & Kruttschnitt, C. (2018). Inmate society in the era of mass incarceration. *Annual Review of Criminology, 1*, 261–283.

Kruttschnitt, C., & Gartner, R. (2003). Women's imprisonment. *Crime and Justice*, 30, 1–81.

Kruttschnitt, C., & Gartner, R. (2005). *Marking time in the Golden State: Women's imprisonment in California*. New York, NY: Cambridge University Press.

Kruttschnitt, C., & Hussemann, J. (2008). Micropolitics of race and ethnicity in women's prisons in two political contexts. *The British Journal of Sociology*, 59(4), 709–728.

Kruttschnitt, C., & Vuolo, M. (2007). The cultural context of women prisoners' mental health: A comparison of two prison systems. *Punishment & Society*, 9(2), 115–150.

Kruttschnitt, C., Gartner, R., & Miller, A. (2000). Doing her own time? Women's responses to prison in the context of the old and the new penology. *Criminology*, 38(3), 681–718.

Kruttschnitt, C., Slotboom, A. M., Dirkzwager, A., & Bijleveld, C. (2013). Bringing women's carceral experiences into the "new punitiveness" fray. *Justice Quarterly*, 30(1), 18–43.

Kubik, J. (2009). Ethnography of politics: Foundations, applications, prospects. In E. Schatz (Ed.), *Political ethnography: What immersion contributes to the study of power* (pp. 25–52). Chicago, IL: University of Chicago Press.

Kutzler, E. A. (2014). Captive audiences: Sound, silence, and listening in Civil War prisons. *Journal of Social History*, 48(2), 239–263.

Kutzler, E. A. (2019). *Living by inches: The smells, sounds, tastes, and feeling of captivity in Civil War prisons*. Chapel Hill, NC: University of North Carolina Press.

Lacey, N. (2008). *The prisoners' dilemma: The political economy of punishment in comparative perspective*. New York, NY: Cambridge University Press.

Lacey, N. (2011). Why globalisation doesn't spell convergence: Models of institutional variation and the comparative political economy of punishment. In A. Crawford (Ed.), *International and comparative criminal justice and urban governance* (pp. 214–250). New York, NY: Cambridge University Press.

Landa, J. T. (1981). A theory of the ethnically homogeneous middleman group: An institutional alternative to contract law. *The Journal of Legal Studies*, 10(2), 349–362.

Landa, J. T. (1994). *Trust, ethnicity, and identity: Beyond the new institutional economics of ethnic trading networks, contract law, and gift-exchange*. Ann Arbor: University of Michigan Press.

Landes, W. M., & Posner, R. A. (1975). The private enforcement of law. *The Journal of Legal Studies*, 4(1), 1–46.

Lappi-Seppälä, T. (2008). Trust, welfare, and political culture: Explaining differences in national penal policies. *Crime and Justice*, 37(1), 313–387.

Lara, A. (2010). Forced integration of gay, bisexual and transgendered inmates in California state prisons: From protected minority to exposed victims. *Southern California Interdisciplinary Law Journal*, 19, 589.

Larson, D. (2013, September 28). Why Scandinavian prisons are superior. *Atlantic*.

Larson, J. H., & Nelson, J. (1984). Women, friendship, and adaptation to prison. *Journal of Criminal Justice*, 12(6), 601–615.

Lee, David S. , & McCrary, J. (2005). *Crime, punishment, and myopia*. NBER working paper #11491. Washington, DC: National Bureau of Economic Research.

Leeson, P. T. (2007a). An-arrgh-chy: The law and economics of pirate organization. *Journal of Political Economy, 115*(6), 1049–1094.

Leeson, P. T. (2007b). Efficient anarchy. *Public Choice, 130*(1–2), 41–53.

Leeson, P. T. (2007c). Trading with bandits. *The Journal of Law and Economics, 50*(2), 303–321.

Leeson, P. T. (2008). Social distance and self-enforcing exchange. *The Journal of Legal Studies, 37*(1), 161–188.

Leeson, P. T. (2014). *Anarchy unbound: Why self-governance works better than you think.* New York, NY: Cambridge University Press.

Leger, R. G. (1987). Lesbianism among women prisoners: Participants and nonparticipants. *Criminal Justice and Behavior, 14*(4), 448–467.

Lessing, B. (2018). *Making peace in drug wars: Crackdowns and cartels in Latin America.* New York, NY: Cambridge University Press.

Lessing, B. , & Denyer Willis, G. (2019). Legitimacy in criminal governance: Regulating a drug empire from behind bars. *American Political Science Review, 113*(2): 584–606.

Levi, M. (1988). *Of rule and revenue.* Berkeley, CA: University of California Press.

Libell, H. P. (2016, March 15). Anders Behring Breivik, killer in 2011 Norway massacre, says prison conditions violate his rights. *New York Times.*

Liebling, A. (2004). *Prisons and their moral performance: A study of values, quality, and prison life.* Oxford, England: Oxford University Press.

Liebling, A., Arnold, H., & Straub, C. (2011). *An exploration of staff–prisoner relationships at HMP Whitemoor: 12 years on.* Revised Final Report. Ministry of Justice, National Offender Management Service. Cambridge Institute of Criminology Prisons Research Centre.

Liebling, A., Hulley, S., and Crewe, B. (2012). Conceptualising and measuring the quality of prison life. In Gadd, D., Karstedt, S., & Messner, S. F. *The SAGE handbook of criminological research methods* (pp. 358–372). London, England: Sage Publications.

Lijphart, A. (2012). *Patterns of democracy: Government forms and performance in thirty-six countries.* New Haven, CT: Yale University Press.

Llana, S. M. (2007, April 11). Serving prison time as a family. *Christian Science Monitor.*

Logan, C. H. (1993). *Criminal justice performance measures for prisons.* US Department of Justice, Office of Justice Programs, Bureau of Justice Statistics.

Lundquist, J. (2004). Andersonville prison headcount rosters. Obtained from the United States National Park Service.

Lustick, I. S. (1996). History, historiography, and political science: Multiple historical records and the problem of selection bias. *American Political Science Review, 90*(3), 605–618.

Macaulay, F. (2017). The policy challenges of informal prisoner governance. *Prison Service Journal, 229,* 51–56.

MacKenzie, D. L., Robinson, J. W., & Campbell, C. S. (1989). Long-term incarceration of female offenders prison adjustment and coping. *Criminal Justice and Behavior, 16*(2), 223–238.

Mahan, S. (1984). Imposition of despair—An ethnography of women in prison. *Justice Quarterly, 1*(3), 357–383.

Mahoney, J., & Rueschemeyer, D. (Eds.). (2003). *Comparative historical analysis in the social sciences*. Cambridge: Cambridge University Press.

Maitra, D. (2013). *Gangs behind bars: Fact or fiction?* (Doctoral Dissertation). University of Cambridge, Institute of Criminology.

Maitra, D. (2015). An exploratory study of prison gangs in contemporary society. In S. Harding & M. Plansinski (Eds.), *Global perspectives on youth gang behavior, violence, and weapons use* (pp. 215–237). Hershey, PA: IGI Global.

Mariner, J. (1998). *Behind bars in Brazil*. New York, NY: Human Rights Watch.

Marvel, W. (1994). *Andersonville: The last depot*. Chapel Hill: University of North Carolina Press.

Mathiesen, T. (1965). *The defences of the weak: A study of Norwegian correctional institution*. London: Tavistock.

Mathiesen, T. (2012). Scandianvaian exceptionalism in penal matters: Reality or wishful thinking? In T. Ugelivik & J. Dullum (Eds.), *Penal exceptionalism? Nordic prison policy and practice* (pp. 13–37). London: Routledge.

Mawby, R. I. (1982). Women in prison: A British study. *Crime & Delinquency, 28*(1), 24–39.

McDonnell, J. (2015). Custody division quarterly report: July–September 2015. Los Angeles County Sheriff's Department.

McDonnell, J. (2017). Custody division public data sharing 2017, Q2 Report. Los Angeles County Sheriff's Department. http://www.lasd.org/public_data_sharing.html

McElroy, J. (1913). *Andersonville: A story of rebel military prisons, fifteen months a guest of the so-called Southern Confederacy. A private soldier's experience in Richmond, Andersonville, Savannah, Millen, Blackshear and Florence*. Wentworth Press.

McLean, R., Maitra, D., & Holligan, C. (2017). Voices of quiet desistance in UK prisons: Exploring emergence of new identities under desistance constraint. *The Howard Journal of Crime and Justice, 56*(4), 437–453.

Meadowcroft, J. (2005). *The ethics of the market*. New York, NY: Palgrave Macmillan.

Medrano, E. (2013, June 21). Tras violación a niña, sugieren anticipar cierre de San Pedro. *La Razon*. http://www.la-razon.com/nacional/seguridad_nacional/violacion-sugieren-anticipar-San-Pedro_0_1855614465.html

Mendoza-Denton, N. (2008). *Homegirls: Language and cultural practice among Latina youth gangs*. Malden, MA: Blackwell Publishing.

Miller, J. (2001). *One of the guys: Girls, gangs, and gender*. New York, NY: Oxford University Press.

Minke, L. K., & Smoyer, A. B. (2017). Prison food in Denmark: Normal responsibility or ethnocentric imaginations? In P. Scharff Smith & T. Ugelvik (Eds.), *Scandinavian penal history, culture and prison practice: Embraced by the welfare state?* (pp. 353–376). London: Springer.

Ministry of Justice. (2017). HM prison population data file, 31 March 2017. https://www.gov.uk/government/collections/offender-management-statistics-quarterly

Mjåland, K. (2014). "A culture of sharing": Drug exchange in a Norwegian prison. *Punishment & Society, 16*(3), 336–352.

Mjåland, K. (2015). The paradox of control: An ethnographic analysis of opiate maintenance treatment in a Norwegian prison. *International Journal of Drug Policy, 26*(8), 781–789.

Moore, B. (1966 [1991]). *Social Origins of Dictatorship and Democracy: Lord and peasant in the making of the modern world.* London: Penguin Books.

Moore, J. (1991). *Going down to the barrio: Homeboys and homegirls in change.* Philadelphia, PA: Temple University Press.

Moyer, I. L. (1980). Leadership in a women's prison. *Journal of Criminal Justice, 8*(4), 233–241.

Munck, G. L., & Snyder, R. (2007). *Passion, craft, and method in comparative politics.* Baltimore, MD: John Hopkins University Press.

Munger, M. C. (2010). Endless forms most beautiful and most wonderful: Elinor Ostrom and the diversity of institutions. *Public Choice, 143*(3), 263–268.

Murtazashvili, I., & Murtazashvili, J. (2014). Anarchy, self-governance, and legal titling. *Public Choice, 162*(3–4), 1–19.

National Park Service. (2015). Camp Sumter/Andersonville Prison. https://www.nps.gov/ande/learn/historyculture/camp_sumter.htm. Copy available on request.

Nelken, D. (2010). *Comparative Criminal Justice.* Los Angeles, CA: Sage Publications.

Neumann, C. B. (2012). "Imprisoning the soul." In T. Ugelivik & J. Dullum (Eds.), *Penal exceptionalism? Nordic prison policy and practice* (pp. 139–155). London: Routledge.

Newburn, T. (2002). Atlantic crossings: "Policy transfer" and crime control in the USA and Britain. *Punishment & Society, 4*(2), 165–194.

Nielsen, M. M. (2012). To be and not to be: Adaptation, ambivalence and ambiguity in a Danish prison. *Advances in Applied Sociology, 2*(2), 135.

Nilsson, R. (2003). The Swedish prison system in historical perspective: A story of successful failure? *Journal of Scandinavian Studies in Criminology and Crime Prevention, 4*(1), 1–20.

North, D. C. (1987). Institutions, transaction costs and economic growth. *Economic Inquiry, 25*(3), 419–428.

North, D. C. (1990). *Institutions, institutional change and economic performance.* New York, NY: Cambridge University Press.

Northrop, J. W. (2013 [1904]). *Chronicles from the diary of a war prisoner in Andersonville and other military prisons of the south in 1864.* Miami, FL: Hardpress Publishing.

Norwegian Correctional Service. (2018). About the Norwegian correctional service. http://www.kriminalomsorgen.no/information-in-english.265199.no.html

O'Donnell, I. (2005). Putting prison in its place. *Judicial Studies Institute Journal 5*(2), 54–68.

Ogilvie, S. (2011). *Institutions and European trade: Merchant guilds, 1000–1800.* Cambridge, UK: Cambridge University Press.

Olivero, J. M. (1998). The crisis in Mexican prisons: The impact of the United States. In R. P. Weiss & N. South (Eds.), *Comparing prison systems: Toward a comparative international penology* (pp. 99–113). Amsterdam, Netherlands: Gordon & Breach.

Olson, M. (1971). *The logic of collective action: Public goods and the theory of groups.* Cambridge, MA: Harvard University Press.

Orbell, J. M., Schwartz-Shea, P., & Simmons, R. T. (1984). Do cooperators exit more readily than defectors? *American Political Science Review, 78*(1), 147–162.

Ortiz, J. (2015, June 23). Shorter California prison officer academy to start next month. *Sacramento Bee.*

Ortiz-Ospina, E., & Roser, M. (2018). Trust. Published online at OurWorldInData.org. https://ourworldindata.org/trust.

Ostrom, E. (1990). *Governing the commons.* New York, NY: Cambridge University Press.

Ostrom, E. (2005). *Understanding institutional diversity.* Princeton, NJ: Princeton University Press.

Otis, M. (1913). A perversion not commonly noted. *The Journal of Abnormal Psychology, 8*(2), 113.

Owen, B. A. (1998). *In the mix: Struggle and survival in a women's prison.* Albany, NY: SUNY Press.

Panfil, V. R., & Peterson, D. (2018). Gender, sexuality, and gangs: Re-envisioning diversity. In S. H. Decker & D. C. Pyrooz (Eds.), *The handbook of gangs* (pp. 208–234). Malden, MA: Wiley-Blackwell.

Pardue, A., Arrigo, B. A., & Murphy, D. S. (2011). Sex and sexuality in women's prisons: A preliminary typological investigation. *The Prison Journal, 91*(3), 279–304.

Parks, B. (2015, May 30). How a US prison camp helped create ISIS. *New York Post.*

Peirce, J. (2019). *Prisoners' perceptions of humane treatment in the Dominican Republic's prison reform process.* Unpublished manuscript, John Jay College.

Petersilia, J. (2003). *When prisoners come home: Parole and prisoner reentry.* New York, NY: Oxford University Press.

Peterson, D., Carson, D. C., & Fowler, E. (2018). What's sex (composition) got to do with it? The importance of sex composition of gangs for female and male members' offending and victimization. *Justice Quarterly, 35*(6), 941–976.

Phillips, C. (2008). Negotiating identities: Ethnicity and social relations in a young offenders' institution. *Theoretical Criminology, 12*(3), 313–331.

Phillips, C. (2012). "It ain't nothing like America with the Bloods and the Crips": Gang narratives inside two English prisons. *Punishment & Society. 14*(1), 51–68.

Pickenpaugh, R. (2013). *Captives in blue: The Civil War prisons of the Confederacy.* Tuscaloosa: University of Alabama Press.

Pogrebin, M. R., & Dodge, M. (2001). Women's accounts of their prison experiences: A retrospective view of their subjective realities. *Journal of Criminal Justice, 29*(6), 531–541.

Pollock, J. M. (2002). *Women, prison, and crime.* Belmont, CA: Wadsworth Thomson Learning.

Poteete, A. R., Janssen, M. A., & Ostrom, E. (2010). *Working together: Collective action, the commons, and multiple methods in practice.* Princeton, NJ: Princeton University Press.

Pratt, J. (2008a). Scandinavian exceptionalism in an era of penal excess: Part I: The nature and roots of Scandinavian exceptionalism. *The British Journal of Criminology, 48*(2), 119–137.

Pratt, J. (2008b). Scandinavian exceptionalism in an era of penal excess: Part II: Does Scandinavian exceptionalism have a future? *The British Journal of Criminology, 48*(3), 275–292.

Pratt, J., & Eriksson, A. (2011). "Mr. Larsson is walking out again." The origins and development of Scandinavian prison systems. *Australian & New Zealand Journal of Criminology, 44*(1), 7–23.

Pratt, J., & Eriksson, A. (2013). *Contrasts in punishment: An explanation of Anglophone excess and Nordic exceptionalism.* New York, NY: Routledge.

Pratt, J., Brown, D., Brown, M., Hallsworth, S., & Morrison, W. (Eds.). (2005). *The new punitiveness: Trends, theories, perspectives.* Portland, OR: Willan Publishing.

Price, J. A. (1973). Private enterprise in a prison: The free market economy of La Mesa Penitenciaria. *Crime & Delinquency, 19*(2), 218–227.

Propper, A. M. (1978). Lesbianism in female and coed correctional institutions. *Journal of Homosexuality, 3*(3), 265–274.

Propper, A. M. (1982). Make-believe families and homosexuality among imprisoned girls. *Criminology, 20,* 127.

Przeworski, A., & Teune, H. (1970). *The logic of comparative social inquiry.* New York, NY: John Wiley & Sons.

Rabuy, B., & Kopf, D. (2015). Separation by bars and miles: Visitation in state prisons. Prison Policy Initiative. https://www.prisonpolicy.org/reports/prisonvisits.html

Radford, R. A. (1945). The economic organisation of a POW camp. *Economica, 12*(48), 189–201.

Ransom, J. L. (1881). *Andersonville diary: Escape, and list of dead, with name, co., regiment, date of death and no. of grave in cemetery.* Auburn, NY: John L. Ransom.

Reiter, K., Sexton, L., & Sumner, J. (2016, February 2). Denmark doesn't treat its prisoners like prisoners—and it's good for everyone. *The Washington Post.*

Reiter, K., Sexton, L., & Sumner, J. (2017). Negotiating imperfect humanity in the Danish penal system. In P. Scharff Smith & T. Ugelvik (Eds.), *Scandinavian penal history, culture and prison practice* (pp. 481–510). London: Palgrave Macmillan.

Reiter, K., Sexton, L., & Sumner, J. (2018). Theoretical and empirical limits of Scandinavian Exceptionalism: Isolation and normalization in Danish prisons. *Punishment & Society, 20*(1), 92–112.

Reuters. (2012, September 25). Six in ten prisons "self-governed" by gangs. *Telegraph.*

Richman, B. D. (2017). *Stateless commerce: The diamond network and the persistence of relational exchange.* Cambridge, MA: Harvard University Press.

Rierden, A. (1997). *The farm: Life inside a women's prison.* Amherst: University of Massachusetts Press.

Robinson, R. K. (2011). Masculinity as prison: Sexual identity, race, and incarceration. *California Law Review, 99,* 1309.

Romero, D. (2014). L.A. jail visitor gets $1 mil-plus for vicious beat-down by deputies. *LA Weekly.* May 30.

Romero, S. (2011, June 3). Where prisoners can do everything, but leave. *New York Times.*

Rosas and Goodwin v Baca. (2012). Complaint for Injunctive Relief Class Action. United States District Court, Central District of California. ACLU Foundation of Southern California.

Rugh, J. S., & Trounstine, J. (2011). The provision of local public goods in diverse communities: Analyzing municipal bond elections. *The Journal of Politics*, 73(4), 1038–1050.

Ruhm, C. J. (2019). Shackling the identification police? *Southern Economic Journal* 84(4): 1016–1026.

Sanhueza, G., Brander, F., & Fuenzalida, F. (2018). First survey on prison life in Chile: A social work call for prison reform. *International Social Work*, 61(6), 1139–1153.

Savage, M. (2018, April 28). Loss of experienced staff leaving prisons unsafe. *Guardian*.

Schaeffer, E. C. (2008). Remittances and reputations in hawala money-transfer systems: Self-enforcing exchange on an international scale. *Journal of Private Enterprise*, 24(Fall), 95–117.

Scharff Smith, P. (2012). A critical look at Scandinavian exceptionalism: Welfare state theories, penal populism and prison conditions in Denmark and Scandinavia. In T. Ugelvik & J. Dullum (Eds.), *Penal exceptionalism? Nordic prison policy and practice* (pp. 38–57). London, England: Routledge.

Scharff Smith, P. (2017). Punishment without conviction? Scandinavian pre-trial practices and the power of the "benevolent" state. In P. Scharff Smith & T. Ugelvik. (Eds.). *Scandinavian penal history, culture and prison practice* (pp. 129–156). London: Palgrave Macmillan.

Scharff Smith, P., & Ugelvik, T. (Eds.). (2017). *Scandinavian penal history, culture and prison practice: Embraced by the welfare state?* London: Palgrave Macmillan.

Schatz, E. (Ed.). (2009). *Political ethnography: What immersion contributes to the study of power*. Chicago, IL: University of Chicago Press.

Schelling, T. (1971). What is the business of organized crime? *Journal of Public Law* 20(71), 71–84.

Schneider, F., Buehn, A., & Montenegro, C. E. (2010). Shadow economies all over the world: New estimates for 162 countries from 1999 to 2007. *World Bank Policy Research Working Paper Series*.

Schuessler, R. (1989). Exit threats and cooperation under anonymity. *Journal of Conflict Resolution*, 33(4), 728–749.

Seawright, J., & Gerring, J. (2008). Case selection techniques in case study research: A menu of qualitative and quantitative options. *Political Research Quarterly*, 61(2), 294–308.

Selling, L. S. (1931). The pseudo family. *American Journal of Sociology*, 37(2): 247–253.

Setty, E. , Sturrock, R., & Simes, E. (2014). *Gangs in prison: The nature and impact of gang involvement among prisoners*. Catch22 Dawes Unit.

Severance, T. A. (2004). The prison lesbian revisited. *Journal of Gay & Lesbian Social Services*, 17(3), 39–57.

Sexton, L., & Jenness, V. (2016). "We're like community": Collective identity and collective efficacy among transgender women in prisons for men. *Punishment & Society*, 18(5), 544–577.

Sexton, L., Jenness, V., & Sumner, J. M. (2010). Where the margins meet: A demographic assessment of transgender inmates in men's prisons. *Justice Quarterly*, 27(6), 835–866.

Shahriari, S. (2014, April 20). Growing up behind bars: 1,500 children being raised by parents in Bolivian jails. *Guardian*.

Shalamov, V. (2018). *Kolyma stories*. New York Review of Books.

Simon, J. (2000). The "Society of Captives" in the era of hyper-incarceration. *Theoretical Criminology*, 4(3), 285–308.

Simon, J. (2014). *Mass incarceration on trial: A remarkable court decision and the future of prisons in America*. New York, NY: The New Press.

Shammas, V. L. (2014). The pains of freedom: Assessing the ambiguity of Scandinavian penal exceptionalism on Norway's prison island. *Punishment & Society*, 16(1), 104–123.

Shortland, A. (2019). *Kidnap: Inside the ransom business*. Oxford: Oxford University Press.

Shortland, A., & Varese, F. (2014). The protector's choice: An application of protection theory to Somali piracy. *British Journal of Criminology*, 54(5), 741–764.

Simmons, E. S., & Smith, N. R. (2019). The case for comparative ethnography. *Comparative Politics*, 51(3), 341–359.

Skaperdas, S. (2001). The political economy of organized crime: Providing protection when the state does not. *Economics of Governance*, 2(3), 173–202.

Skarbek, D. (2008). Putting the "con" into constitutions: The economics of prison gangs. *The Journal of Law, Economics, & Organization*, 26(2), 183–211.

Skarbek, D. (2010). Self-governance in San Pedro prison. *The Independent Review*, 14(4), 569–585.

Skarbek, D. (2011). Governance and prison gangs. *American Political Science Review*, 105(4), 702–716.

Skarbek, D. (2012). Prison gangs, norms, and organizations. *Journal of Economic Behavior and Organization*, 82(1), 96–109.

Skarbek, D. (2014). *The social order of the underworld: How prison gangs govern the American penal system*. New York, NY: Oxford University Press.

Skarbek, D. (2016). Covenants without the sword? Comparing prison self-governance globally. *American Political Science Review*, 110(4), 845–862.

Skocpol, T. (1979). *States and social revolutions: A comparative analysis of France, Russia and China*. New York, NY: Cambridge University Press.

Skocpol, T. (1984). Emerging agendas and recurring strategies in historical sociology. In T. Skocpol (Ed.), *Vision and method in historical sociology* (pp. 356–391). New York, NY: Cambridge University Press.

Snortum, J. R., & Bødal, K. (1985). Conditions of confinement within security prisons: Scandinavia and California. *Crime & Delinquency*, 31(4), 573–600.

Snyder, R. (2001). Scaling down: The subnational comparative method. *Studies in Comparative International Development*, 36(1), 93–110.

Solzhenitsyn, A. (1973). *The Gulag archipelago: An experiment in literary investigation* (Vol. 2). New York, NY: Harper Perennial Modern Classics.

Sparks, R., Bottoms, A. E., & Hay, W. (1996). *Prisons and the problem of order*. Oxford: Clarendon Press.

Stemple, L., Flores, A., & Meyer, I. H. (2017). Sexual victimization perpetrated by women: Federal data reveal surprising prevalence. *Aggression and Violent Behavior*, 34, 302–311.

Stringham, E. (2015). *Private governance: Creating order in economic and social life*. New York, NY: Oxford University Press.

Sturge, G. (2018). UK Prison Population Statistics. Briefing Paper: Number CBP-04334, July 23. https://researchbriefings.parliament.uk/ResearchBriefing/Summary/SN04334

Sumner, J., & Sexton, L. (2015). Lost in translation: Looking for transgender identity in women's prisons and locating aggressors in prisoner culture. *Critical Criminology*, 23(1), 1–20.

Sutter, J. R. (2012, May 24). Welcome to the world's nicest prison. *CNN*.

Sykes, G. M. (1958 [2007]). *The society of captives: A study of a maximum security prison*. Princeton, NJ: Princeton University Press.

Teasdale, B., Daigle, L. E., Hawk, S. R., & Daquin, J. C. (2016). Violent victimization in the prison context: An examination of the gendered contexts of prison. *International Journal of Offender Therapy and Comparative Criminology*, 60(9), 995–1015.

Tilly, C. (1984). *Big structures, large processes, huge comparisons*. New York, NY: Russell Sage Foundation.

Tilly, C. (1985). War making and state making as organized crime. In P. Evans, D. Rueschemeyer, & T. Skocpol (Eds.), *Bringing the state back in* (pp. 169–191). Cambridge, England: Cambridge University Press.

Tittle, C. R. (1969). Inmate organization: Sex differentiation and the influence of criminal subcultures. *American Sociological Review*, 34(4): 492–505.

Tischler, C. A., & Marquart, J. W. (1989). Analysis of disciplinary infraction rates among female and male inmates. *Journal of Criminal Justice*, 17(6), 507–513.

Thompson, H. A. (2017). *Blood in the water: The Attica prison uprising of 1971 and its legacy*. New York: Vintage.

Tonry, M. (Ed.). (2007). *Crime, punishment, and politics in comparative perspective*. Chicago, IL: University of Chicago Press.

Trammell, R. (2009). Relational violence in women's prison: How women describe interpersonal violence and gender. *Women & Criminal Justice*, 19(4), 267–285.

Trammell, R. (2011). Symbolic violence and prison wives: Gender roles and protective pairing in men's prisons. *The Prison Journal*, 91(3), 305–324.

Trammell, R. (2012). *Enforcing the convict code: Violence and prison culture*. Boulder, CO: Lynne Rienner Publishers.

Trammell, R., & Chenault, S. (2009). "We have to take these guys out": Motivations for assaulting incarcerated child molesters. *Symbolic Interaction*, 32(4), 334–350.

Trammell, R., Wulf-Ludden, T., & Mowder, D. (2015). Partner violence in women's prison: The social consequences of girlfriend fights. *Women & Criminal Justice*, 25(4), 256–272.

Tullock, G. (1967). The welfare costs of tariffs, monopolies, and theft. *Economic Inquiry*, 5(3), 224–232.

Ucar, Ani. (2014, November 18). In the gay wing of L.A. men's central jail, it's not shanks and muggings but hand-sewn gowns and tears. *LA Weekly*.

Ucar, Ani. (2015, January 22). How the Beatles saved the gay inmates of L.A. men's central jail. *LA Weekly*.

Ugelvik, T. (2011). The hidden food: Mealtime resistance and identity work in a Norwegian prison. *Punishment & Society*, 13(1), 47–63.

Ugelvik, T. (2012). The dark side of a culture of equality: Reimagining communities in a Norwegian remand prison. In T. Ugelvik & J. Dullum (Eds.), *Penal exceptionalism? Nordic prison policy and practice*. London: Routledge.

Ugelvik, T. (2014a). "Be a man. Not a bitch." Snitching, the inmate Code and the narrative reconstruction of masculinity in a Norwegian prison. In I. Lander, N. Jon, & S. Ravn (Eds.), *Masculinities inthe criminological field; control, vulnerability and risk-taking* (pp. 57–70). Abingdon: Ashgate.

Ugelvik, T. (2014b). *Power and resistance in prison: Doing time, doing freedom*. London: Palgrave Macmillan.

Ugelvik, T., & Dullum, J. (Eds.) (2012). *Penal exceptionalism? Nordic prison policy and practice*. London: Routledge.

Ungar, M. (2003). Prisons and politics in contemporary Latin America. *Human Rights Quarterly*, 25(4), 909–934.

Uniform Crime Report. (2012). Crime in the United States, 2012. Available: https://ucr.fbi.gov/crime-in-the-u.s/2012/crime-in-the-u.s.-2012/tables/42tabledatadecoverviewpdf/tab42overview.pdf

U.S. Department of State. (2001). Country Reports on Human Rights Practices, Bureau of Democracy, Human Rights, and Labor 2001.

U.S. Department of State. (2006). Country Reports on Human Rights Practices, Bureau of Democracy, Human Rights, and Labor 2006.

Useem, B., & Piehl, A. M. (2008). *Prison state: The challenge of mass incarceration*. New York: Cambridge University Press.

van Wormer, K. S. (1981). Social functions of prison families: The female solution. *Journal of Psychiatry & Law*, 9, 181.

Vanberg, V. J., & Congleton, R. D. (1992). Rationality, morality, and exit. *American Political Science Review*, 86(2), 418–431.

Varella, D. (1999). *Lockdown: Inside Brazil's most dangerous prison*. London: Simon & Schuster.

Varese, F. (1994). Is Sicily the future of Russia? Private protection and the rise of the Russian mafia. *European Journal of Sociology*, 35(2), 224–258.

Varese, F. (2001). *The Russian mafia: Private protection in a new market economy*. New York: Oxford University Press.

Varese, F. (2010). What is organized crime? *Organized crime: Critical conepts in criminology* (Vol. 1, pp. 11–33). London: Routledge.

Varese, F. (2011). *Mafias on the move: How organized crime conquers new territories*. Princeton, NJ: Princeton University Press.

Vigil, J. D. (2008). Female gang members from East Los Angeles. *International Journal of Social Inquiry*, 1(1), 47–74.

Vogel, S. K. (2018) *Statecraft: How governments make markets work*. New York, NY: Oxford University Press.

Von Zielbauer, P. (2005, December 30). New York set to close jail unit for gays. *New York Times*.

Wacquant, L. (2002). The curious eclipse of prison ethnography in the age of mass incarceration. *Ethnography, 3*(4), 371–397.

Wacquant, L. (2003). Toward a dictatorship over the poor? Notes on the penalization of poverty in Brazil. *Punishment & Society, 5*(2), 197–205.

Wacquant, L. (2008). The militarization of urban marginality: Lessons from the Brazilian metropolis. *International Political Sociology, 2*(1), 56–74.

Wang, P. (2017). *The Chinese mafia: Organized crime, corruption, and extra-legal protection.* New York, NY: Oxford University Press.

War of the Rebellion: A Compilation of the Official Records of the Union and Confederate Armies, 1880–1901. (Series 2, Vol. VII). Washington, D.C.: U.S. Government Printing Office.

War of the Rebellion: A Compilation of the Official Records of the Union and Confederate Armies, 1880–1901. (Series 2, Vol. VIII). Washington, D.C.: U.S. Government Printing Office.

Ward, D. A. (1972). Inmate rights and prison reform in Sweden and Denmark. *The Journal of Criminal Law, Criminology, and Police Science, 63*(2), 240–255.

Ward, D. A., & Kassebaum, G. G. (1964). Homosexuality: A mode of adaptation in a prison for women. *Social Problems, 12*(2), 159–177.

Ward, D. A., & Kassebaum, G. G. (1965). *Women's prison: Sex and social structure.* Piscataway, NJ: Transaction Publishers.

Weegels, J. (2017). Prisoner self-governance and survival in a Nicaraguan city police jail. *Prison Service Journal, 229,* 15–19.

Weiner, J. (2014). *The beak of the finch.* New York, NY: Vintage Books.

Wilkinson, W. V. (1990). An exploration of the Mexican criminal justice system: Interviews with incarcerated inmates in a Mexican prison. *International Journal of Comparative and Applied Criminal Justice, 14*(1–2), 115–122.

Williams, R. J. (2018). Finding freedom and rethinking power: Islamic piety in English high security prisons. *The British Journal of Criminology, 58*(3), 730–748.

Williamson, O. E. (1985). *The economic institutions of capitalism: Firms, markets, relational contracting.* New York, NY: Free Press.

Wood, J. (2006). Gang activity in English prisons: The prisoners' perspective. *Psychology, Crime & Law, 12*(6), 605–617.

Wood, J., & Adler, J. (2001). Gang activity in English prisons: The staff perspective. *Psychology, Crime and Law, 7*(1–4), 167–192.

Wood, J., Moir, A., & James, M. (2009). Prisoners' gang-related activity: The importance of bullying and moral disengagement. *Psychology, Crime & Law, 15*(6), 569–581.

Woolf, L. J. (1991). Prison disturbances, April 1990. *London: HM Stationery Office.*

World Prison Brief. 2018. World prison brief data. http://www.prisonstudies.org/world-prison-brief-data

Young, R. (2009, 1 May). Personal correspondence.

Young, R., & McFadden, T. (2003). *Marching powder: A true story of friendship, cocaine, and South America's strangest jail.* New York, NY: St. Martin's Griffin.

Zingraff, M. T., & Zingraff, R. M. (1980). Adaptation patterns of incarcerated female delinquents. *Juvenile and Family Court Journal, 31*(2), 35–47.

INDEX

Tables, figures, and boxes are indicated by an italic t, f, and b following the page number.

For the benefit of digital users, indexed terms that span two pages (e.g., 52–53) may, on occasion, appear on only one of those pages.

Chief Inspector of Prisons, 126
community responsibility system
　absence of, 91–92, 104, 122,
　　130–31, 159–60
　characteristics of, 15–17, 159
　defined, 15–16
comparative method, 154–57, 161
　case selection, 164–66
　explanatory power, 149–50, 156–57,
　　162, 163–64
　limitations to, 155, 161–64
　precedents in other disciplines, 154–55
　use of ethnographies, 162–64, 195n8,
　　195n9, 195n11
　use of typologies, 155–56
convict code, 10, 95, 96–97, 98–99, 151, 156
Crewe, Ben, 115

Darwin, Charles, 1–2
debt, 10, 13, 30, 34, 38–39, 54, 103, 113,
　114, 116
Denmark, 50, 52–53, 60
DiIulio, John J., 152–53
Dolovich, Sharon, 134–35, 136,
　139–40, 141–42
Dowd (Andersonville prisoner), 82–83

Ecuador, 4–5, 25, 26–27, 59–60
England and Wales prison system
　benefits of small prisons, 109–10
　cliques, 118, 120–21, 123–24
　decentralized governance in, 112–21
　differences with California, 107–11, 120–21,
　　122–25, 130–32
　friendships in, 118
　housing estates, 118–19, 120, 158–59
　Islam religious influence inside,
　　125–30, 131–32
　location of prisons, 110–11, 111f
　norms, 113, 116–17
　population, 107–10, 108f, 109f
　pre-prison social networks, 111, 118–20, 122
　prison gang absence, 111, 113–15,
　　121–25, 127
　prison size, 109–10, 109f, 112, 115,
　　121–22, 127
　race and ethnicity, 114, 120–21, 122, 130–
　　31, 189n125
　radicalization, 125–30

　similarities to California, 106–7
　underground economy in, 113, 114–15,
　　117–18, 123
Evans, Rhoda D., 102

fictive kinships. See prison families
Finland, 44–45, 48, 59–60
Forbes, Eugene, 64, 74–75, 79, 80, 84
Forsyth, Craig J., 102
Futch, Ovid, 64, 73, 80, 81

Gambetta, Diego, 13
Gartner, Rosemary, 90, 93–94
gay and transgender housing unit
　classification process, 135–38
　co-governance in, 140–41
　criticisms of, 134–35, 138, 192n29
　danger in, 144, 145
　House Mouse, 140–41, 156
　norms, 140, 141–42
　official governance in, 139–42
　population, 135–36, 139–40, 142
　prison families, 141, 142–43
　prison gang absence, 140, 144–45
　sexual activity in, 141, 192–93n45
　social distance, 134, 138, 142–43, 144–46
　social networks, 134, 138, 143, 144–46
Giallombardo, Rose, 184n25
Global Prisons Research Network, 164
governance institutions in prison
　defined, 6–7
　degree of centralization, 12–18, 12t, 17f
　effects, 6–7
　official providers of, 7
　private crime control, 7
　private providers of, 7
　reasons for lack of official provision, 8–9, 12
　regime types, 9–10
　supply and demand of, 10–12
Gulags, 155–56

Hay, Will, 112
Heffernan, Esther, 100–1
HMP Albany prison, 112–15
HMP Long Lartin prison, 112–15
HMP Maidstone, 121–22
HMP Oakwood, 109–10
HMP Rochester, 121–22
HMP Wellingborough, 115–21

San Pedro prison (*cont.*)
  self-governing, 32–42
  sex offenders in, 38–39, 41
  violence in, 36–37, 38–39
Shasta County, 157–58
Simon, Jonathan, 164
Skocpol, Theda, 166–67
social distance
  defined, 15
  Los Angeles County Jail, in, 15, 134, 138,
    142–43, 144–46
  promote cooperation, 15, 16–17, 17f,
    56, 57, 152, 154–55, 156, 158–59,
    164–65, 171n45
social networks
  English prisons, in, 14, 111, 118–19,
    120–21, 131
  facilitate information acquisition, 13, 14, 16–
    17, 50–51, 52–53, 57
Sparks, Richard, 112
Straub, Christina, 127
Substance Abuse Treatment Facility and State
  Prison, 109–10
Sweden, 44–45, 60, 175n4
Sykes, Gresham, 1, 5

Texas "building tenders", 9–10, 172n34
Tiebout competition, 43
Tijuana Mexico, 3–4
Trammell, Rebecca, 94

Ugelvik, Thomas, 50–51
United Kingdom Ministry of Justice, 127

U.S. Bureau of Justice, 110
U.S. Department of State, 34–35, 38–39
U.S. Supreme Court, 63, 107

Valley State Prison for Women, 93–94
Varella, Drauzio, 1, 21, 30, 36
Varese, Federico, 13
Venezuela, 3–5, 25–28

Wacquant, Loïc, 26–27, 164
Ward, David, 92–94, 96–97
Williams, Ryan, 127
Winder, General John Henry, 65, 66, 67–68,
    70–71, 84
Wirz, Captain Henry, 63, 72–73, 75–76, 77,
    79–80, 83–85
women's prisons
  compared to men's prisons, 90–91, 92f, 95,
    96–97, 98–99, 102, 103, 104–5
  decentralized governance institutions, 95–99
  enforcement mechanisms, 97–98
  norms, 95–98
  play families. *See* prison families
  prison gang absence, 90–91, 102–5
  prison population, 90, 91–92, 92f
  sex in, 185n63
  street gang participation, 91
  victimization in, 185n63
  violence in, 91
World Bank, 33
World War II, 53
World Values Survey, 59–60
War of the Rebellion collection, 64